Aristophanes is the most important Greek comic dramatist and one of the greatest comic playwrights of all ages. Little is known about his life except that he was of Athenian parentage and either lived or owned land on Aegina. He composed about fifty-five comedies, of which only eleven plays and numerous fragments remain. Aristophanes' comedies continue to be a valuable aid to an appreciation of the Athenian culture of the late fifth century B.C.

Paul Roche, a distinguished English poet and translator, is the author of *The Bible's Greatest Stories*. His other translations include *Euripides: Ten Plays; Sophocles: The Complete Plays;* and *The Orestes Plays of Aeschylus.*

FOUR PLAYS BY ARISTOPHANES

Lysistrata
The Frogs
A Parliament of Women
Plutus (Wealth)

The New Translations by
Paul Roche

A SIGNET CLASSIC

SIGNET CLASSIC
Published by New American Library, a division of
Penguin Group (USA) Inc., 375 Hudson Street,
New York, New York 10014, U.S.A.
Penguin Books Ltd, 80 Strand,
London WC2R 0RL, England
Penguin Books Australia Ltd, 250 Camberwell Road,
Camberwell, Victoria 3124, Australia
Penguin Books Canada Ltd, 10 Alcorn Avenue,
Toronto, Ontario, Canada M4V 3B2
Penguin Books (NZ), cnr Airborne and Rosedale Roads,
Albany, Auckland 1310, New Zealand

Penguin Books Ltd, Registered Offices:
80 Strand, London WC2R 0RL, England

First published by Signet Classic, an imprint of New American Library,
a division of Penguin Group (USA) Inc.

First Printing, June 2004
10 9 8 7 6 5 4 3 2 1

Library of Congress Catalog Card Number: 2003063328

Printed in the United States of America

Acknowledgments

My debt to Jeffrey Henderson, editor of the Loeb Classical Library and Professor of Classical Studies at Boston University, knows no bounds. His translations of Aristophanes in the Loeb series with accompanying Greek text is scrupulously faithful and expressed in language that is wholly contemporary. I was guided and steadied by him throughout and I found his footnotes invaluable.

Contents

Introduction

The dates of Aristophanes' birth and death are variously given, but 445–375 B.C. is a possibility. We know that he was considered too young to present his first three plays in his own name: the lost *Daiteleis* (*The Banqueters*), which won second prize at the Lenaea in 427 B.C., when he would only have been about eighteen; the lost *Babylonians*, which won second prize in 426 B.C.; and *The Archarnians*, which brought him first prize in 425 B.C. when he was barely twenty. These plays and the four that followed over the next four years are the work of a very young man endowed with the courage to level unrelenting attacks on no less than the head of state—the demagogic Cleon.

Like the great tragedians Aeschylus, Sophocles and Euripides (and, I expect, the poets of all ages), he decried the destructiveness and sheer stupidity of war, and in his most celebrated plays he warned and pleaded against it. Yet for twenty-seven years of his writing life, with one brief interval, Athens was at war with Sparta in an internecine struggle that finally left her exhausted and shorn of her glory, never fully to recover.

Aristophanes had no respect for shoddy politicians like Cleon, who plunged Athens into campaigns that led to defeat and decline, and he lampooned them without mercy. He himself came from a landowning family and his political outlook was conservative. Not necessarily in favor of oligarchy, he believed that democracy was best served by the brightest minds and not by selfish, clamorous demagogues. He was conservative too in his general thought, defending religion though he laughed at the gods, and he was suspicious of contemporary philosophy. He mocked Socrates as a Sophist knowing full well he was as anti-Sophist as Aristophanes himself; it was just too easy to use him as a scapegoat because he was well known and easy to parody. Aristophanes' conservatism did not extend to his language, which is almost unimaginably rich and varied. The obscenity that crops up here and there is funny because it is unexpected. When one considers the milieu in which the plays were presented—"under the auspices of the state, to the entire population, at a religious festival under the presidency of a priest and on consecrated ground"*—how could it not be hilariously incongruous? It was as if somebody (preferably the grandest dignitary present) trumpeted a fart in a solemn moment at high mass.

But it is incongruous too because the rest of Greek literature from Homer to Thucydides (if we except Sappho) is so well behaved. Yet we ought not to be surprised by the phallic thrust of Aristophanes' jokes, because the origins of comedy are undoubtedly found in fertility rites at the dawn of drama. Sex, after all, is the oldest human hobby.

Having said all this, it is important to add that the plays of Aristophanes are serious. In them he confronts and dares to laugh out of court some current

*Moses Hadas in his introduction to *The Complete Plays of Aristophanes,* Bantam Books, 1982.

trend or action or human aberration. He recognized that the prime function of the poet is to reduce to order—Shelley's "unacknowledged legislator of this world"—in other words, to preserve a world worth living in, with the greatest political and personal freedom consonant with order, and the leisure to enjoy it all.

This is essential teaching at an organic level, and it is done not by giving information—the way of prose—but by lifting the spirit to a new plane of truth and beauty. *"Ut doceat, ut demonstrat, ut delectat."** Such is the brief of the poet, and it is this last, "to please," which is the touchstone of lasting poetry. This does not mean that poetry deals only with the beautiful but that when it deals with ugliness it remains in itself beautiful.

Not only was Aristophanes one of the greatest poets of antiquity but, in the words of Lempriere's *Classical Dictionary,* "the greatest comic dramatist in world literature: by his side Molière seems dull and Shakespeare clownish."

Be that as it may, the lyrics of Aristophanes present the translator with an irresistible but crippling challenge, and the best he can do to meet it—if he is really trying to translate and not just to paraphrase or adapt—is ineluctably doomed to be a poor reflection of the original. Nevertheless, even this pittance is well worth trawling for.

THE PLAYS

Of Aristophanes' forty-four comedies, only eleven have come down to us: *The Archarnians,* which won

---

*To teach, to show, to please.

first prize at the Lenaea in 425 B.C. when he was about twenty; *The Knights,* a courageous attack on Cleon, then at the height of his power, which also won first prize, in 424 B.C; *The Clouds,* in 423 B.C., which for some reason was not a success and which he rewrote (it is this second version that survives); *The Wasps,* winning second prize in 422 B.C.; and *Peace,* again with second prize, in 421 B.C.

After this comes a gap of six years in which what he wrote is unknown to us, but in 414 B.C. came *The Birds,* perhaps his masterpiece and another second-prize winner. Thereafter we have no record of prizes, but we do know that he produced *Lysistrata* in 411 B.C.; the *Thesmorphoriazusae* (*Women at the Festival of Demeter*) in 411 B.C.; *The Frogs* in 405 B.C.; *Ecclesiazusae* (*A Parliament of Women*) in 392 B.C.; and *Plutus* (*Wealth*) in 388 B.C. (There were two additional comedies of which we do not even have the titles.)

In the *Ecclesiazusae,* produced when Aristophanes was about fifty-three—not old in our day but comparable to sixty-five or seventy then—there is a slackening of the youthful zest of his earlier comedies, and the choruses that were so essential to their lyric ebullience are greatly reduced. This perhaps is the first step in the evolution of what is known as Old Comedy into New. In *Plutus,* some four years later, the transmogrification is complete.

The chief features of New Comedy are that it virtually did away with the choruses, turning them into musical interludes (a direction already taken by Euripides); it presented characters as types rather than as individuals; it constructed elaborate plots rather than letting the context itself of a story dictate the setting; it discarded topical allusions, political satire and direct attacks on individuals, and it introduced the ups and downs, the torture and the ecstasy, of romantic love.

As to this last, New Comedy was the progenitor of the boy-meets-girl story, as well as all the clever Cox-and-Box mix-ups of mistaken identity. It is in fact the blueprint of drama such as we know it, with its complex but logical plots, its love entanglements, and its domestic comedy of manners. The chief exponent of New Comedy was Menander (ca. 342–292 B.C.), the Aristophanes of his generation, of whose work we have extensive fragments and one almost-complete play, *Dyskolos* (*The Grouch*). It is, however, mainly through Roman adaptors, Plautus and Terence, that we know his work.

CHORUS, COSTUMES, STRUCTURE, MUSIC

There were twenty-four actors in the chorus, which was divided into two sets of twelve that could sing and dance against each other. The chorus members were elaborately dressed in costumes on which large sums of money were spent. The choruses wore masks suitable to their parts—birds, frogs, wasps—and these masks in themselves must have generated a good deal of merriment. One can imagine the laughter that must have greeted the appearance of the "dog" Cleonacur in *The Wasps,* almost certainly wearing a mask that was an unmistakable caricature of the despised Cleon. Reflecting back to the Dionysiac fertility rituals of the Comus—the origins of comedy—the members of the chorus wore long floppy phalluses strapped to them, but these need not have been always visible and could be hidden if need be by a variety of clothing.

Though the members of the chorus were not professional actors, as were the leading players, they were rigorously trained in dance and song—at least six months' preparation being thought necessary. Music, dance, and song were at the heart of the performance, and one wouldn't be far wrong in regarding an Aristophanic comedy more as a musical than a play.

All parts, including female, were played by men. The naked flute girl Dardanis, for instance, in *The Wasps,* would have been a boy or young man dressed in tights with female breasts painted on him.

As to its general structure, the Aristophanic comedy followed this pattern: (1) Prologue, which could be a dialogue; (2) Parados, or entry of the Chorus, singing and dancing in character; (3) the Agon, or debate; and (4) the Parabasis, or address of the Chorus to the audience in the name of the author. Each of these sections was characterized by its own particular meters and system of prosodic repetition akin to the strophe and antistrophe of Tragedy. The music was provided by flute, lyre and kettledrum.

Strophe literally means "turning (one way)," so *antistrophe* would mean "turning the other." These refer to movements of the Chorus: either the whole Chorus or the Chorus split into two, each part balancing the other. Normally strophe and antistrophe are identical in the number, meter, and length of lines.

THE TRANSLATION

Aristophanes is not easy to translate: He stretches the Greek language—that most elastic of tongues—to the breaking point and uses a vocabulary almost Shakespearian in its variety and richness: five or six times as large as Aeschylus, Sophocles, and Euripides. And as if it were not enough, he puns and coins words at the drop of an iota subscript. Moreover, the plays are in verse that shifts from one intricate meter to another throughout.

Some translators have valiantly set out to reflect this teeming prosody by using rhyme, but the results for the most part seem merely forced or fussy. My own solution is first of all to reflect the meter as far as I can, and then to echo rhyme more often than to use it, though I do use it fairly strictly in the choral parts where the sound pattern of the Greek becomes emphatic and condensed. Did Aristophanes himself use rhyme? Yes, but not in the way we do.

Greek versification compared to English is more like a plum pudding than a blancmange. In blancmange you get what you see. In a plum pudding you get what you don't see. Greek prosody is stuffed with every kind of syllabic analogy—assonance, consonance, alliteration, rhyme—but because Greek is a polysyllabic language these sounds are buried in the middle of words, and even if they are at the end of lines they don't get the same stress that they would in English. Consequently, this matching of sound with sound, Greek with English, is not subtle enough, especially when it comes to rhyme.

Putting Aristophanes into the straitjacket of English versification is like trying to turn plum pudding into a blancmange; perhaps this is a misleading simile, though, for English, far from being a blancmange, shares with Greek the delight in a rich variation of sounds. The difference ultimately is between a constantly polysyllabic language and a seldomly polysyllabic one.

To use rhyme in an attempt to reflect Aristophanes' verbal effulgence produces something that is not nearly subtle enough. For this reason, I use rhyme warily, though I do use it, and instead I put the burden of capturing Aristophanes' variations of sound, tone, and rhythm on a novel system of prosody that I call, rather grandly, "sonic intercoping." This means that the end syllable of every line is "coped," that is, topped with or tied into the endings of other lines before and after. Thus one gets the effects of verse without actually using verse.

Let me demonstrate this by taking a page at random from *Lysistrata* and showing how all the lines are sonically linked. One need not be conscious of this while reading the play. It will have its effect willy-nilly, so long as the flow of a passage reads naturally and the tie-ins of the preceding and succeeding lines do not seem forced. If on occasion they do, the fault is mine.

> …that comes with women.
> MEN'S LEADER: Wait till you hear how they've
> gone
> completely beyond the pale with their jars of
> water
> and almost drowned us, so that
> we had to wring out our clothing later
> as if we'd peed in it.
>
> MAGISTRATE: Great briny Poseidon, we get
> exactly what we deserve.
> We ourselves collaborate with our
> womenfolk
> and abet them in behavior that's absurd.
> What follows is a blooming herbacious
> border of nonsense.
> We go into a jeweler's shop and say
> something like:
> "Goldsmith, you know that torque

> the one you made my wife,
> she was dancing with it on
> the other night, and the prong
> slipped out of its groove.
>   I have to go to Salamis, so do you think
> you could spare the time one evening
> to pop into her
> and fit the prong inside her groove?"

Any reader who wants to stop and analyze the system will see that sonic intercoping is based on a play of consonance, assonance, and alliteration, occasionally bolstered by rhyme.

Let me take five lines of Greek from *A Parliament of Women* and trawl them for these sometimes hidden gems, then trawl in my English translation and see how much can be retrieved. But first, let us be clear about the following.

> Assonance: the same vowel sound enclosed by different consonants: *boat, soul*
> Consonance: the same consonants enclosing different vowels: *boat, but*
> Alliteration: syllables beginning with the same consonants or vowels: *watered, wine; angry, assassins*
> Rhyme: the same vowel sound preceded by different consonants: *boat, coat; at, bat*

1 τουτου γε τοινυν την ἐπιουσαν ἡμεραν.
2 τολμημα τολμωμεν τοσουτον ὁυνεκα,
3 ἠν πως παραλαβειν της πολεως τα πραγματα
4 δυνωμεθ᾽ ὡστ᾽ ἀγαθον τι πραξαι την πολιν
5 νυν μεν γαρ ὁυτε θεομεν ὁυτ᾽ ἐλαυνομεν.

Line 1: 9 assonances: του-του-ους, γε-επ-ερ, νη-την-ήμ

2 half consonances: την-αν

6 alliterations: του-του-τοι-την, ἐπ-ερ

2 rhymes: σαν-ραν

Line 2: 7 assonances: μων-ων, νεκ-μεν, τους-ουτ-ουν

6 half consonances: τολ-τολ-το-τον, ουτ-ουν

2 full consonances: μωμ-μημ

9 alliterations: τολ-τολ-τος, μημ-μεν-μα-μω, ουτ-ουν

2 rhymes: μα-κα

Line 3: 4 assonances: ην-της-βειν-ην

8 half consonances: πως-παρ-ραλ-λαβ-τα-τα-πραγ-ματ

9 alliterations: πως-παρ-πραγ-πολ, της-τα-τδ, λαβ-λεως

7 rhymes: παρ-ρα-λα-τα-πρα-μα-τα

Line 4: 5 assonances: δγ-αθ-πραξ, νωμ-ώστ

4 half consonances: δυν-θον-την-λιν

6 alliterations: ἰαγ-την, θ'ωστ-θον, πραξ-πολ

Line 5: 8 assonances: μεν-μεν-μεν, ουτ-ουτ, τε-θε-ελ

4 half consonances: νυν-μεν-μεν-μεν

7 alliterations: μεν-μεν-μεν, ουτ-ουτ, ομ-ομ

Sonic intercoping line endings: ραν-λιν-μεν, κα-τα

The English translation

> If he can do it, I swear by this dawning day
> that we too can carry out a coup and essay
> something for our city, but as things are
> we lie stuck in the doldrums
> with power of neither sail nor oar.

Line 1: 4 assonances: if, it, -ing, this
           2 half consonances: can, dawn
           5 alliterations: if, it, I; do, dawn, day

Line 2: 6 assonances: that, can, car, and; too, coup
           4 half consonances: can, car; that, out
           3 alliterations: can, carry, coup
           4 rhymes: too, coup; day, say

Line 3: 5 assonances: thing, things, cit; our, are
           5 half consonances: thing, things; for, our, are

Line 4: 2 assonances: stuck, drums
           2 half consonances: stuck, drums
           2 alliterations: dol, drums

Line 5: 4 half consonances: power, neither, nor, oar
           2 alliterations: neither, nor
           2 rhymes: nor, oar
Sonic intercoping line endings: day, essay; are, oar.

Perhaps the most perennial and greatest difficulty of all is that Greek, compared to English, is devilishly condensed. A single word often can only be done justice by a phrase, or sometimes only by a whole sentence. Mere transcription is not enough. One is trying to bring over not only words but thoughts, feelings, and connotations, which the words themselves sometimes merely adumbrate. And here lies a pitfall difficult to avoid: when one discovers that in one's efforts to bring out the fullness of the Greek one has leapt from the legitimate boundaries of translation and landed in the realm of mere paraphrase.

Fidelity to the original, too, can be a stumbling block. Fidelity, yes, but this should not mean being a slave to the literal, which can put one on the high road to the absurd. For instance (to take a current language), one wouldn't translate the name of the Spanish newspaper *Ultima Hora* as *The Last Hour,* which is the literal meaning, but by what the idiom means: *Up to the Minute.* Sometimes the translator feels compelled for the sake of clarity to add a phrase or sentence that is not actually in the original. Is this being unfaithful? Not necessarily, not if the addition makes explicit that which was truly implicit in the original. One might even go as far as saying that to leave it out is not so much fidelity as pedantry.

Perhaps the final challenge of attempting to translate Aristophanes is that, unlike the three great tragedians, he did not deal with grand universal themes ineluctably germane to the human scene, but with the here and now of a particular place and particular people, with particular problems, and at a particular time in history. It's almost as if an Athenian of the fifth century B.C. were asked to put into Attic Greek the antics, absurdities, the cleverness and sparkle of a Gilbert and Sullivan operetta.

The miracle is that, even if one is only half successful in doing justice to the letter and spirit of Aristophanes, and even if many of the names and places he mentions mean nothing to us, we *still* find him funny—so original is the cast of his imagination and so delightful his penchant for rank nonsense.

LYSISTRATA

Lysistrata was produced by Callistratus in the early spring of 411 B.C., probably at the Lenaea. He had already presented four plays of Aristophanes, the last being *The Birds*. It is not known how it was received or if it won a prize.

THEME

It was a bad time for Athens. The grandiose armada invasion of Sicily had proved a disaster. She lost her fleet, her army, and a great deal of money. Meanwhile, the Spartans were on her doorstep and many of her allies were seizing the opportunity to defect from the Athenian hegemony. Aristophanes, who in his last three plays had done his best to show the stupidity, the waste, the corruption of war, now courageously writes a comedy with a brilliantly unexpected slant: funny enough to get around the warmongers, and serious enough to make them think.

CHARACTERS

LYSISTRATA, young Athenian wife
CALONICE, young Athenian wife
MYRRHINE, young Athenian wife
LAMPITO, young Spartan wife
MAGISTRATE, Athenian, with servants
THREE OLD WOMEN, of the marketplace
FOUR WIVES, citizens of Athens
CINESIAS, husband of Myrrhine

3

BABY, of Cinesias and Myrrhine
HERALD, from Sparta
SPARTAN DELEGATES, with servants
ATHENIAN DELEGATES, with servants
TWO LOUTS, of Athens
PORTER, of gate to Acropolis
CHORUS, twelve old Athenian men
CHORUS, twelve old Athenian women

Others: Spartan and Athenian wives, a Corinthian wife, Ismenia (a Theban wife), young Theban woman (Miss Boeotia), Scythian girl (servant of Lysistrata), more old women, four Scythian archer police, women friends of Calonice and Myrrhine.

THE STORY

To put an end to war Lysistrata hits on a startlingly simple way of forcing husbands to stay at home and become pacifists: deny them sex. Not all the husbands, of course, are immediately subject to this radical treatment because they are already away fighting, but even these would come home on leave—with one thought on their minds. Withholding sex from panting young husbands is the strategy Lysistrata has devised for their wives, but she has a different one for the older women: to make an assault on the Acropolis and seize and freeze the assets that fund the war.

OBSERVATIONS

"Lysistrata" (pronounced LySIStrata) means in Greek "the Demobilizer," and if one wanted to be clever in English one could simply call her Lisa. But there is more to it than that. The "lys" part of the name is from the verb "luō," "to loosen," and one of the powers women possess is that of loosening the loins of men.

Lysistrata herself is something of a grande dame and is treated with decided respect by the other women. It is also noticeable that though she is the organizer of "Operation Prick," she is not in the least bawdy, unlike her friend Calonice. In her initial conversation with Calonice, when she describes her enterprise as pressing, huge, and weighty, she is being quite literal; it is Calonice who is thinking of something very different.

Lampito, a Spartan, speaks in a Greek the Athenians would consider a dialect. Her words have shorter syllables than Attic Greek. The Spartans, or Lacedaemonions, from Laconia (another name for Sparta), were noted for their brevity—from which we get the word "laconic"—and their speech must have had the same relation to Attic Greek as, say, Catalan Spanish has to Castillian. Aristophanes takes pains to have Lampito speak in short clipped syllables, and translators do their best to follow suit and tend to put her into broad Scots. I don't know what the American equivalent would be (perhaps Hillbilly), but for my part I would speak her lines in London cockney,* because Cockneys also go in for swallowing their words in a language that is faster than the Queen's English. The same applies to the Spartans.

As to my intentions as translator, let me say again what I think I said before: This rendering is strict translation, neither paraphrase nor adaptation. I try to keep as close to the Greek of Aristophanes as I can. This is not simply a matter of being faithful to mean-

*Key to London cockney: A becomes i: e.g., name=nime
                       I becomes oi: e.g., time=toime
                       O becomes ow: e.g., home=howm
                       U becomes oe: e.g., you=yoe
                       H is mute

ings but of organizing them into patterns of sound
that reflect the original, which entails keeping a steady
watch on the way phrases and sentences hit the ear.

TIME AND SETTING

A street in Athens in the early morning, with the
Acropolis in the background. LYSISTRATA is pacing up
and down impatiently, and finally bursts out:

LYSISTRATA: Honestly, if they'd been invited to a Bacchic party
  or a do at Pan's or those goddesses of fucking, the
     Genetilides,
the streets would be jammed and tambourines at the
   ready. . . .
      Just look, not a female in sight!

[*she continues to pace, then sees someone approaching*]

      Ah, at last! My neighbor at least.
      Good morning, Calonice.
CALONICE: And to you too, Lysistrata. . . . But, my dear,
   what a state you're in—all tensed up!
      It doesn't suit you, lovey.
LYSISTRATA: Calonice, I'm absolutely furious—and
   with us women.
No wonder men think we're an impossible group.
CALONICE: Well, aren't we?
LYSISTRATA: Asked to come to a crucial meeting of
   no piffling import,
   and they're all asleep and don't turn up.
CALONICE: They'll be here all right, my sweet,
   but you know what a business it is to get out in
      the morning:

There's a husband to pack off, a maid to wake up,
a baby to bathe and give something to eat.
LYSISTRATA: I know, but some things are more pressing.
CALONICE: Like what you've summoned us to hear?

Well, I hope what's pressing is something really big,
Lysistrata dear.
LYSISTRATA: It's huge.
CALONICE: And weighty?
LYSISTRATA: God, it's huge, and God, it's weighty.
CALONICE: Then why aren't they all here?
LYSISTRATA: Oh, it's not that; if it were
there'd be a stampede. No,
it's something that sticks in my mind hard as a shaft
and keeps me from sleeping, though I tease
it and tease it night after night.
CALONICE: By now the poor thing must be floppy.
LYSISTRATA: It's collapsed.

Which leaves us women to save Greece.
CALONICE: Us women? Some hope!
LYSISTRATA: All the same, the salvation of our State
rests with us,
even if it's the end of the Pelopponnese. . . .
CALONICE: Ah! That would be a help.
LYSISTRATA: . . . and the Boeotians are wiped out.
CALONICE: Wait a minute, not the eels, please!*
LYSISTRATA: And I won't mention the Athenians,
but you know what I mean. . . . If all us women
united en masse—Boeotians, Spartans, and us,
we all together could save Greece.
CALONICE: What on earth could we women do?

Anything brilliant and clever is beyond females like us.
We're just household ornaments in flaxen dresses

*The eels from Lake Copais in Boeotia were a famous delicacy.
Boeotia is pronounced *Bec-o-sha.*

and negligees you see through,
all nicely made up in pretty come-hither flats.
LYSISTRATA: Precisely, that's
   exactly what we're going to need to save Greece:
a seductive wardrobe, our rouge, our negligees and
   our pretty flats.
CALONICE: But what's it all meant for?
LYSISTRATA: To stop every living man
   from ever raising a spear against another and . . .
CALONICE: I'll have a frock dyed crocus yellow.
LYSISTRATA: . . . from ever lifting a shield or . . .
CALONICE: I'll make myself completely see-through.
LYSISTRATA: . . . springing a dagger.
CALONICE: I'm off shopping for new shoes.
LYSISTRATA: But oughtn't the women to have come?
CALONICE: They should have flown here long ago.
LYSISTRATA: I know, sweetie, but they're Athenians
   and can't do anything on time.
      No one has exactly raced here
on the *Paralus* and *Salaminia*.*
CALONICE: All the same,
   I bet they've been properly manned and coming
since early morning.
LYSISTRATA: Even the women I counted on to be the
      first to appear
   are not here.
CALONICE: I happen to know that Theogenes'† wife
   has been skimming this way at the tip of her plough-
      ing skiff.
      But look, here are some more of your ladies.
LYSISTRATA: And there are others over there.

*The two swift Athenian galleys used for state missions.
†A nouveau riche politician, also mentioned (derogatively) in
Wasps, Peace and *Birds*.

[MYRRHINE* *and a group of women enter*]

CALONICE: [*wrinkling her nose*] Ugh! Where are they from?

LYSISTRATA: Anagyrus—Stink City.†

CALONICE: I thought we'd just made someone fart.

MYRRHINE: [*breathless*] Lysistrata, I hope we're not too late.

[*a critical pause*]

Speak, damn it! Say something.

LYSISTRATA: I do not approve, Myrrhine . . . um . . . of people who turn up late when there's so much at stake.

MYRRHINE: Dear, I'm sorry.
Couldn't find my girdle in the dark.
But at least we're here,
so what's cooking?

LYSISTRATA: Wait a bit till the women from Boeotia and the Peloponnese appear.

CALONICE: Right— . . . But look, here's Lampito coming.

[LAMPITO, *a robust young woman, arrives with other Spartan wives, a wife from Corinth, and* ISMENIA, *a Theban wife*]

LYSISTRATA: Good morning, Lampito, my Spartan darling!
How luscious you look! Quite stunning!
Such clear skin, and that firm body,
why you could strangle a bull.

---

*The name means "myrtle," a plant associated with Aphrodite.
†*Anagyrus foetida*, the bean trefoil: a plant noted for its unpleasant smell.

LAMPITO: By Castor and Pollux,* that I could.
   It's the work I do in the gym, buddy,
jump-kicking and bumping my tail.
LYSISTRATA: [*putting out a hand to feel*]
   My, what marvelous tits!
LAMPITO: Hey, lovey, you feeling me up for sacrifice?
LYSISTRATA: And who's this young lady here?
LAMPITO: By Castor and Pollux, would you believe it, it's
   no less than Miss Boeotia.
MYRRHINE: Miss Boeotia? What a surprise! Lovely as
   a meadow.
CALONICE: [*gazing at her crotch*]
   Yes, when the hay's just been cut.
LYSISTRATA: And this other girl?
LAMPITO: She's from Corinth. A bit o' all right
   by Castor an' Pollux, real cute.
CALONICE: One can see that, back and front.
LAMPITO: But who called us all together?
LYSISTRATA: Me, right here.
LAMPITO: Pray tell, what for?
CALONICE: Yes, dear lady, do explain
   what makes this so important.
LYSISTRATA: Explain I shall, but first I have a small
   question.
CALONICE: Then out with it.
LYSISTRATA: Don't you all miss your kiddies' dads
   when they're at the front?
      I expect that every one of you has a man away
      from home.
CALONICE: My man's been away five months in
   Thrace—how I miss him!—

---

*The heavenly twins, brothers of Helen and Clytemnestra. They
were patrons of the Spartans.
   For the key to rendering Lampito's speech in cockney, see foot-
note on p. 5.

keeping an eye on Eucrates.*

MYRRHINE: Mine's been seven months at Pylos.

LAMPITO: As for mine, hardly is he in the door
  when he's strapping on his shield again.

CALONICE: What's more,
  there's not the shadow of a lover left for us,
and since the Miletus crisis,†
not a dildo in the offing.
    That at least would be better than nothing.

LYSISTRATA: Well, suppose I hit on a way to stop
    the war,
  would you be with me?

CALONICE: Holy Demeter and Persephone! Absolutely.
  Even if I have to pawn this blouse

[*sotto voce*]

  and spend the proceeds on booze.

MYRRHINE: And I'm ready to slit myself down the
    middle
  like a mackerel and give half to support the cause.

LAMPITO: I'd clamber to the tiptop of Mount Tagetus‡
  just to get a wee peep at peace.

LYSISTRATA: Then let me disclose.
  In a word, dear ladies,
to make the men make peace
we've got to forgo . . .

CALONICE: Oh, what, please?

LYSISTRATA: Are you ready for it?

CALONICE: You bet. Even if death is the price.

---

*Athenian commander suspected of collaborating with the enemy.
†After the Athenian disaster in Sicily, Miletus seized the opportunity to break away from the federation. One of Miletus' exports was leather dildos.
‡The highest mountain in Laconia (Sparta).

LYSISTRATA: All right,
  what we're going to have to forgo is—*phallus*.*

ALL: Oh no!

LYSISTRATA: Hey, don't turn away. . . . Where are you
    off to
  so dolefully with clamped lips, ashen cheeks and
    shaking heads?
    Will you or won't you do it? What's bugging you?

CALONICE: This is where I stick. . . . Let the war
  drag on.

MYRRHINE: Me too. I couldn't for the life of me. Let
  the war drag on.

LYSISTRATA: That coming from you, Miss Mackerel, is
    against the odds.
  Weren't you saying just now that you were ready
    to slit yourself in two?

CALONICE: Ask for anything else, just anything you like,
  I'll walk through fire if you want,
but I simply can't give up prick.
    Lysistrata, darling, there's nothing to compare.

LYSISTRATA: And what about you?

MYRRHINE: Fire for me too.

LYSISTRATA: Oh, what a low-down randy lot we are!
  No wonder we're the subject of tragedies,
like "Poseidon and the Tub" of Sophocles:†
have fun with a god, then dump the brats.
    But, Lampito, Spartan dear,
even if only you side with me, that's

---

*An anomaly that must have occurred to Aristophanes, which per-
haps he hoped nobody would notice, is: if all the males are at the
front and not even lovers left (which we've just been told), there
are no throbbing pricks around to abstain from!

†Sophocles wrote two tragedies on the subject. Tyro, a beautiful
young woman, is seduced by Poseidon, who turns himself into her
lover for the occasion. Tyro exposed the twin boys that resulted in
a tub by the river.

enough for us to make a go of it—so please!

LAMPITO: Eh, but it's tough on a woman
   not to sleep side by side with an erection.
    All the same, we do need peace,
so . . . well . . . oh, all right!

LYSISTRATA: You perfect darling, the only real woman
   of the lot.

LAMPITO: But if we do give up . . . er . . . what you
    suggest,
   which God forbid, is there any guarantee
that peace will result?

LYSISTRATA: By Demeter and Persephone, absolutely!
   Imagine it: us lolling around all tarted up,
our pussies' sweet little triangles neatly plucked,
and we float past them in our see-throughs,
and our men get stiff as rods and want to screw,
but we elude them and hold ourselves aloof—why,
   they'll sue
for peace real quick. That you can bet.

LAMPITO: Like Meneláus at the sight of Helen's
    melons,
   chucking away his sword when he meant to slay her
    on the spot.*

CALONICE: I know, darling, but say the men just ignore us?

LYSISTRATA: That would be like—as old Pherecrates†
    said—
   skinning the same dog twice.
    We'd just have to take dildos to bed.

CALONICE: Substitutes are so disappointing.

---

*After the Trojan War, when the sinning Helen was brought home
to Sparta by her husband, Meneláus, and he was ready to put an
end to her, she disarmed him quite simply by her beauty.
†A comic poet and older contemporary of Aristophanes. The point
of the quote is obscure (at least to me!).

Anyway, what if they grab us and drag us
into the bedroom by brute force?

LYSISTRATA: Hang on to the door.

CALONICE: What if they hit us?

LYSISTRATA: Then give in, but start sulking.

Men don't enjoy sex by force,
and you can get at them by other means.

Have no fear, they'll soon kowtow.

No man's happy with an uncooperative wife.

CALONICE: Well, if you two agree with this, we do too.

LAMPITO: There'll be no problem with our Spartan
men;

they'll agree to a fair and honorable peace,
but those crazy Athenian roughs—good grief!—
how does one knock any sense into them?

LYSISTRATA: Don't worry. We'll get them to go along
with us.

LAMPITO: I don't see how:

not with triremes all primed for sea
and bottomless holds of brass in Athena's treasury.

LYSISTRATA: That's all been taken care of now.

We're raiding the Acropolis today:
a job the older women will undertake,
and while the rest of us carry out our peace work
here below
they'll capture the Acropolis up there
on the pretext of coming to sacrifice.

LAMPITO: My, but you've got it all wrapped up real
nice!

LYSISTRATA: Lampito, in that case
why don't we ratify everything right now
and make it binding with a vow?

LAMPITO: Yes, a vow: we're all agog to swear.

LYSISTRATA: Fine! Where's that Scythian girl?

[*she calls and her maid, a swarthy Scythian girl, appears carrying a shield and glancing about her open-eyed*]

Hey, girl, what's making you stare? . . .
  Put your shield down in front of us, bottom up,
    right there. . . .
  Somebody fetch me the sacrificial bits and pieces.
LAMPITO: What sort of oath are we going to swear?
LYSISTRATA: What sort? One like Aeschylus's,
  with the victim slaughtered over a shield.*
LAMPITO: My dear Lysistrata, not over a shield,
  not when we're making a vow about peace.
LYSISTRATA: Then how should the vow proceed?
CALONICE: How about getting hold of a white stallion
  and slicing a piece off him?
LYSISTRATA: A white stallion? Come on!
CALONICE: How are we going to swear then?
LYSISTRATA: I've got an idea that you might like:
  we put an enormous black wine bowl in position
and over it we slaughter a skin of Thracian wine,
swearing not to . . . add a drop of water.
LAMPITO: Yeah! That's an oath you couldn't better.
LYSISTRATA: Will somebody go inside and bring out
  a wine bowl and a skin of wine.

[*the Scythian girl goes into the house and brings out a bulging wine skin and an enormous bowl*]

MYRRHINE: My word, girls, what a whopper!
CALONICE: Merely to touch it is to hiccup.
LYSISTRATA: Now lay your hands with mine on this
  mighty beast.

---

*In his tragedy *Seven Against Thebes,* where the Seven swear to take Thebes or die in the attempt.

[*solemnly intoning*]

My lady Persuasion and you good Convivial Cup,
deign to accept this sacrifice from us.

[*she opens the wine skin and lets the dark red wine
bleed into the bowl*]

CALONICE: What a robust and richly colored spurt!
LAMPITO: The aroma's superb without a doubt.
MYRRHINE: Girls, I beg be first to take the oath.
CALONICE: By Aphrodite, not so fast.
    Wait and see if your lot comes first.
LYSISTRATA: Hold your hands over the bowl—
    Lampito, are you listening?—now,
one of you repeat after me this vow:
"No man whatsoever
whether husband or lover, shall . . ."
CALONICE: No man whatsoever
    whether husband or lover, shall . . .
LYSISTRATA: . . . "come near me with a rampant
    cock . . ." Speak up.
CALONICE: Come near me with a rampant cock.
    Oh, Lysistrata, my knees are buckling!
LYSISTRATA: "I'll live at home in continence
    unrutting."
CALONICE: I'll live at home in continence unrutting.
LYSISTRATA: "All tarted up in my saffron frock . . ."
CALONICE: All tarted up in my saffron frock . . .
LYSISTRATA: "so that my husband is bursting to
    erupt . . ."
CALONICE: so that my husband is bursting to erupt . . .
LYSISTRATA: "while I stay aloof and adamant."
CALONICE: while I stay aloof and adamant.
LYSISTRATA: "And if he exercises force . . ."

CALONICE: And if he exercises force . . .

LYSISTRATA: "I'll receive him coldly; won't waggle my hips or grunt . . ."

CALONICE: I'll receive him coldly; won't waggle my hips or grunt . . .

LYSISTRATA: "nor lift slippered feet to make it easy, nor of course . . ."

CALONICE: nor lift slippered feet to make it easy, nor of course . . .

LYSISTRATA: "crouch like a lioness waiting to be grated."*

CALONICE: crouch like a lioness waiting to be grated.

LYSISTRATA: "And only if I keep this vow may I quaff from this cup."

CALONICE: And only if I keep this vow may I quaff from this cup.

LYSISTRATA: "And if I don't keep this vow may the wine be watered."

CALONICE: And if I don't keep this vow may the wine be watered.

LYSISTRATA: Now let all of you swear, all united.

THE WOMEN: We swear, we swear.

LYSISTRATA: Good. I'll consecrate the cup.

[*she takes a long draught*]

CALONICE: Darling, not more than your share . . . Surely we're all on equal footing.

[*while they quaff the sound of cheering from the older women reaches them*]

Whatever is that cheering?

*In the Greek it is ". . . like the lioness on the cheesegrater." The meaning, though obscure, is obviously intended to be sexual.

LYSISTRATA: It's what I told you:
 we women have seized the Acropolis and the tem-
    ple of the goddess.
 Therefore, Lampito, get cracking
and go and do what you have to do back home.
 We can use your Spartan friends here as hostages.

[LAMPITO *leaves*]

 Meanwhile, let's join the other women on the
    Acropolis
and help them to barricade the gates.
CALONICE: But won't the men launch an attack on us?
LYSISTRATA: If they do, I don't give a damn.
 Just let them try with threats and fire to unbar
    those gates,
we'll make them come to heel.
CALONICE: So help me, Aphrodite, so they will!
 Or else we women are an impossibly hopeless breed.

[*All the women disappear into the Acropolis and the*
MEN'S CHORUS *enters in a slow shambling dance.*
They are old and shabby. They carry logs, unlit
torches, and live coals in earthen pots as they shuffle
toward the Acropolis.]

MEN'S LEADER: Forward, Dracus,* though your shoulders
 ache from carrying logs of green and heavy olive wood.

---

*The names given to members of this semichorus are generic for old
men. (Loeb) [*Loeb* stands for the Loeb Classical Library founded by
James Loeb in 1911 and published by Harvard University Press and
William Heinemann Ltd., London. This unique corpus of translations comprises almost the whole of Greek and Latin literature that
has come down to us. The translations are literally faithful and are
faced on the page by the original text.]

STROPHE

MEN'S CHORUS:

Live a long life and much will surprise you,
    such as we elders
Are witnessing now. Oh yes, Strymodorus,
    can you believe we'd
Ever be told these pestilent females
    reared in our homes
  Had taken possession of Pallas's image
  On the Acropolis and now have control.
  And that's not the end of their damnable damage:
  They've bolted and blocked every entry and portal.

MEN'S LEADER:

To the Acropolis, forward Philurgus,
    as fast as you can.
Let us arrange around these women
    logs in a circle.
They are the ones who have thought up this
    deplorable plan.
Let's make a bonfire and sizzle them up
    with our own hands,
Yes, every one of them, starting with Lycon's
    lecherous wife.*

ANTISTROPHE

MEN'S CHORUS:

Holy Demeter, I'll not have them laughing
    while I have life,
Especially not Cleomēnes,† the first
    who ever besieged
This place, and in spite of the bellicose Spartan
    spirit he breathed

---

*Because Lycon's wife had a reputation for promiscuity, the men imagine (wrongly) that she must be the ringleader. (Loeb)
†A Spartan king who in 508 B.C. held the Acropolis for two days before being induced to leave by the Athenians.

He surrendered to us and scurried away
In the flimsiest jacket without his arms.
Dirty, disheveled, and needing a shave:
For six years he hadn't deigned to wash his limbs.

MEN'S LEADER:
Yes, I was fierce and that's the way
    I dealt with this fellow.
We camped before the gates in ranks
    of seventeen.
And now will I simply stand and watch
    these brazen women,
Enemies of Euripides*
    and of heaven? Oh,
I might as well wipe out
    the glories of Marathon.

STROPH

MEN'S CHORUS:
A little bit more and the slogging is done.
The steepest stretch is the last to come
Before the Acropolis, and I strain to reach the spot.
How can we lug these logs along?
We need a donkey—that's for sure.
This log is making my shoulders sore
But I've got to reach that blessed gate
And also keep this fire alight;
I simply mustn't let it go out
Until I'm where I should be at.
    Phew! Phew!
Fuck! Fuck! The smoke, the smoke!

ANTISTROPHE

Lord Heracles help me—this bloody smoke

*Because of the desperate characters of Euripides' women it was
assumed (probably wrongly) that he hated them.

Plunges out of the bucket and bites
Both my eyes like a bitch gone mad, a bitch in heat,
The fire's a volcano. Yuk! Yuk!
My poor eyes, how they ache!
They must be a couple of bloodshot holes.
But I've got to get to the Acropolis,
And run, run, run if I can
To rescue the goddess Pallas Athena.
Laches, could the time be better?
          Phew! Phew!
Fuck! Fuck! The smoke, the smoke!

MEN'S LEADER: This fire's a lively thing, thank heavens
    it's awake.
  Let's put our logs down here
and dip our torches in the coals to get them lit.
    Then we'll batter
the gates like rams and summon the women to surrender.
    But if they won't and refuse to open the gates,
we'll set the doors on fire
and smoke them out. But first, let's set the logs
        down here.
    Phew! Phew! This bloody smoke!
    I wish some of you admirals at Samos* could
lend us a hand with this damned wood.

[*the old men unshoulder the logs and lay them down*]

    Oh brother! At last I've freed my poor back!
    Now it's all yours, you coals in the bucket.
    My lady Victory, secure us a triumph over this
        womanhood
on the Acropolis. Bring us luck,
it is high time to punish them for their cheek.

*An island on the southwest coast of Asia Minor, between Ephesus
and Miletus. "Since the end of summer 412 Samos had been the
headquarters of the Athenians' Aegean fleet." (Loeb)

[*the* CHORUS OF WOMEN, *middle aged and elderly, comes into view. They are better dressed than the old men and carry pitchers of water. When names are used they are, as with the men, generic*]

WOMEN'S LEADER: Women, I can see sparks and smoke. There's a bonfire somewhere. Hurry.

STROPHE

WOMEN'S CHORUS: Wings, wings, Nicodīcé,
    Fly to Critilla, Calīcé,
    And quench the galloping flames
    Fanned by malevolent breezes
    And nasty old men whose aims
    Are to kill us. But are we
    Too late for the crisis?
    We've come from the well with our pitchers
    And filled them to the brims:
    A task that was hardly easy
    With the crush and the clatter and din,
    And elbowing maids from the homesteads
    And branded slaves, but I heaved my
    Pitcher on my head,
    Rushing to help my neighbor
    And rescue her with water.

ANTISTROPHE*

Fanatic old men, it appears
Are gadding about with timbers
Costing a lot, and heading
Toward the Acropolis, stokers
Bawling their heads off, saying:
"We'll burn you women to cinders."
Grant, O Pallas Athena,
We'll not be set on fire.
See us as heroines rather,

*I have followed Aristophanes in not making strophe and antistrophe exactly symmetrical or of equal length.

Saving Hellas from warfare
And folly. That is the reason,
O golden helmeted one.
Defender of your temple,
They've pounced on your holy shrine.
Divinity, I implore
You to be our helper
And if they should light a bonfire
Be nearby with water.

[WOMEN'S LEADER *steps forward just as the old men
are about to charge the gates*]

WOMEN'S LEADER: Stop it, you disgusting men!
What d'you think you're doing?
No decent men would behave the way you are.

MEN'S LEADER: We've got an unexpected problem—
women
outside the gates, simply swarming.

WOMEN'S LEADER: Worried are you? Don't tell me we're
too hot to handle? You aren't seeing
a thousandth part of our forces yet.

MEN'S LEADER: Phaedrus, are we going to let
them go on blabbing?
It's time we got those logs and conked them on
the nut.

WOMEN'S LEADER: Women, put your pitchers down
and free your hands.
We may have to withstand a charge.

MEN'S LEADER: Two or three hefty socks in the jaw,
ye gods,
would shut them up.

WOMEN'S LEADER: Okey-doke, here's my mug, I
won't budge.
Have a sock and see if it quells.
But if you do, I'm the bitch that bites off balls.

MEN'S LEADER: Shut your damned gob,
or I'll bang you out of your ancient hide.

WOMEN'S LEADER: Just lift a little finger, slob,
and I, Stratyllis,* will . . .

MEN'S LEADER: Will what? Got a secret weapon to stop
me knocking you flat?

WOMEN'S LEADER: I'll tear your chest wide
apart and rip your entrails out.

MEN'S LEADER: Euripides got it right:
"no beast's so bloody as a woman," he said.

WOMEN'S LEADER: [*calling to the others*]
Rhodippe and everybody, get your pitchers ready.

MEN'S LEADER: So, you god-detested crone, you've
brought water, have you?

WOMEN'S LEADER: So, up yours too!
You've brought fire for a funeral, have you?

MEN'S LEADER: Not mine. The pyre's for your cronies.

WOMEN'S LEADER: [*thrusting out her pitcher*]
And I'll put it out with this.

MEN'S LEADER: You'll put out my fire, will you?

WOMEN'S LEADER: That's what you're going to witness.

MEN'S LEADER: While I roast your backside with my
torch.

WOMEN'S LEADER: Need a bath? Got soap?

MEN'S LEADER: You give me a bath—you witch?

WOMEN'S LEADER: A bath for the bridegroom, creep.

MEN'S LEADER: The barefaced impudence!

WOMEN'S LEADER: I'm quite free, you know, to be
the bride.

MEN'S LEADER: I'll put a plug in your loudmouthed
insolence.

WOMEN'S LEADER:
If that puts a stop to your jury work don't be
surprised.†

---

*The name means "militant one."
†The State paid a small stipend to impoverished old men to serve
on juries.

MEN'S LEADER: Forward, troops! Fire—her hair.
WOMEN'S LEADER: Ready, girls—the river.

[*the* WOMEN *raise their pitchers and souse the* MEN
with a flood]

MEN'S LEADER: I'm drowning.
WOMEN'S LEADER: Water's right temperature, I hope?
MEN'S LEADER: Right temperature? Stop it!
  What d'you think you're doing?
WOMEN'S LEADER: Watering you to make you sprout.
MEN'S LEADER: I'm shivering dry.
WOMEN'S LEADER: [*in mothering accents*] You've got
    fire,
  haven't you? Sit and warm yourself, you dope.

[*a* MAGISTRATE *arrives attended by his servants and
four Scythian archer police*]

MAGISTRATE: So, once again we have the glaring libidi-
    nous show
  of women's excesses:
bongo drums, Bacchic hymns, rooftop Adonis séances.
  I've heard it all before.
    Once when I was sitting in Parliament
and that bore Demostratus was telling us
that an armada to Sicily should be sent,
his wife was on the top of a roof, bleating:
"Adonis, oh, the poor poor youth!"*
    Then while Demostratus was trying
to get a bill passed
enlisting Zakynthian infantry, his wife,

---

*Adonis was famous for his beauty and Aphrodite fell in love with
him, but he was killed by a wild boar. Lamentations for his death
became a female cult and took place in midsummer on rooftops.

half sozzled up there on a roof,
was moaning: "O . . . h, women, beat your breasts
    for Adonis!"
    He took no notice
and just went on with his blithering motions.
    What a godforsaken lousy, mouth-frothing, blus-
    tering ass!
    That's the kind of topsy-turvy nonsense
that comes with women.

MEN'S LEADER: [*pointing to the* WOMEN'S CHORUS]
  Wait till you hear how they've gone
completely beyond the pale with their jars of water
and almost drowned us, so that
we had to wring out our clothing later
as if we'd peed in it.

MAGISTRATE: Great briny Poseidon, we get
  exactly what we deserve.
    We ourselves collaborate with our womenfolk
and abet them in behavior that's absurd.
    What follows is a blooming herbacious border
of nonsense. We go into a jeweler's and say some-
    thing like:
"Goldsmith, you know that torque,
the one you made my wife,
she was dancing with it on
the other night, and the prong
slipped out of its groove.
    I have to go to Salamis, so do you think
you could spare the time one evening
to pop into her
and fit the prong inside her groove?"
    Or a husband tells a cobbler—
a young jock with a strapping cock—
"Hey, cobbler, my wife's sandal cord
is pinching her wee tootsy and making it sore;

do you think you could come—sometime after
  luncheon—
I mean could you stretch it a bit and fit it
into smoother play with the puncheon?"
      That's the sort of thing that is apt to harden
into the climax we face now.
      Here am I, a magistrate,
with a commission to buy timber for oars,
who comes here to get the necessary brass
and finds himself standing outside the gate
locked out by women. So,

  [*to the servants*]

bring on the crowbars and I'll put a stopper to this
  farce.

  [*to one policeman and then another*]

      What are you gawking at, you damn fool?
      And you? See something interesting? A wine
        bar? Ale?
      I said "crowbars," that's all.
      Wedge those crowbars under the gates and start
        levering on your side.
      I'll do the same on mine.
LYSISTRATA: No levering, if you don't mind.
  I'm here of my own accord
and I don't see why you have to lever.
      It's not levers you want but nous and common
        sense.
MAGISTRATE: Is that so, you minx? . . . Where's the
        police?

  [*to First Policeman*]

Grab her and handcuff her hands behind her.

LYSISTRATA: If he so much as touches me with his little finger

I swear by Artemis he's heading for a breakdown.

MAGISTRATE: [*to First Policeman*] Don't tell me that you're scared.

Hey you [*to Second Policeman*], give him a hand.
Seize her by the middle and tie her up so she won't come undone.

[FIRST OLD WOMAN *advances from the gates*]

FIRST OLD WOMAN: So help me, Pandrosus,* I'll batter the shit out of you

if you dare touch her.

MAGISTRATE: Batter the shit? You there, officer [*to Third Policeman*],

tie up the foulmouthed old crone.

SECOND OLD WOMAN: [*advancing*] Raise a finger,

so help me Hecate,† and you'll get a black eye.

MAGISTRATE: What the hell! Is there an officer anywhere?

[*to Fourth Policeman*]

Hey you, arrest that one and put her at least out of action.

THIRD OLD WOMAN: [*advancing*] Take a step in her direction,

and, by Artemis, I'll tear your hair out by the roots.

MAGISTRATE: God help us, I've gone through our police.

---

*Another name for Artemis and also of a minor Attic goddess who had a shrine on the Acropolis.
†Artemis as the moon goddess.

But men must never succumb to women.
Fall in, men, we'll charge them.

LYSISTRATA: Holy Demeter and Persephone!
You'll find out very soon
that we too have our troops:
four battalions of fully armed fighting women—
at the ready.

MAGISTRATE: Archer police, buckle their arms behind
their backs.

LYSISTRATA: Women of the reserve, sally forth:
you market-gardeners-garlic-vendors-grain-dispensers-
hacks.
You bakers-lettuce-growers-barmaids, show your
teeth.*
Punch them, pound them, reel at them with horrid names,
the nastier the better.

[*the Scythian archer police retreat as a horde of old
women swarm out from the gates of the Acropolis*]

MAGISTRATE: Good heavens! It's insane!
My archer police—look, they scatter!

LYSISTRATA: Well, what did you expect?
Did you imagine you were up against a pack of slaves,
or that we women had no guts?

MAGISTRATE: They've got guts, all right, especially
when it gets
to filling them with booze.

MEN'S LEADER: You're a fine one to talk, Magistrate:
magistrate of the realm wasting effort and time
heckling animals like these.
Don't you realize

---

*Two lines in which Aristophanes coins two stupendous words:
"spermagoraiolekitholaxanopolides" and "skorodopandokeuttiar-
topolides."

that we've just been hosed in our clothes
and given a bath—without soap?

WOMEN'S LEADER: You poor dope!
    You shouldn't lift a hand against your neighbor
and not expect to get a black eye yourself.
        I'd much rather,
to tell the truth about myself,
sit quietly at home like a sweet little lass,
troubling no one and not disturbing a blade of grass.
        But if somebody ruffles me up
and pillages my nest, they've got themselves a wasp.

STROPHE*

MEN'S CHORUS:
    O Zeus, how can we possibly deal with gorgons
        like these?
    It's beyond the pale. . . . But the time has come
        to analyze
    What has occurred, you with me and see
    If we can tell what they wanted to fulfill
    When they captured the citadel
    And the rocky perch of the Acropolis
    A most sacrosanct place.

MEN'S LEADER: Question her closely, don't believe her:
    examine every syllable.
Not to be thorough in this sort of thing
    is totally deplorable.

MAGISTRATE: First of all I'd really like you to tell us
    what on earth you hoped to achieve
by barring and bolting the gates of the Acropolis
        against us?

LYSISTRATA: To stop you from being able to remove
    money from the treasury to spend on war.

*The antistrophe does not occur until p. 34.

MAGISTRATE: So you think it's money that funds the war?

LYSISTRATA: It certainly is.

And that's what fouls up everything else.

It's the reason Pisander,*

and all the rest of them scrambling for office,

sets everything astir.

Well, let them stir up all the trouble they want to,
they're not getting a single drachma out of here.

MAGISTRATE: So what do you intend to do?

LYSISTRATA: You want to know?

We'll take charge of the funds for you.

MAGISTRATE: You'll take charge of the funds?

LYSISTRATA: What's so odd about that?

Don't we look after the household budget as it is?

MAGISTRATE: It's not the same.

LYSISTRATA: Why not?

MAGISTRATE: These funds are for the war.

LYSISTRATA: But there shouldn't be a war.

MAGISTRATE: How else can we protect ourselves at home?

LYSISTRATA: *We'll* protect you.

MAGISTRATE: You?

LYSISTRATA: Indeed we shall.

MAGISTRATE: What downright gall!

LYSISTRATA: Yes, you'll be protected even against your will.

MAGISTRATE: This is too much.

LYSISTRATA: It upsets you, does it? But it must be done.

MAGISTRATE: By Demeter, you're out of step!

LYSISTRATA: My dear sir, you have to be saved.

MAGISTRATE: But that's exactly what I want to stop.

LYSISTRATA: Which makes the issue all the more grave.

---

*Pisander was an admiral who took to politics. He played a part in setting up an oligarchy in Athens. When it collapsed he took refuge with the Spartans.

MAGISTRATE: What is it that compels you to meddle
  with war and peace?

LYSISTRATA: Let us explain.

MAGISTRATE: Do just that, or else . . .

LYSISTRATA: Then listen, but kindly restrain
  those fists of yours.

MAGISTRATE: I can't. I can't keep my hands down. I'm
  so furious.

OLD WOMAN: Then for you it'll make it all the worse.

MAGISTRATE: You can croak that malediction on yourself, old crow.

[to LYSISTRATA]

  And you, start talking now.

LYSISTRATA: Of course.
  Before today and long before then
we women went along in meek silence with everything done
by you men.
  We weren't allowed to speak back,
though you yourselves left a lot to be desired
and we knew pretty well what was going on.
  Many a time at home we heard
of some idiotic blunder you'd made
in a major political issue,
and we'd smother our anguish, put on a demure smile
  and say:
"Hubby, I wish you'd
tell me how you got on in Parliament today.
  Any change in the notice stuck up
on the pillar about the peace?"* and Hubby would snap:

*The notice repudiating the Peace of Nicias made in 421 B.C. on
the grounds that "The Spartans have not abided by their promises."

"Stick to your job, wife, and shut your gob."
    So I did shut up.

OLD WOMAN: I wouldn't have.

MAGISTRATE: Then you'd have got a walloping.

LYSISTRATA: Exactly. So I didn't say a thing—
    at least for a time.
        But it wasn't long before you made an even sil-
            lier gaffe
and we'd say: "I'd like to hear
why you people are being so dim."
        And he'd glare and snarl:
"Stick to your embroidery, woman,
or you'll get a thick ear.
        'War is the business of men.' "*

MAGISTRATE: I'd say that's right on the ball.

LYSISTRATA: How could it be right, you nit,
    when we weren't allowed to speak at all
even when you were making a mess of things.
        Then when we heard you proclaiming in the
            streets and lanes:
"In the whole land there's not a man,"†
and someone else confirming this: "No, not one,"
we decided there and then
to take matters into our own hands
and all of us together to rescue Greece.
        What was the point of waiting a moment more?
        Which means, it's your turn now to listen to
            good advice
and to keep your mouths shut as we had to,
and if you do we'll get you out of the mire.

MAGISTRATE: You'll do what? I won't stand for such
    brass.

LYSISTRATA: Silence!

*Quoting Hector in the *Iliad*.
†Meaning, presumably, that all the menfolk were at war.

MAGISTRATE: Silence, for you?
  A confounded woman with a veil on your head?
  I'd rather be dead.
LYSISTRATA: All right, if you find my veil "not nice"
  I'll take it off and put it on your own head;
then be quiet.
OLD WOMAN: And here's a sewing basket for you too.
LYSISTRATA: [*merrily chanting and dancing*]
    Hitch up your petticoat, do.
    Card the wool and chew
    These beans, they're good for you.
    War is women's work now.
WOMEN'S LEADER: Ladies, we don't need these pitch-
    ers anymore.
  Let's discard them and go and help our friends.

ANTISTROPHE*

WOMEN'S CHORUS:
    As for me I'll dance with a passion that knows no
      ends.
    And an energy that never can tire my knees.
    Nothing is too much for me to endure
    When I'm with women with courage equal to these,
    Whose character, grace and sheer pluck
    Is matched by both feeling and wit
    Patriotic and quick.

WOMEN'S LEADER: Rise, you bristling mommies and
    grannies to the attack
  Now's not the moment to let down your guard or
    to slack.
LYSISTRATA: If honey-hearted Eros and Aphrodite of
    Cyprus
  instill our loins and bosoms with desire,
and infect our men with ramrod fits of cudgelitis,

*Answering the strophe on p. 30.

then I truly think that one day Hellas will call us
Demobilizers of War.

MAGISTRATE: How will you accomplish that?

LYSISTRATA: Well, for a start,
  by putting a stop to oafs in full armor
clonking around the agora.

OLD WOMAN: Three cheers for Aphrodite of Paphos!*

LYSISTRATA: At this very moment, armed to the teeth,
  in the vegetable stalls and pottery shops all over
    the market,
they're clanking around like dummies out of their
    minds.

MAGISTRATE: Lord above! A man's a man for all that.

LYSISTRATA: Which is laughable when you see a great
    hunk with
  a blazing Gorgon shield† shopping for sardines.

OLD WOMAN: That's the truth.
  I once saw a gorgeous long-haired fellow riding a
    stallion,
a cavalry captain,
buying porridge from an old crone
and stuffing it into his brass hat.
    Another time I saw a Thracian‡
brandishing his shield and spear like Tereus in a state§
and making the fig lady faint
while he gobbled down her ripest fruit.

---

*Another name for the island of Cyprus, near which Aphrodite was
born and rose from the sea. ("Aphros," genitive "aphroditos," is
the word for foam.)
†The head of the Gorgon Medusa writhing with snakes. The sight
of it turned people to stone. Perseus cut off her head using a mirror.
‡The Thracians, from the wilds north of the Aegean and east of
Macedon (now part of European Turkey), were viewed by the
Athenians as big, brawny, brave, and brash.
§Tereus, King of Thrace, raped Philomela, daughter of King Pandion
of Athens, and then cut out her tongue so that she could never tell.
She, however, did manage to tell by weaving the crime into a tapestry.

MAGISTRATE: But how will you women unravel the general muddle
of the present international situation?

LYSISTRATA: Dead easy.

MAGISTRATE: Really? Explain.

LYSISTRATA: [*taking a ball of wool from the* MAGISTRATE's *basket*]
It's not unlike a skein of wool in a tangle.
We hold it up like this
and carefully sort out the strands
this way and that way as we wind them onto a spindle.
That's how we'll unravel this war if you'll let us,
sending out envoys this way and that way.

MAGISTRATE: If you really imagine
that a policy based on balls of wool and spindles can settle
the present terrible crisis—you're insane.

LYSISTRATA: Oh, but I do! And if *you*
had a speck of sense you'd handle
the international situation
as we handle our tangled yarn.

MAGISTRATE: How exactly? I'm all ears.

LYSISTRATA: Think of the State as a newly shorn fleece;
so the first thing to do is to give it a bath and wash out the muck.
Then spread it out and paddle out the parasites with a stick,
and you pick out the burrs.
Next, you comb out the knots and snarls of those nasty little cliques
that tangle up the Government:
you pick them off one by one.

Then you card out the wool into a basket of
   goodwill,
unity and civic content:
   And this includes everyone:
resident aliens, friendly foreigners, and even
those in debt to the Treasury—mix them all in.
   Finally, bring together the bits and pieces of fleece
lying around that are supposed to be part
of Athens's colonies, bring them all together and
   make a tight
ball of wool, from which you weave for the People
a splendid new coat.
MAGISTRATE: Don't you think it's insufferable
   for you women to be playing around with distaffs
      and sticks
and doing not a thing for the war?
LYSISTRATA: Not a thing? You stupid old prick!
   We do more than our share—far more.
   We produce the sons, for a start,
and off we send them to fight. . . .
   On top of that,
when we are in our prime and ought to be enjoying life,
we sleep alone because of the war.
   And I'm not just talking about
us married ones . . . it pains me even more
to think of the young girls
growing into lonely spinsters in their rooms.
MAGISTRATE: Men grow old too, don't you know!
LYSISTRATA: Hell's bells! It's not the same.
   When a man comes home,
even if he's old and gray he can find a girl to marry
      in no time,
but a woman enjoys a very short-lived prime,
and once that's gone she won't be wed by anyone.

She mopes at home
full of thwarted dreams.

MAGISTRATE: But any man still able to rise to the
occasion . . .

LYSISTRATA: [*losing patience and deciding to have
some fun*]
Why don't you shut up and die?
There's a nice graveyard nearby
And you'll need a coffin it seems.
I'll bake you some funeral rolls.

[*taking off wreath and plonking it on his head*]

You might as well have these frills.

OLD WOMAN: And here are some ribbons from me.

SECOND OLD WOMAN: And from me this wreath.

LYSISTRATA: Ready? Got everything? Get on board.
Charon is calling*
And you're keeping him waiting.

MAGISTRATE: Good grief! Isn't it scandalous to treat
me like this?
I'm going to the other magistrates at once
to show myself and what I have endured.

[MAGISTRATE *leaves in high dudgeon with his servants.* LYSISTRATA *calls after him*]

LYSISTRATA: And you'll complain no doubt
That you weren't properly laid out.
Don't worry, we'll be with you soon:

*Charon was a minor but important deity who, for a fee, ferried
the souls of the dead across the rivers Acheron and Styx to the
infernal realms. The fee was a coin slipped between the lips of the
dead. He is represented as a gloomy and shabby old man.

The day after tomorrow to be exact,
And we'll complete the funeral at your tomb.

[LYSISTRATA *and the* OLD WOMEN *go into the Acropolis*]

MEN'S LEADER: No free man, you fellows, should be slumbering now.
Roll up your sleeves and confront this menace.

STROPHE

MEN'S CHORUS:

I think there's a whiff of something that cer-
tainly is
The unmistakable stink of a tyrant near
Like Hippias* was and it reduces me to an ab-
ject fear
That a group of men from Sparta is about to appear
In the house of Cleisthenes† and conjure there
A plot to set these god-awful women astir,
And make them seize the treasury and my jury
pittance,
My only remittance.

MEN'S LEADER:

Yes, it's disgraceful the way they're hectoring the
citizens,
these miserable women: frothing at the mouth
and fussing about disarmament.
Not only that, but holding forth
on the need to make peace with the men of Sparta,
who can't be trusted any more than a hungry wolf.
If I may bring to you men's

*The last Athenian tyrant, expelled in 510 B.C.; his name (based on *hippos*, "horse") suggests the equestrian position in sexual inter-course (woman on top). (Loeb)
†A formidable politician who, after the fall of Hippias, steered Ath-ens toward democracy.

attention this plot of theirs—what they are really
   after—
is tyranny. . . . All right, that's enough,
they won't tyrannize *me*.
      I'll be on the watch and camouflage my sword
in a bouquet of myrtles and go to market attired
in full armor and pose next to the statue of
   Aristogiton*
like this . . . a good position
for slamming this godforsaken old gorgon right on
the muzzle.
WOMEN'S LEADER: Come along, dear girls, on the
   double
and leave our wrappers on the ground.

[they take their jackets off]

ANTISTROPHE

WOMEN'S CHORUS:
      Citizens of Athens, we owe it to our town
      To begin by telling you something for your good;
      Which is only right, for she reared me in luxurious
         splendor.
      I was barely seven when I became an Arrephoros†
      And at ten a grinder for Demeter,‡ then later
      As a Bear I shed my yellow dress for Artemis,
      And as a slip of a girl I carried a necklace
      Of dried figs in a hamper.

---

*Aristogiton and Harmodius were the two young men who assassi-
nated Hipparchus, the brother of the tyrant Hippias. Their statues
stood in the marketplace.
†The Arrephoroi were two girls between the ages of seven and
eleven who were chosen every year to live on the Acropolis and
serve Athena-of-the-city. They helped to weave her mantle and later
carry it in the Panathenaic procession.
‡That is, they helped to grind the flour for Demeter's ritual cakes.

WOMEN'S LEADER: As you've heard, I owe my city
     some advice;
   but don't let my being a woman be a thing adverse,
or my telling you how to make conditions better
than they are at present. For that matter,
I'm an essential part of our way of life:
My donation to it is men, and it pisses me off
that you frigging creeps contribute nothing—
you've thrown away just about everything
we won in the Persian Wars, and you pay no tax,
     to boot.
          Worse, your extravagance has reduced us all to
             naught.
          Got an answer to all this? No doubt you can grunt!
          But any more lip from you and I'll clunk
you with this very solid shoe.

[*she wrenches off a shoe and threatens him with it*]

STROPHE

MEN'S CHORUS:
     Wouldn't you say that this is the height of hubris?
     And it seems to me it's not going to get any better.
     It's up to every fellow with balls to resist.
MEN'S LEADER:
     We'll take off our shirts and give off our manly smell.
     A man shouldn't be swaddled and bound like a parcel.
MEN'S CHORUS:
     Be Whitefoot* again and remember
     How once we toppled a despot.
     Those were the days we were something.
     Now to be young again, now to take wing

---

*"Whitefeet" was the nickname given to those who rose against the
tyrant Hippias ca. 511 B.C., perhaps because they wore white
sandals.

Is what our old carcass requires to slough off
  this skin.

MEN'S LEADER: If any of us men lets these women
  get so much as a toehold, there'll be no stopping them.
    They'll be building a fleet and launching ships
as fiercely as Artemisia* against us.
    And you can forget about our cavalry once they
    become equestrian.
    When it comes to riding cock-horse
nothing can match a woman: ·
she never slips off no matter how hard the ride is—
witness the Amazons† in the paintings of Mikon,‡
astride their chargers in their battles with men.
    Our duty is obvious:
grab these pests by their necks and clamp them in
  the stocks.

[*he marches threateningly toward* WOMEN'S LEADER]

ANTISTROPHE

WOMEN'S CHORUS:
    By Persephone and Demeter, if you molest us

*Artemisia, Queen of Caria in Asia Minor. Though a Greek, she fought
on the Persian side during the Persian invasion and contributed five
ships. At the battle of Salamis in 480 B.C., when pursued by an Athenian
trireme, she was blocked by two Persian ships and to get away rammed
them. Xerxes, the Great King, watching the battle from a hillside, ex-
claimed in admiration (according to Herodotus): "See how my women
have become men and my men women." He probably would have said
something else if he'd known that the rammed ships were his!
†The Amazons were a nation of female warriors who lived in the
eastern regions of Asia Minor. They cut off their right breasts in order
to more easily handle bow or javelin, hence their name, *a mazos*
("without breast"), though some say it is from *a maza* ("without cereal
food"), for they were meat eaters. Their only association with men
was to procreate girls. The boys they gave to their fathers. They were
ruled by queens and often warred with men.
‡I could not find anything about the painter Mikon.

I'll charge you like a sow that's gone berserk
And you'll run home today with your pubes
   clipped bare.

WOMEN'S LEADER:
   Off with our blouses and give forth the scent of
      our dugs.
   That'll show them that we're ready to rear.

WOMEN'S CHORUS:
   Come on, someone, attack.
   It'll be the end of garlic
   For you, and haricots verts*
   If you dare to utter a word against me, you mugs,
   I'll be the beetle that wrecks your couple of eggs.†

WOMEN'S LEADER: You fellows don't bother me in
      the least
   so long as my Lampito and my Ismenia are alive—
that wellborn Theban girl.
   You can't do a thing against
us even if you manage to contrive
another set of seven decrees;
they'll only show the loathing for you that people
   feel,
especially those next door.
   Yesterday, when I threw a party
for the girls in honor of Hecaté
and asked a girl who means a lot to me—my neighbor,

---

*Green beans, pronounced "arico vair."
†In this fable of Aesop, an eagle grossly offended a dung beetle by
catching and devouring his friend the rabbit. So the dung beetle
took to climbing up to the eagle's nest and tossing out her two eggs.
After this happened several times the eagle (the bird of Zeus) laid
her eggs in Zeus' lap, but when the dung beetle rolled a ball of
dung there Zeus sprang up and the eggs smashed. This is what the
CHORUS WOMEN imply they'll do to the twin eggs of the MEN.

a genuine Boeotian eel*—
they prevented her from coming because of some
      bloody decree.
    Oh, those decrees of yours, yuk! Yuk!
    Will you never stop passing them until
someone trips you up, lands you flat, and breaks
      your neck?

[LYSISTRATA *emerges from the Acropolis. The next
ten lines are a pastiche in mock high tragedy*]

    Dear mistress of this ruse and enterprise,
why come you from the palace with such doleful
      eyes?
LYSISTRATA: 'Tis because the feeble heart of woman
    sets me pacing because it yearns for man.
WOMEN'S LEADER: Say you that? Not surely that?
LYSISTRATA: In very truth, 'tis that.
WOMEN'S LEADER: How so? Pray tell it to your
    friends.
LYSISTRATA: 'Twere disgrace to speak it but calamity
    to keep it.
WOMEN'S LEADER: Conceal not from me whatsoever
    hurt impends.
LYSISTRATA: The issue I'll no further duck: we have
    to fuck.
WOMEN'S LEADER: Holy Zeus!
LYSISTRATA: It's no use calling Zeus,
    and in any case, the fact is thus.
    Frankly, I can't control them anymore:
they're running off every which way to their men.

---

*Lake Copais—now Limne—in Boeotia was famous for its eels.
To call someone "a genuine Boeotian eel" was calling her a first-
class person.

I caught the first trying to slip into Pan's grotto
over there.*
The next was doing her best to let herself down
with rope and pulley over the barrier.
And yesterday one of them got on to the back of
a sparrow†
and was hoping to make it to Orsilochus' house of
ill fame.
I dragged her off by the hair.
They're inventing every kind of pretext to go
home.

[FIRST WIFE *comes running from the Acropolis*]

Hey there! Where are you off to?
FIRST WIFE: I simply must return to the house.
Moths in the closet are after my Milesian woolies,
stripping them to the marrow.
LYSISTRATA: Moths be damned! Get back inside.
FIRST WIFE: I won't be long, I promise;
just let me lay them out on the bed.
LYSISTRATA: Don't you dare do any laying.
FIRST WIFE: So I'm to let my woolies be stripped?
LYSISTRATA: If necessary, yes.

[SECOND WIFE *runs out from the Acropolis*]

SECOND WIFE: Heavens above! I forgot to shuck my
flax
when I left the house.
LYSISTRATA: So you're off to shuck your flax?
Get back inside.

---

*This was the grotto in which Apollo raped Creusa and she became
the mother of Ion. The whole story is told in Euripides' play *Ion*.
†Sparrows are well known for lechery.

SECOND WIFE: By Our Lady of Light,* I'll return in
    a trice;
  all I want is a little f . . . I mean shucking.
LYSISTRATA: No, shucking is out,
  or they'll all want a little "f . . . I mean shucking."

[THIRD WIFE *runs out from the Acropolis*]

THIRD WIFE: [*with hands pressed against her abdomen*]
  Good holy Hileithya,† go slow on the baby,
I can't have it here.
LYSISTRATA: What nonsense is this?
THIRD WIFE: I'm about to deliver.
LYSISTRATA: You weren't pregnant yesterday.
THIRD WIFE: But I am today.
  Send me home to the midwife at once—
Oh, please, Lysistrata.
LYSISTRATA: [*prodding her*] That's a whopper!
  What's in there? It's hard.
THIRD WIFE: It's a boy.
LYSISTRATA: What it is is something metallic and
    hollow.
  Let's have a dekko.

[*she uncovers an enormous helmet*]

  Silly girl! . . . My word!
  You're pregnant with the helmet of Athena.
THIRD WIFE: I swear it: I really am enceinte.
LYSISTRATA: So you're doing what?
THIRD WIFE: Well, when I began
  to go into labor in the citadel here,

---

*Artemis (Roman Diana).
†The goddess of childbirth. Giving birth in shrines like the Acropolis was taboo.

I thought I could crawl into the helmet like a pigeon
and have the baby there.
LYSISTRATA: That's a tall one and it doesn't wash.
It's quite clear what you're doing.
You'll have to stay here till the helmet's
christening.*
THIRD WIFE: But I have absolutely no wish
to sleep on the Acropolis ever since
I saw the snake that guards the sanctuary.†

[FOURTH WIFE *runs out from the Acropolis*]

FOURTH WIFE: Has any of you thought of poor me,
all the long night listening
to the owls going: Toowit toowhoo?‡
LYSISTRATA: You wacky women, you miss your men,
of course you do, and they miss you:
think of the lonely and lustless nights they're
spending.
Be good girls, have patience
and bear with this a little longer,
it'll soon be ending, since
there's an oracle predicting that we'll conquer,
but only if we stick together.
Look, I have it here: the very thing.

[*she produces a scroll*]

THIRD WIFE: Gee! What's it say?
LYSISTRATA: Silence!

[*she begins to read*]

*Not really an anachronism. It is the nearest equivalent to the cere-
mony that took place on "naming day" about ten days after the
baby's birth.
†Pure invention by the THIRD WIFE. No such snake existed.
‡Colonies of owls (mainly the screech owl) lived on the Acropolis
and the owl became the emblem of Pallas Athena.

On the day the swallows muster together alone
Away from the hoopoe that chases them* away
    from the cocks,
Then all will be solved and thundering Zeus will turn
Up into down . . .

THIRD WIFE: You mean we'll be on top while it's
being done?

LYSISTRATA:

But if there's any dissension among the swallows'
    flocks
And they fly from the holy shrine in search of cocks,
All will say: "such randy birds as these we've
    never seen."

THIRD WIFE: Ye gods, that's blunt enough!

LYSISTRATA: So, dearest women,
    let us go into the Acropolis again.
    It would be such a pity to let the oracle down
just because the going's a little tough.

[*all enter the Acropolis*]

STROPHE

MEN'S CHORUS:

I'd like to tell you a tale I heard a long time ago
When I was only a lad.
Once upon a time there lived a young man by
    the name of Meilanion
Who fled to the desert to escape from having to
    woo.
He lived on a crag
And he had a dog,
And to catch hares

---

*Recalling the story of Tereus and Procne, a married couple, in
which Tereus rapes his wife's sister, Philomela, and cuts out her
tongue. The gods change Tereus into a hoopoe and Procne into
a swallow.

He constructed a noose.
His hatred was such that he never went home again:
That is, he hated women
The same way as us,
So we're as smart as Meilanion.

MEN'S LEADER: [*stepping toward* WOMEN'S LEADER]
Give us a kiss, haggy dear.
WOMEN'S LEADER: [*slapping him*]
You won't need an onion to make you cry.
MEN'S LEADER: And I'll shake a leg and let fly with
a kick.

[*he pulls up his tunic for action*]

WOMEN'S LEADER: [*pointing and giggling at his
exposure*]
My my! Not a bad forest you have down there.
MEN'S LEADER: [*breaking into song*]
Myronides* down there was also thick
And had a hairy bottom,
Phormion† too,
Which sent their enemies into a panic
Whenever they came at 'em.

ANTISTROPHE

WOMEN'S CHORUS:
I've got a tale I'd like to tell you too
To go with your Meilanion.
Once upon a time lived a footloose man called
Timon‡
With a face as prickly as a cactus, spawn of the
Furies, who

---

*An Athenian general who in 458 B.C. defeated the Corinthians
at Megara.
†Athenian general, remembered for his vigor and toughness.
‡A proverbial misanthrope who appears in several comedies.

Went his way, this Timon,
Meandering off
And holed up in the desert,
Growling and gruff,
Saying how evil men were and how much he
    took part
With women's hatred of them
And that this would never end,
But that he was fond of women.

WOMEN'S LEADER: [*advancing on* MEN'S LEADER]
    Like a clip on the jaw?
MEN'S LEADER: [*in sarcasm*] Now you're really scar-
    ing me.
WOMEN'S LEADER: [*lifting her skirt to free a leg*] Or
    would you prefer
    a good straight kick?
MEN'S LEADER: With a glimpse of your pussy?
WOMEN'S LEADER: [*singing*]
    Old though I may be
    It's not lank and thick
    It's singed and slick.

[LYSISTRATA *appears on the walls of the Acropolis*]

LYSISTRATA: [*shouting*] Hey there, women, join me on
    the double.
WIFE: [*shouting back*] What's up? Why the shouting?
LYSISTRATA: A man approaches, and in dire trouble.

[*a group of women including* MYRRHINE *crowd
around* LYSISTRATA]

He's obviously inflamed with aphrodisiac desires—

Cyprus, Cytherea, Paphos, all in one*—
I can see by the way he walks he's a truly upright man.

WIFE: Where's he now, whoever he is?

LYSISTRATA: Down by Chloe's shrine.

WIFE: Now I can see him. But who is he?

LYSISTRATA: Look hard. . . . Know who he is?

MYRRHINE: Dear God, I do! It's my husband, Cinesias.

LYSISTRATA: So you know what you have to do.
    Set him on fire with pangs of desire.
        Tantalize him to the hilt
with "at last we'll come together . . .
No no, I have to go."
        Promise him his every want
except what on the wine cup we swore we wouldn't.

MYRRHINE: I'll do just that, have no fear.

LYSISTRATA: And I won't be far . . . I'll help you to stoke up his fire.
    Now, everyone, disappear.

[*the wives move out of sight as* CINESIAS *enters with his servant Manes, who carries a baby*]

CINESIAS: [*moaning and groaning*] Ouch! Ah! Such pangs,
    I'm stretched on the rack!

LYSISTRATA: Who goes there,
    penetrating our defense line?

CINESIAS: I do.

LYSISTRATA: A man?

*Cyprus, the island near which Aphrodite was born; Cytherea, the island in the Ionian Sea that also claims that honor; Paphos, a city on Cyprus near which Aphrodite rose from the foam.

CINESIAS: [*pointing to his obvious erection*] Of course,
   a man!

LYSISTRATA: Then off with you.

CINESIAS: Who d'you think you are to order me away?

LYSISTRATA: The watch of the day.

CINESIAS: Then in the name of the gods, do fetch
   Myrrhine out here to me.

LYSISTRATA: [*mimicking*] Hark at him! "Do fetch
      Myrrhine. . . ."
   Who, pray, are you?

CINESIAS: Her husband, from the town of Screw.

LYSISTRATA: Oh, darling, how d'you do!
   Your name's well known to us and mentioned often:
it trips on your wife's tongue.
      She can't eat an apple or an egg
without murmuring: "For Cinesias."

CINESIAS: Ye gods!

LYSISTRATA: I swear by Aphrodite, yes;
   and whenever the talk turns to men
your wife pipes up and says:
"Compared to my Cinesias, the rest are nonentities."

CINESIAS: Really? Oh, do call her out.

LYSISTRATA: Well, got anything for me?

CINESIAS: Yes yes, of course: anything you want . . .
   Will this do? . . . it's all I've got.

[*he tosses her a purse*]

LYSISTRATA: Fine! I'll come down and get her for you.

CINESIAS: As quickly as you can.

[LYSISTRATA *descends from the walls and hurries off*]

   I've not had a speck of pleasure or of fun
ever since she left the house.

Coming home's sheer agony.
The place seems like a wasteland to me.
All food is tasteless too,
and of course, I'm screw-loose and randy as the
   deuce.

[MYRRHINE *appears on the walls and addresses* LY-
SISTRATA, *unseen*]

MYRRHINE: I love that man, I really do,
   but he's indifferent to my love—
don't make me go to him.
CINESIAS: Sweet little Myrrie darling, don't be dumb,
   come down here to me.
MYRRHINE: Come down there? Not on your life!
CINESIAS: You won't come down? I'm summoning
   you, Myrrhine.
MYRRHINE: You can summon me all you like but you
   don't really want me.
CINESIAS: Not want you? I'm going crazy without you.
MYRRHINE: I'm off.
CINESIAS: No, stop. Listen to the baby.

[*sotto voce as he pinches the infant*]

Come on, you brat, howl for Mommy.
BABY: Mamma, Mamma, Mamma!

[MYRRHINE *doesn't stir*]

What's come over you? Have you no feelings for
   the baby?
It's been three days since he's been washed or fed.
MYRRHINE: Has it indeed?
I feel sorry his father has such careless ways.

CINESIAS: [*peremptorily*]
Come down at once, you baggage, to your child.
Please!

MYRRHINE: What it is to be a mother! I must go down.

[*she descends from the walls*]

CINESIAS: [*to himself*] Lord, how she affects me!
She seems even younger and sexier than she was
before.
That look of disdain,
that hoity-toity glance,
that bristly grace,
make me want her even more.

[MYRRHINE *emerges from the Acropolis and takes
the baby from Manes*]

MYRRHINE: Honey, let me hug you! Mommy's little
sweet pea,
who's got such a naughty daddy.

CINESIAS: And such a naughty mommy,
who listens to silly women and makes everything so
hard for Daddy,
and for Mommy.

[*he takes a step toward her*]

MYRRHINE: Don't you dare lay a hand on me.

CINESIAS: Darling, everything in the house, your things
and mine,
is all higgledy-piggledy.

MYRRHINE: I don't care a hoot.

CINESIAS: You don't care if the chickens are pecking
apart
your precious woolies?

MYRRHINE: Not in the least.

CINESIAS: And when did we last
  celebrate Aphrodite's rites? . . . Oh, come home,
  please!
MYRRHINE: Not likely!
  Not until you men do something to stop the war.
CINESIAS: Right, you've made your point. We'll do
  just that.
MYRRHINE: Very well, once that's settled I'll come
  home;
  meanwhile I've taken an oath to stay here.
CINESIAS: Meanwhile, lie down with me for a bit.
  It's been so long.
MYRRHINE: No, thank you. But that doesn't mean my
  love's gone numb.
CINESIAS: You love me? So what's wrong? . . .
  Oh, do lie down, Myrrie darling!
MYRRHINE: Right in front of the baby? Are you
  joking?
CINESIAS: Not at all! . . . Manes, take it home.

[*Manes takes the baby and leaves*]

  So the kid's out of the way. Now will you lie down?
MYRRHINE: But where, dear one, can it be done?
CINESIAS: Where? Pan's shrine would be absolutely
  fine.
MYRRHINE: But where could I purify myself before
  going back to town?
CINESIAS: The spring of Clepsydra* would be the best
  place to wash.
MYRRHINE: But, darling, that would mean breaking
  my oath.
CINESIAS: Be that on my head. The oath's a lot of tosh.

*A spring on one of the slopes of the Acropolis.

MYRRHINE: All right. Let me go and get something to lie on.

CINESIAS: Not necessary. The ground is good enough.

MYRRHINE: So help me, Apollo, even if you were the worst man on earth
I wouldn't dream of letting you lie on the crude ground.

[*she goes into the Acropolis*]

CINESIAS: My, how she loves me! There's no doubt about that.

MYRRHINE: [*returning with a folding cot*] All set . . .
Lie down now while I undress. . . . Oh, drat it!
We need a mattress.

CINESIAS: A mattress? I'll be darned!

MYRRHINE: By Artemis, yes!
It's beastly lying on bare cords.

CINESIAS: Then, give us a kiss.

MYRRHINE: There.

CINESIAS: Yummy yummy! . . . Come back at once.

[MYRRHINE *goes into the Acropolis and returns with a mattress*]

MYRRHINE: There we are!
Just lie back and relax while I undress. . . .
Oh, Lord, you don't have a pillow!

CINESIAS: I don't need one.

MYRRHINE: But *I* do.

CINESIAS: By Heracles the Glutton,* have I got a hard-on!

---

*Heracles was reputedly endowed with a gargantuan appetite for food and sex.

MYRRHINE: [*returning with a pillow*] Head up! That's it!

Have we got everything now?

CINESIAS: You bet! . . . Come here, my little honeypot!

MYRRHINE: Just a minute while I remove my bra . . . and no reneging on your promise to end the war.

CINESIAS: Zeus strike me dead if I do!

MYRRHINE: Oh, dear, you don't have a blanket!

CINESIAS: I don't want a damned blanket. I want a screw.

MYRRHINE: [*running off*] And that's what you're going to get . . .

I'll be back in a minute.

CINESIAS: The woman'll drive me round the bend with all her bedding.

MYRRHINE: [*returning with a blanket*] Up a little.

CINESIAS: I'm up all right.

MYRRHINE: A dash of scent?

CINESIAS: Apollo, no! And I'm not kidding.

MYRRHINE: Aphrodite, yes! Whether you want it or not.

CINESIAS: Zeus above! Make her spill the bottle.

MYRRHINE: Hold out your hand and rub in a little.

CINESIAS: This stuff doesn't appeal to me at all.

It stinks of delayed action, not of sex.

MYRRHINE: Dear me, I must be bats:

this is Rhodian. I've brought the wrong bottle.

CINESIAS: It'll do, you devastating witch!

MYRRHINE: [*dashing out again*] Don't be silly!

CINESIAS: [*as she returns with a long elegant bottle*]

Blast the man who invented perfume!

MYRRHINE: Really? Here, try a little from this bottle.

CINESIAS: Thanks, but I've got a bottle of my own, so lie down

and don't go getting anything else, you bitch.

MYRRHINE: Shan't! See, I'm shedding my shoes . . .
  but, darling, don't forget—you're voting for peace.
CINESIAS: Of course.

[*she runs off again to the Acropolis*]

  Drat it, the woman's just about finished me.
  She's inflated me, then left me flat.

[*he breaks into a mournful little song*]

  Bereft of a screw, what shall I do?
  Lord, I'm through! What am I at?
  The loveliest of the lot has gone.
  My poor little cock is all forlorn.
  Things couldn't be worse.
  Hey, you pimp out there,
  Bring me a nurse.

MEN'S LEADER:
  Poor agonized soul! Poor bereft prick!
  So hoodwinked and stretched upon the rack!
  I'm full of concern for your soul, your balls,
    your gall.
  What loins or crotch could bear so much,
  So distended but suspended?
  What bad luck—deprived of a morning fuck!

CINESIAS: [*shooting a hand to his phallus*]
  Holy Zeus, another spell!

MEN'S LEADER: See what she's reduced you to,
  The abominable and beastly shrew.

CINESIAS: No, the most lovable sweetie pie.

MEN'S LEADER: Sweetie pie indeed—she's absolutely
    horrid.

CINESIAS: Yes, Zeus, great Zeus, absolutely horrid.
  Send a whirlwind, sweep her away,

Up and up like a wisp of hay.
Twirl her high into the sky
Then let her plummet to the earth headlong
On to my upstanding prong.

[*a* HERALD FROM SPARTA *arrives, a young man who like* CINESIAS *himself shows acute signs of priapism because of the boycott of sex by the women of both Athens and Sparta*]

HERALD: Where's this 'ere Athenian Senate or Parliament? I got news.
CINESIAS: [*staring at his crotch*]
And what might you be, a phallic symbol?
HERALD: I'm a 'erald, mate, from the Peloponnese.
Come about the truce.
CINESIAS: Truce? With a bayonet in your trews!
HERALD: That ain't so, by Zeus!
CINESIAS: Ain't so you're turning your back,
screening your weapon with your cloak?
Get a bit stiff from hard riding?
HERALD: 'e's off his rocker is this jerk.
CINESIAS: Got a nice hard-on, you trouser snake?
HERALD: 'aven't got bleeding nuffin. Give over babblin'.
CINESIAS: [*pointing*] Well, is that thing yours, or what?
HERALD: That there's a Spartan cipher rod.*
CINESIAS: I've got a Spartan cipher rod as well. Ain't that odd!
But let's come to the point:
how are things in Sparta?
HERALD: The 'ole bloody Peloponnese 'as arisen

*Cipher messages were written on strips of parchment wound around a rod that exactly matched the rod of the recipient, who was the only one, therefore, who could decode the message.

and all our allies 'ave erected themselves and
 we've sorta

set our 'earts on a bit o' twat.

CINESIAS: Who brought this affliction on you? Was
it Pan?*

HERALD: No. I 'ave some info it was Lampito.

All the Spartan lasses as one

joined 'er from the word go

and refused us men entrance to their pussies.

CINESIAS: And how are you getting on?

HERALD: We're 'avin a 'ard time. We walk about the
town

all 'unched up like we was carryin' lanterns in a gale.

 The women won't as much as let us touch their
  myrtle berries†

unless we make peace with the 'ole of Greece.

CINESIAS: So this crisis is caused by a worldwide female plot.

 Now I understand, so go back to Sparta as quickly
  as you can

and get them to send plenipotentiaries here to make
treaties;

I'll tell our Assembly they've got

to send some special envoys. This prong of mine is
witness number one.

HERALD: I'll scoot. Yer gumshion, man, is a bloomin'
treat.

[HERALD *and* CINESIAS *go off in different directions*]

MEN'S LEADER: No beast is so ineluctable as
  womankind,

 not even fire. No panther is so fierce.

---

*Pan, half man, half goat, was a nature god: playful, lascivious and
unpredictable. He could cause Panic. He invented the panpipe.
†The myrtle berry is small, purple, and delicious.

WOMEN'S LEADER: If that's not beyond your intelligence,
   why must you persist in fighting me, you goose,
when we could be as friend to friend?
MEN'S LEADER: Because my dislike of women knows
   no end.
WOMEN'S LEADER: Have it your own way, meanwhile
   I don't intend
   to watch you going around half naked.
   You've no idea how silly you look,
I'm coming over to help you put your shirt on again.

[*she steps toward him and does so*]

MEN'S LEADER: Thank you. That was generous of you,
   I'm flattered,
and it was ungenerous of me to take it off and lose
   my temper.
WOMEN'S LEADER: Now you look like a man once
   more and not a comic.
   And if you hadn't been so mean to me before
I'd have removed that insect from your eye.
MEN'S LEADER: So that's what's been stinging me!
   Do scoop it out and let me see.
   It's been annoying me for some time.
WOMEN'S LEADER: I'll do just that, though you're a
   difficult man.

[*she comes up to him and twists out a gnat with her
handkerchief*]

   My god, what a monster you've been harboring!
      See this? It's gargantuan!
MEN'S LEADER: Bless you for coming to my rescue.
   That thing's been excavating my eye for ages
and the well it gouges
is now overflowing with tears.

WOMEN'S LEADER: And I'll wipe them away and kiss you, you old sod.

MEN'S LEADER: No kisses, please!

WOMEN'S LEADER: I'll darn well kiss you whatever your fears.

MEN'S LEADER: Then be it on your own head.

You women are by nature such cajolers:
the old proverb didn't get it wrong:
"We can't live with the blighters
and we can't live without them."
    So let me make peace with you then:
I'll no more mishandle you, and you'll not be a shrew.
    Come, let's get together and begin our song.

[*the two* LEADERS *join hands and the two* CHORUSES *become one*]

STROPHE

CHORUS:
    Fellows, we do not want to say
    Nasty things about a citizen,
    Anything slanderous or unbidden.
    We'll do and say quite the reverse:
    You've got enough upon your plate—
    Quite enough that is adverse.
    We'd like every man and woman,
    If they could do with a penny or two,
    To let us know and plainly state
    If they'd like some minas, two or three
    (We've certainly got them on the premises),
    As well as the purses to put them in.
    And if peace erupts you needn't repay
    The money you borrowed,
    Because you never got it anyway.

ANTISTROPHE

We're getting ready to receive
Some guests from Carýstus,* they
Are gallant and good-looking men.
We have an excellent soup to give
Them, and there's sucking pig, the one
We sacrificed, so it's nice
And succulent; so come to my house
Today. . . . Get up early, bathe,
Bring the brats and come along.
No need to report to anyone,
Just head for the house and walk right in
As if you were entering your own home.
That's the way I want you to behave.
Don't hesitate.
But the door'll be bolted when you come.

[*The* SPARTAN ENVOYS *arrive with their servants. It
is clear that the sex boycott has affected them too
with acute ithyphallic problems.*]

CHORUS LEADER: Here come the envoys from Sparta,
     stooping
   with beards astraggle and wearing
what looks like a fence to confine swine, around
     their middle.
     Men from Sparta, how are you doing?
SPARTAN: Cut the twaddle.
   Yer can see very well 'ow we're doing.

[*they drop their swine guard*]

*A seaside town in south Euboea famous for its marble and its
lustful young men.

CHORUS LEADER: My word! What development!
What tension!

SPARTAN: There ain't a word for it. Best not to mention.
Just get some'un to fix up a peace at any price.

[*the* ATHENIAN ENVOYS *arrive in similar condition*]

CHORUS LEADER: And here come the Athenians, native born.
They're also covering their middle with their cloaks,
crouching like wrestlers as if they were nursing acrobatic pricks.

ATHENIAN: Can anyone tell us where Lysistrata is?
You can see the shape our men are in.

[*they open their cloaks*]

CHORUS LEADER: As I thought: the same symptoms,
the same crouching spasms . . .
Are they at their worst just before dawn?

ATHENIAN: They are. Then we're in the tenderest
condition
and there's nothing we can do
except go and fuck Cleisthenes.*

CHORUS LEADER: If I were you I'd cover up.
You don't want any herm dockers† to spot you.

SPARTAN: By them twain goddesses, chum,
that's the right step.

---

*Beardless and homosexual, frequently ridiculed for his effeminacy.
†A herm was a short rectangular pillar surmounted by a bust of the
god Hermes, with an erect phallus at its base. They were set up at
street corners, in front of houses, and on high roads, as emblems
of good luck. One night just before the Sicilian armada set sail, all
the herms in Athens were mutilated, with phalluses and heads
chopped off. The mystery of the outrage exercised the Athenians
for years with no explanation.

ATHENIAN: Hey there, Spartan, we've had a hard time!
SPARTAN: Yeah, pal, a real tense time,
  an' if them herm fellas saw us fidgeting down
    there . . .
ATHENIAN: You're right, but let's talk business:
  Why are you here?
SPARTAN: Me? I'm a peace delegate.
ATHENIAN: Good, we're the same,
  so let's get hold of Lysistrata, no one but her
can settle the peace terms between us.
SPARTAN: By them twain goddesses, yer right,
  and why not a Lysistratus too, what's in a name?

[LYSISTRATA *enters from the gates of the Acropolis*]

  No need t' ask for 'er; she must 'ave 'eard us.
CHORUS LEADER: Welcome, Lysistrata, most dauntless
    of women!
  The time has come to be pliable yet adamant,
high class yet common,
meek yet arrogant,
because the foremost men of Hellas,
dazzled by your glamor, have all come together
and unanimously submit their dissensions to your
  arbitration.
LYSISTRATA: That's not difficult if one gets them be-
    fore their anger
flares into action.
    I'll soon find out. . . . Where's Reconciliation?

[RECONCILIATION *appears in the form of a beautiful
girl, completely naked.* LYSISTRATA *addresses her.*]

  Handle the Spartans first, dear, and bring them here.
  Don't be rough or bossy with them or boorishly prod

them like our husbands handle us
but with a sweet, homely, womanly touch.
    If your Spartan won't take your hand,
lead him by his life line; then fetch
the Athenians and lead them by whatever part they
    proffer
and bring them here.

[RECONCILIATION *proceeds to assemble the* SPARTANS
and ATHENIANS]

LYSISTRATA:*
Now you Spartans come and stand this side of me,
and you Athenians this, and listen carefully.
    Yes, I am a woman but I have a mind,
and I know I'm not of mean intelligence,
I've common sense. Besides I've sat at my father's
    feet
and knelt to the Elders. My education was complete.
    Now I've got you here I'm going to give you both
the lashing that you're asking for—the two of you.
    At Olympia you go around and are not loath
to sprinkle libations like buddies from the same
    cup—
as you do at Thermopylae, Pytho, and umpteen
    places:
and yet when Greece's enemies are at our doorstep
in barbarian hordes, it's Greek men and Greek
    cities
you want to undermine. . . . That's my first point.

---

*The following passage (to the end of the speech) is couched in the
form and meter of Greek tragedy—i.e., a twelve-syllable line divided
into two sets of three, with six stresses in each line and known as
iambic trimeter.

ATHENIAN: [*with eyes on* RECONCILIATION]
　　Point indeed! Mine's bubbling and I'm dying.
LYSISTRATA:
　　And you Spartans—I'm talking to you now—do you
　　　　forget how
your Pericleidas came to us here at Athens
and crouched at our altars in his scarlet trappings,
white-faced and begging us to send a force
to rescue you from the onslaught of Messenia*
after you'd had an earthquake, and also how
Cimon went with four thousand foot soldiers and
　　　　rescued Sparta?
　　Do you really want to repay this kindness, after
such generous help, by plunging Athens in disaster?
ATHENIAN: They couldn't be more wrong, Lysistrata.
SPARTAN: [*ogling* RECONCILIATION]
　　Perishin' wrong! Spot on! Eh, but, look at that be'ind!
LYSISTRATA: [*resuming the iambic trimeter line*]
　　I'm not letting you Athenians off, need I remind
you how when you were dressed like slaves, the
　　　　Spartans in return
came in force and slew the foreign mercenaries
from Thessaly and the partisans of Hippias?†
　　Or how in that day their one concern
was to help you drive him away so you could again
be free and wear the livery of liberty like free
people instead of the tatters of slavery?
SPARTAN: [*still ogling* RECONCILIATION]
　　I ain't never seen a nattier female.
ATHENIAN: Ditto. Nor I a neater twat-hole.

---

*The inhabitants of Messenia in the Peloponnese, after the earth-
quake of 464 B.C., took the opportunity to revolt against the hegemony of Sparta.
†The Spartan king Cleomēnes helped expel the Athenian tyrant
Hippias in 510 B.C. (Loeb)

LYSISTRATA: [*as if she hasn't heard*] Well, gentlemen,
    after all
the nice things you've done for one another, must you
persist in fighting? Why can't you put an end to
such lunacy? What's wrong with peace, pray tell?
    Come on, what's blocking you?

[SPARTAN *and* ATHENIAN *finally do what they're itch-
ing to do: they sidle up to* RECONCILIATION *and start
pawing and fingering*]

SPARTAN: We're all for it if ye fellas'll just let go
    of this wee promontory.
LYSISTRATA: What wee promontory, sir?
SPARTAN: This wee Pylos gate right 'ere:*
    we'd like fur ter squeeze it and go through.
ATHENIAN: By Poseidon, no! Absolutely not!
LYSISTRATA: Come on, chum, let them have it.
ATHENIAN: Then what will we be left to sport with?
LYSISTRATA: Just ask him for a swap.
ATHENIAN: Let's think. . . . Yes, this pubis of Echi-
    nous here,
    and these buttocks of Malia with their inlet,
and the two legs of Megara—I mean the walls.
SPARTAN: Gee, fella, is that all?
    Yer askin' for most everythin'.
LYSISTRATA: Get on with you, you're not going to
    scrap
    over a pair of legs, are you?

*The Bay of Pylos in the western Peloponnese and the island of
Sphacteria that almost closes the mouth of the bay were a bone of
contention between Athens and Sparta. It was there in 425 B.C. that
the Athenians defeated the Spartans. "Literally *gate*, exploiting the
stereotype of Spartan predilection for anal intercourse with either
sex; the Athenians will opt for the vagina, and so the settlement
will be mutually satisfactory." (Loeb)

[SPARTAN *shrugs his shoulders in reluctant agreement*]

ATHENIAN: I'm stripping, ready for ploughing.

SPARTAN: Me too, damn it. I'm fertilizin'.

LYSISTRATA: Hold on, the two of you, you know you must
   ratify the treaty first,
so if you're really serious about a settling
go back and tell your allies.

ATHENIAN: Allies, dear girl, we can't delay for that.
   Surely they all want the same as us—to fuck.

SPARTAN: Spot on, by them twain gods!

ATHENIAN: And I can vouch for those horny Carystian lads.

LYSISTRATA: You've convinced me but will you just hold on
   a little longer till we women
prepare a supper for you on the Acropolis
from the ample provisions we've brought with us,
and after you two have promised to trust each other
you can each get your wife back and go home with her.

ATHENIAN: Right, the sooner the better!

SPARTAN: I'm be'ind yer, mate, don't linger.

[*Everyone leaves except the* CHORUSES. *Various servants loll about outside the Acropolis, where there is also a* PORTER.]

STROPHE

WOMEN'S CHORUS:
   Spangled designs on costly stuffs,
   Superb dresses and beautiful gowns,
   The golden jewelry I own:
   The whole lot—there's quite enough—

I'll give away to anyone
Whose daughter may be walking in
The basket ritual procession.
So allow me to urge you to take whatever you want
Of whatever you find inside my house.
There is nothing so adamantly locked you can't
Break the lock and carry away
Whatever you discover it has.
But let me say: there's not a thing for you to spy
Unless you have a better eye than I.

ANTISTROPHE

MEN'S CHORUS:

If any of you is out of bread
And has a score of slaves to feed,
Not to mention sundry brats.
In my house is flour that's
Perhaps not really up to scratch,
But a pound of the stuff is quite enough
To make a really splendid loaf.
So come to my house you stricken ones, and if
You bring your sacks to fill with flour
My houseboy Manes'll come to your help and pour
The flour out for you, but do take care:
There's something I must warn you of—
It might be better after all not to come at all:
There's a hungry watchdog in the hall.

[*It is now evening and a banquet is going on inside
the Acropolis, just as* LYSISTRATA *has promised. Two
Athenian* LOUTS *arrive and want to get in. The* POR-
TER *tries to stop them.* They carry torches.*]

---

*The text here is hopelessly muddled and it's anybody's guess as to
who is speaking. My selection makes sense, though it is difficult to
square with that of the Loeb Classics.

LOUT 1: Hey, you, open the damned door.

[*he punches the* PORTER]

Yer shoild 'ave got out of the way.

[*he stares at the* CHORUSES]

　　What are yoe nerds 'anging around for?
　　Like me to tickle yer tails with a flare?
　　A bit vulgar that? Aye,
but I will if yer insist.
LOUT 2: An' I'll give yer a 'and.
PORTER: Off with the two of yer. Git aht of it!
　or yer'll get yer long locks untressed.
　　Them Spartan delegates're coming out of their
　　　feast
'an I don't want yer to molest
them. . . . Better scram.

[*the two* LOUTS *slink away as two* ATHENIAN DELE-
GATES, *well fed and slightly sozzled, come out of
the Acropolis*]

ATHENIAN: Quite a party, what! Never seen the like.
　And those Spartans—hiccup—weren't they a delight!
　　We were in pretty good form too.
　　Oh, boy—hiccup—that vino!
SECOND ATHENIAN: Don't I know!
　When we're sober we're not at our best.
　　Know what, I'd tell our Gov'ment—hiccup—
ter make sure evry damn ambassador
is well and truly loaded.
　　Now the way things go,
we t-turn up in Sp-a-arta stone sober and stupid
an' picking for a fight.

We're not list'ning t' what they say
an' we're reading nasty things—hiccup—inter what
  they don't say.
An' we come home
wi' a pack o' nonsense as to what went on
an' dis-dis-kushuns—hiccup—riddled with contradik-
  shun.
But on this occashun
everything was handled with such—such . . . charm.
  Even when somebody began singing "Long Long
    Ago"
when he orta be singing "The Bluebells of Sparta,"
we all clapt shoutin' Encore! Encore!

[*the two Athenian* LOUTS *return and the* PORTER
rounds on them]

PORTER: Will yer not git aht of it, yer two yobs!
LOUT: Not 'arf! More of 'em 'igh-ups is comin' out.

[*The two* LOUTS *skedaddle as a group of* ATHENIAN
and SPARTAN DELEGATES, *well dined and wined,
come out of the Acropolis. They are accompanied
by a young piper carrying bagpipes.*]

SPARTAN: [*to the piper*] Mah darlin' lad, take up yer pipe
  an' I'll carol aht a jingle full o' pep
fer yous Athenians and fer us 'uns.
ATHENIAN: By all means do.
  I just love to see you people dance.

[*the piper improvises a tune as the* SPARTAN *sings
and dances*]

SPARTAN*: Memory, tell us again of when we were young,

*Here the actor should adopt the cockney pronunciation previously
used by this character.

Be our very own Muse in song:
The Muse who knows most everything,
Whether we're Athenians or Laconians.
Remember Artemisium on that day*
When we hoisted sail, we and they,
Against the armada sent from Persia.
Remember how we routed the Medes,
Leonidas our leader in the lead,
And we as savage as forest boars
Baring our tusks and foaming at the jaws
While our limbs were covered in shining sweat.
More numerous than the sands of the shores
Were the Persian hordes, and yet
Great glory was ours. So, goddess of woodlands,
    Artemis,
Killer of beasts, come to us
And seal our pact,
And keep our friendship long intact
In cordial amity so that we,
Free from disagreement and enmity,
Stop our shennanigans so foxy and so silly.
Come to us, come,
Illustrious huntress, virgin dame.

[LYSISTRATA *comes out of the Acropolis leading the
Spartan and Athenian wives*]

LYSISTRATA: Now that everything's worked out so well

---

*Artemisium was a promontory of Euboea where Artemis had a
shrine. On August 7, 480 B.C., the Greek fleet, composed mainly of
Athenian ships, inflicted heavy losses on the Persian navy, which
was further buffeted by a storm. At the same time, three hundred
Spartans led by their king, Leonidas, held up the entire Persian
army at the pass of Thermopylae for three consecutive days, fighting
to the last man till all were dead. Simonides, one of the greatest of
Greek lyric poets, composed a famous epitaph for the fallen:
    "Go tell the Spartans, you who are passing by,
    That faithful to their word here we lie."

it's time you Spartans got back your wives and you
     Athenians yours.
     So, my dears,
let each husband stand beside his woman while
each wife stands beside her husband.
     And let us celebrate this happy bond
and thank the gods with dance.
     And let us swear
never to make the same mistakes again and be so
     dense.
ATHENIANS: Bring on the dance, invite the Graces,
     Not forgetting Artemis
     And her brother the healer, gracious Apollo,
     And Bacchus, of course, all aglow
     Among his bacchantes,
     And Zeus with his bolts of fire,
     And Hera his consort—excellent lady—
     Call on every celestial power
     To witness this contract with humanity,
     Conceived by the goddess Aphrodite.
       Alalai, leap high
       With a victory cry.
       Apollo, be nigh.
     Alalai alalai alalai!
LYSISTRATA: Dear Spartans, can you match that music
     and cap it with a brand-new song?
SPARTANS: Laconian Muse from the magic
     Mountain of Tagetus, please come back
     To celebrate this pact
     And sing a hymn to the god of Amyclae,*
     And to Athena in her Spartan guise,
     And Tyndareus' stalwart sons†
     Galloping by

*Apollo.
†Castor and Pollux.

The river Erotas. . . . Hey there, hi!
Foot it featly, prance
And chant a canticle to Sparta,
Nursery of the god-directed dance
And the twinkle of feet by the river
Erotas of blossoming girls
Frolicking like fillies, tossing their curls,
Waving their wands and churning up whorls
Of dust, like maenads in their gambols,
Led by Helen, Leda's daughter,
Chaste and pure.*

UNITED CHORUS: [*the whole cast line up for the trium-
    phant exodus dance out of the theater*]
Come along now, let your fingers bind up your hair
And your feet tread as nimble and light as a deer,
With shouts of success that quicken the dance.
So, sing to Pallas, all-winning Athena—
Goddess of the Brazen House.

---

*The Spartans did not go along with the story of Helen as the
adulterous wife of Meneláus of Sparta dazzled by the good-looking
Paris. To them she was the chaste bride forcibly abducted.

THE FROGS

The Frogs was produced at the Lenaea in January 405 B.C. by Philemedes, who had previously presented two of Aristophanes' plays. It won first prize.

THEME

If one can accept that poetry is the apprehension of Being through the beauty of words, the next step is to realize that this implies reducing the seeming chaos of existence to some kind of order. The function of the poet becomes the showing of what lies behind the flux of textures that unite whatever is unique in the habits, tendencies, and vicissitudes of human behavior. Once again the poet is seen, in Percy Bysshe Shelley's memorable phrase, as the "unacknowledged legislator of the world."

In *The Frogs,* Aristophanes goes further than merely enunciating principles and examines piecemeal the tools of the poet's trade. But beyond the discussion of the intricacies of prosody, there looms the specter of what all this is used to illustrate—namely, the tragedy of the human scene, now being manifested in the decline of Athens and the decline of tragedy itself as a supreme art.

CHARACTERS

XANTHIAS, servant of Dionysus
DIONYSUS, god of nature and wine
HERACLES, deified hero
CORPSE, in the Underworld
CHARON, divine ferryman of the dead
AEACUS, doorkeeper of Hades
MAID, of Persephone
BISTROKEEPER, of street in Hades
PLATHANE, her assistant
EURIPIDES, the tragic poet
AESCHYLUS, the tragic poet
PLUTO, god of the Underworld
CHORUS, of frogs
CHORUS, of Mystery initiates (the Novices)

SILENT PARTS

DONKEY, of Dionysus, carrying Xanthias
PALLBEARERS, of the corpse
TWO MAIDS, of the bistrokeeper
SERVANTS, of Aeacus
SERVANTS, of Pluto
ARCHER POLICEMEN: DITYLAS (Camelface)
                  PARDOCAS (Wet-blanketface)
                  SCEBYLAS (Shitface)

THE STORY

Aeschylus, Sophocles, and Euripides are all dead, the latter two quite recently, and there are no more good poets or good theater; so Dionysus, patron of the stage, decides to go down to Hades with his servant Xanthias (mounted on a donkey) and bring back a great poet. Once there, after a journey full of diversion, they can't decide whether to bring back Aeschylus or Euripides and become involved in a detailed discussion of the nature of the poetic art. But it is not only the plight of poetry and drama that needs to be redressed but the plight of Athens itself. Was it not high time that the war with Sparta was brought to an end and that hawkish demagogues like Cleophon were removed and more responsible and better educated leaders were elected?

OBSERVATIONS

It might be wondered why Dionysus and Xanthias debate bringing back Aeschylus or Euripides from Hades, but not Sophocles. The answer is not simply that Aeschylus and Euripides are easier to parody but that Sophocles was still alive when the play was first written. He died in 406 B.C., when the acting draft of *The Frogs* was ready for production. There wasn't time to write a whole new draft incorporating Sophocles in the lengthy discussions on the art of poetry; the best Aristophanes could do was to insert a few references.

The Athenian audience that thronged to the Lenaea on that winter morning of 405 B.C. must have been in dire need both of distraction from the deplorable plight Athens found herself in and of being bluntly told a few hard truths. As to the first, matters could hardly have been worse. The Spartan army had devastated much of Attica, commandeering cattle, destroying crops, and cutting down the sacred olive trees. The citizens, were it not for the Athenian fleet, were in danger of starvation. Unfortunately, that fleet—though victorious in the recent, costly engagement off Arginusae*—was in no state to meet a counteroffensive that Sparta, backed by the Persians, was preparing for the spring. The heavy losses that the fleet had suffered, both in the battle and in the storm that followed, needed to be made good and a rigorous program of shipbuilding begun. But where was the money to come from? The treasury was empty and the sacred objects of the temple had been melted down to provide coinage.

On top of all this, the one man who could help Athens by his advice and diplomacy, the one man who understood the needs of the navy—for since 411 B.C. he had been in charge of it—the aristocratic and versatile Alcibiades, was not to be had. The shoddy treatment he'd received from the Assembly had made him wash his hands of Athens and tuck himself away in his stronghold on the Hellespont, where he was parleying with the Persians.

It is not surprising, therefore, that one of the hard truths that Aristophanes was to tell the Athenian people in the parabasis† of *Frogs* was that they had chosen as their leaders not the best men in the state but the worst. There had been a chance of peace after the victory at Arginusae and the Spartans had offered

*Three small islands in the northeast of the Aegean off the coast of Lesbos.
†That part of a comedy where the author speaks directly to the audience in his own person or through the Chorus.

honorable terms, but the Assembly was persuaded by the right-wing hothead Cleophon to turn the offer down.

What remains to be said about this remarkable play is that, given the range and seriousness of the discussions on poetry and the place of the poet in society, it becomes obvious that the Athenian people from high to low enjoyed an exceptional degree of literacy. They knew their Homer as we know our Bible and they could pick up on any reference from their Classics.

TIME AND SETTING

It is early afternoon and DIONYSUS, with his servant XANTHIAS, is seen walking down a street in Athens. DIONYSUS is disguised as HERACLES, a most incongruous camouflage, HERACLES being the supermacho male of all time and DIONYSUS being notably endowed with much of the sensitivity of a female. Over one shoulder he has draped the lionskin of HERACLES—which partly hides the somewhat epicene yellow of his smock—and he carries (with some difficulty) HERACLES' giant cudgel. XANTHIAS rides a donkey laden with baggage and he holds a pole in one hand from which dangles a bag with their provisions. They halt for a breather outside the house of HERACLES.

XANTHIAS: Hey, boss, like me to perk things up a bit
  with one of those corny cracks
that always gets the audience laughing?
DIONYSUS: Go ahead if you must,
  so long as it's not: "I'm in a jam."
    It's so old hat it sucks.

XANTHIAS: Then want a real gem?

DIONYSUS: So long as it's not: "Squashed as I am."

XANTHIAS: This one, then, and you'll be rolling?

DIONYSUS: Out with it, but it had better not be . . .

XANTHIAS: Be what?

DIONYSUS: About your having to shift your pack and
have a crap.

XANTHIAS: What the heck! I can say, surely,
that if somebody doesn't come and help,
my bottom's going to let out a yelp.

DIONYSUS: I'll thank you to keep that until I'm ready
to spew.

XANTHIAS: It's a bit tough, don't you think, to have to
carry all this stuff
and not be allowed to do what Phrynichus does
and all the others too—like Lycis and Ameipsias?*
They all tote bags in their comedies.

DIONYSUS: Well, just don't go on about it.
Whenever I see that silly cliché trotted out
I'm more than twelve months older when I leave
the theater.

XANTHIAS: Some neck mine must be—and you can
multiply by three—
if it's saddled by a choker
and I'm not even allowed to make a crack.

DIONYSUS: The nerve! What a pampered brat!
Here am I, Dionysus, son of Tipple, plodding along
on foot
so *he* won't get tired or have to carry.

XANTHIAS: And aren't I carrying?

DIONYSUS: What, carrying just sitting?

XANTHIAS: I'll have you know I *am* carrying something.

*Phrynichus, Lycis, and Ameipsias were fellow competitors with Ar-
istophanes. Phrynichus won second prize with his *Muses*.

DIONYSUS: Really?

XANTHIAS: And mighty heavy.

DIONYSUS: So it's not the donkey that's doing the carrying?

XANTHIAS: The donkey's not exactly carrying what I'm loaded with.

DIONYSUS: How can you be loaded with anything when someone else is carrying everything?

XANTHIAS: All I know is that this shoulder of mine sorely bears the brunt.

DIONYSUS: All right, since you say the donkey's no help to you, aren't
you going to pick him up and take your turn at helping *him*?

XANTHIAS: God, how I wish I'd been in that battle at sea,
then I'd be able to say to you—Scram!

DIONYSUS: Get down, prodigy!
I've plodded along and we've arrived at our first stop.

[*They halt outside the house of* HERACLES. DIONYSUS *knocks with his club.*]

Hi there, boy! Open up, boy!

HERACLES: [*as he comes out*] Who on earth's battering down my front door?
Some bleeding centaur?*

[*trying not to laugh at first sight of* DIONYSUS *in his getup*]

---

*The centaurs were a race of creatures living in the wilds of Thessaly, half man and half horse. HERACLES had numerous encounters with them.

My goodness, what's this creature?

DIONYSUS: [to XANTHIAS] Laddie?

XANTHIAS: What?

DIONYSUS: Didn't you notice?

XANTHIAS: Notice what?

DIONYSUS: The shock I gave him.

XANTHIAS: Yes, the shock of seeing you'd gone off your rocker.

HERACLES: [staring at DIONYSUS and shaking with laughter]

Sorry, can't stop, though I'm biting my lip in two!

DIONYSUS: Come, my fine fellow, I want a word with you.

HERACLES: [still convulsed] I simply . . . can't . . . gag this laughter. . . .

It's that lionskin . . . atop . . . that crocus yellow . . .
frock . . . and a cudgel married to . . . girlie booties!

What's the big idea?

What on earth have you been up to?

DIONYSUS: I've been on board with Cleisthenes.*

HERACLES: See any action?

DIONYSUS: Sure did. Sank several enemy ships—twelve or thirteen.

HERACLES: The two of you?

DIONYSUS: Apollo's my witness, yes!

XANTHIAS: [out of nowhere] And then I awoke.

DIONYSUS: You see, I was on deck
    reading *Andromeda*,† when I was struck
with an overwhelming urge; I can't tell you how strong.

---

*A public figure mocked for his effeminacy. DIONYSUS' remark is probably a euphemism for "I buggered him."
†Another lost play of Euripides, produced in 412 B.C.

HERACLES: An urge? How overwhelming?

DIONYSUS: As big as Moton*—really tiny.

HERACLES: For a woman?

DIONYSUS: No.

HERACLES: For a laddie?

DIONYSUS: No such thing!

HERACLES: For a man?

DIONYSUS: Boy oh boy!

HERACLES: So you came . . . with Cleisthenes? Ho ho ho!

DIONYSUS: O brother, you're making fun of me,
and I'm in a real mess.
That's how strong my passion is.

HERACLES: Passion for what, kid brother?

DIONYSUS: I don't have words for it exactly,
but let me give you some idea by analogy.
Have you ever had a sudden craving for bean soup?

HERACLES: Good heavens yes, constantly!

DIONYSUS: Do I make myself clear, or do I need to recoup?

HERACLES: No, you're quite clear. I have no problem with the bean soup.

DIONYSUS: My point is, that's the way I'm craving for Euripides.

HERACLES: Though he's a goner?†

DIONYSUS: Maybe, but nothing on earth will stop me chasing after him.

HERACLES: What, down to Hades?

DIONYSUS: Absolutely, and if necessary even lower.

HERACLES: What are you after?

DIONYSUS: I need a proficient poet,

---

*A famous actor, remarkable for his huge size.
†Euripides had died only the year before, at the court of King Archelaus of Macedon. Sophacles, in his nineties, brought on his choruses in mourning. He died himself the next year.

for "the good are gone and the present ones are
   dim."*

HERACLES: What d'you mean? Isn't Iophon alive?†

DIONYSUS: Yes, he's the only consolation; if it is a
   consolation,
   I'm not quite sure.

HERACLES: If you must have a candidate for
   resurrection,
   why not Sophocles? He's superior to Euripides.

DIONYSUS: Because I want to give young Iophon a
   chance to prove
   himself on his own without his dad, Sophocles.
      Besides, Euripides is a bit of a rascal
and could probably help us to pull off some dirty work
whereas Sophocles was always a gentleman here up
   above
and must be a gentleman down below.

HERACLES: Oh! . . . Then Agathon?‡

DIONYSUS: Gone! Deserted me. A fine poet and a
   real pal.

HERACLES: Gone where, the poor jerk?

DIONYSUS: Gone to install
   himself among the happy ones.§

HERACLES: And Xenocles?‖

DIONYSUS: Less said the better!

---

*Fragment from Euripides' lost *Oeneus*.
†A son of Sophocles and a successful playwright.
‡Agathon, victorious in his debut in 416 B.C. (commemorated in
Plato's *Symposium*) and famous both for his innovative style and
his personal beauty, had left Athens with his lover Pausanias for
the court of Archelaus of Macedon around 408 B.C. He is portrayed
in *Women at the Thesmophoria*. (Loeb)
§At the court of King Archelaus.
‖A son of Carcinus who defeated Euripides' Trojan trilogy in 415
B.C. (Loeb)

HERACLES: And that goes for Pythangelus.*

XANTHIAS: What about poor me,
  with my shoulder being worn to the bone?

HERACLES: [*ignoring the remark*]
  But don't we have a whole horde of babies today
churning out tragedies and out-babbling Euripides
  by the mile?

DIONYSUS: They're nonentities, all,
  like swallows twittering away
and murdering their art; and though they have the gall
to wangle themselves a Chorus,†
after they've pissed all over Tragedy they're never
      heard of again.
      Meanwhile, you can hunt for a poet of con-
      sequence,
someone capable of a memorable line,
and you won't find a single one.

HERACLES: A poet of consequence?

DIONYSUS: Yes, consequence in that he can invent
  a striking phrase, like "Ether, the bedroom of Zeus,"
or "the footstep of Time," or "a heart that won't
go along with what the tongue is willing to swear."‡

HERACLES: You like such piffle?

DIONYSUS: I'm crazy about it.

HERACLES: You know as well as I do it's pure baloney.

DIONYSUS: "My mind is my own care. Mind your
  own affair."

HERACLES: No, seriously, it's utter twaddle.

---

*Unknown.
†To be given a Chorus meant that a wealthy patron had undertaken
to fund a production.
‡A paraphrase of the famous line (612) in Euripides' *Hippolytus*:
"It was my tongue that swore, my heart remained aloof." The other
quotations are also from Euripides.

DIONYSUS: Stick to teaching me how to be greedy.*

XANTHIAS: But about me—not a syllable.

DIONYSUS: [the remark is again ignored]
   Now the reason for the outfit I wear,
copying yours, is that I'm going to have to confront
   Cerberus,†
like you did, and I need a few tips.
      Also, do you have any good contacts down there?
      And I'd like to know about ports, towns, brothels,
         bakeries,
restrooms, roads, where to get a drink, landladies,
and lodgings with the fewest creepy-crawlies.

XANTHIAS: But what about me? Not a word!

HERACLES: Don't tell me you've the nerve to go there
   too, you poor kid?

DIONYSUS: Never mind that, just tell me how to get
   there:
   the quickest route down to Hades.
      And I don't want one that's too muggy or too
         chilly.

HERACLES: Well now, let me see . . . hm . . . What
   should I recommend first?
   There's one past the Rope and Gallows, where you
      could hang out.

DIONYSUS: And strangle. . . . Not that!

HERACLES: Then there's a shortcut,
   paved by suicides.

DIONYSUS: Hemlock addicts?

HERACLES: I'm afraid so!

DIONYSUS: That's too upsetting. I can feel the chill:
   turns shanks into blocks of ice.

HERACLES: You might prefer a speedier route—all
   downhill.

*Heracles was famous for his gargantuan appetite.
†The three-headed dog that guarded the entrance to Hades.

DIONYSUS: Not so nice if you don't freewheel.

HERACLES: Oh! . . . But you could take a stroll
through the potteries.

DIONYSUS: What for?

HERACLES: To climb the tower there, the high one.

DIONYSUS: Then what?

HERACLES: Watch the torch race start,
and at the words "Ready, set, go" you go too.

DIONYSUS: Where?

HERACLES: Down.

DIONYSUS: I'd rather not. . . . It would be a waste
of brain.

HERACLES: So, how will you go?

DIONYSUS: The same way you went.

HERACLES: A long trip by water.
First you come to a huge lake—quite bottomless.

DIONYSUS: How do I get across?

HERACLES: You'll be ferried across by an ancient tar
in a tiny bark the size of this—no bigger.
Two obols is the fare.

DIONYSUS: My goodness, obols everywhere!
How did these two get down there?

HERACLES: Brought there by Theseus. . . .*
After that you come to an arena
horribly alive with snakes and beasts—really beastly!

DIONYSUS: Don't try to scare me off. You won't
succeed.

HERACLES: You'll run into a mass of mud and a river
of excreta
in which you'll see quite a lot of people flounder:
those who wronged a stranger,

*An early legendary king of Athens, involved in any number of
heroic exploits. He went down to Hades to rescue Persephone,
whom Pluto had abducted while she was picking flowers in the
meadows of Enna in Sicily.

those who screwed a comely lad out of his fee or
    lashed out at his mother,
or socked his father in the jaw,
or anyone who was a perjurer
or copied out a speech by Morsimus.*

DIONYSUS: And you should put on the list too
    anyone who has learnt that stupid war dance by
        Cinesias.†

HERACLES: Then the soft airs of the flute will breathe
        about you
    and sunbeams play as beautiful as ours
amid myrtle groves where happy bands
of men and women throng to the sound of clapping
    hands.

DIONYSUS: And who are they?

HERACLES: The Mystery novices.

XANTHIAS: And I'm the damn donkey toting mysteries,
    but I've had enough. I'm not going to play.

[he dumps the baggage off his back]

HERACLES: [ignoring him] They'll tell you all you need
    to know;
    in fact they live on the way you have to go
right outside the entrance to Pluto's house.
        So good-bye, brother, and best of luck!

*A playwright despised by Aristophanes. He is similarly ridiculed
in Knights and Peace.
†A dance in full armor.
    Cinesias was a contemporary of Aristophanes and came from
Thebes. He was a dithyrambic poet, the dithyramb being a pas-
sionate type of choral lyric dedicated to Dionysus. The word possibly derives from Thriambus (another name for Dionysus, also
meaning triumphant) and di, meaning twice. Aristophanes elsewhere makes fun of Cinesias for his wispy physique and his "unor-
thodox" music.

[HERACLES *goes into the house*]

DIONYSUS: [*calling after him*] And to you too.
[*to* XANTHIAS] Pick up that luggage, you louse.
XANTHIAS: Just a tick . . . I've just put it down.
DIONYSUS: Just make it quick.
XANTHIAS: Have a heart, boss. Hire someone else.

[*he sees a procession of mourners carrying corpses*]

Why not one of those?
They're heading in the same direction.
DIONYSUS: Not so easy to get hold of one.
XANTHIAS: Very well, take me.
DIONYSUS: I will.

[*a cortege passes with a corpse laid out on a bier*]

DIONYSUS: Look, here comes a body being taken away.

[*he approaches the bier*]

Hey you, corpse, I mean. . . . Say, stiff,
how'd you like to cart some bags to Hades?
CORPSE: [*sitting up*] How many?
DIONYSUS: This lot—see?
CORPSE: Three drachmas, I'd say.
DIONYSUS: Far too much.
CORPSE: Bearers, move on.
DIONYSUS: Wait a minute, corpsy, I'm sure we can reach
a sum within reason.
CORPSE: Two drachmas down, or go to blazes.
DIONYSUS: Here's one and a half.
CORPSE: I'd sooner come to life.

[CORPSE *flops back on the bier and is carried away*]

XANTHIAS: Bloody cheek, the creep!
Good riddance! I'll do it.
DIONYSUS: Good of you—real nice!
Let's proceed to the skiff.

[*They move on, and in the distance* CHARON *is visible handling his boat. They walk toward him and can just hear him.*]

CHARON: Whoa there! Make her secure.
DIONYSUS: [*gazing into the horizon*] What's over there?
XANTHIAS: A lake, boss.
DIONYSUS: Yes, of course.
It's the lake he told us of, and there's the dinghy.
XANTHIAS: Holy Poseidon, and there's Charon.
DIONYSUS: [*drawing up to him*] How do you do, Charon?
XANTHIAS: Hi there, Charon.
DIONYSUS and XANTHIAS: [*together, shouting*] Charon, good day to you.
CHARON: [*ignoring them*] Anybody for Amnesia or Peacehaven?
Anybody for the Savannahs of Oblivion?
Step this way if you want to see the famous painting of Oeneus*
down there plaiting ropes for 'is donkey,
or the spot where 'eracles grappled with Cerberus.
DIONYSUS: I do.
CHARON: Come along then, on board.
DIONYSUS: Where to?
CHARON: 'ell.

*The painting was by Polignotus, to be seen at Delphi.

DIONYSUS: Good Lord!

CHARON: On board if you want to: for you it's special.

DIONYSUS: [*to* XANTHIAS] On board, kid.

CHARON: I'm not taking 'im.
No slaves unless they fought at Arginusae.*

XANTHIAS: Would have, but had eye trouble.

CHARON: Yer'll 'ave ter go round the lake, m'boy, and
on the double.

XANTHIAS: Where shall I meet you then?

CHARON: By Rotting Rock and the Rest in Peace 'otel.

DIONYSUS: Got it?

XANTHIAS: Sure do, worse luck!
Ever since leaving the house it's not been my day.

[XANTHIAS *meanders off into the shadows*]

CHARON: [*as* DIONYSUS *gets into the boat*] Sit 'ere by
the oar.
'urry up; any more for the trip?
'ey you, what yer doing?

DIONYSUS: What me? Just what you told me to:
sitting by the oar.

CHARON: Not *on* the oar, fat'ead, 'ere.

DIONYSUS: Fine.

CHARON: Now open yer 'ands and stretch out yer arms.

DIONYSUS: Done.

CHARON: Not like that, dummy.
Brace yer feet against the board and row like 'ell.

DIONYSUS: All very well,
but what do you expect? I'm no sailor,
I'm from terra firma, I'm not a rower.

CHARON: 'ain't nothing to it. And once yer start rowing
yer'll 'ear beautiful singing.

*The Athenian naval victory off the isles of Arginusae, after which
any of the crewmen who were slaves were given their freedom.

DIONYSUS: Singing?

CHARON: Yeah, frogswan songs—real spellbinding.

[as the boat begins to move off the FROG CHORUS is heard from afar]

DIONYSUS: Why, it's in time with my rowing!

CHARON: Yeah: in . . . out, in . . . out . . . in . . . out.

[The FROG CHORUS has now entered. They follow the boat leaping and swimming.]

CHORUS: Brekekekex koax koax
    Brekekekex koax koax
    Of lake and stream we are the brats
    And this is the music we chatter that's
    In tune with the fifes. It is our song.
    It's beautiful, koax koax.
    We sang it once for Zeus's son
    Dionysus in the bogs
    On the Festival of the Fen.*
      That was when
    Revelers rollicked home befogged
    Through the precincts of our shrine.
    Brekekekex koax koax.

DIONYSUS: My poor bottom's getting worn.
    Koax to you, koax koax.

FROGS: Brekekekax koax koax.

DIONYSUS: For you people of course it lacks
    Any importance—koax koax.

FROGS: Brekekekax koax koax.

DIONYSUS: Damn you and your ceaseless croaks!

*This was a three days' Feast of Flowers in honor of Bacchus-of-the-Marshes held between the end of February and beginning of March. Heavy drinking was one of its attractions.

All you amount to is koax.
FROGS: As you say, you fussy old man.
    Meanwhile we're loved by the lyre-playing Muses
    And cherished by reed-piping goat-footed Pan.
    And the harp of Apollo also seduces
    Us in thanks for the reeds which we coax
    To grow in the lake, and these he uses
    To wrap round his lyre. Brekekekex
    Koax koax.
DIONYSUS: And I've got blisters on my arse
    My bottom's bleeding till it soaks.
    Don't be surprised if up it pokes
    Uttering this sodding curse.
FROGS: Brekekekex koax koax!
DIONYSUS: I'll thank you melody-making frogs to
    stop it.
FROGS: Not a bit of it, we're all set
    To rasp out our lungs when the sun shines
    And we frolic and leap in the sedgy reeds
    Drowning the water with our songs.
    Or on the days when Zeus's rain
    Is pattering down and we are sheltering
    Under the water, we are spattering
    Our musical jewels deep in the wet.
DIONYSUS and FROGS: Brekekekex koax koax.
DIONYSUS: I've caught the disease from you.
FROGS: Not a good idea.
DIONYSUS: Not as bad as what
    This rowing's doing to my rear.
FROGS: Brekekekex koax koax.
DIONYSUS: Koax away, I don't care.
FROGS: Have no fear,
    We'll koax all day
    Until we blow
    Our lungs asunder.

DIONYSUS and FROGS: Brekekekex koax koax.

DIONYSUS: You're not going to beat me in this.

FROGS: And you'll never never beat us.

DIONYSUS: You'll never never beat me
  And if necessary
  I'll brekekekex all day.
  Brekekekex koax koax.

[*the* FROGS *retire*]

DIONYSUS: I knew I'd out-koax you out of the way.

CHARON: [*bringing his boat alongside the jetty as he
  and* DIONYSUS *arrive in the port of Hades*]
  Whoa there, 'ave a care, use your oar . . .
  Now give me the fare.

DIONYSUS: Two obols, here you are.
  Xanthias, where's Xanthias? Xan . . . thi . . . as!

XANTHIAS: [*calling from the shadows*] Yoho . . . o!

DIONYSUS: I'm over here.

XANTHIAS: [*appearing and looking a little distraught*]
  Gee, boss!

DIONYSUS: How did it go?

XANTHIAS: Blackness and mire.

DIONYSUS: But did you catch a glimpse
  of those hooligans and perjurers he warned us of?

XANTHIAS: No, did you?

DIONYSUS: [*looking straight at the audience*] I certainly did,
  and I can see them right now.
  What's the best thing to do?

XANTHIAS: The best thing, guv? Beat it from here.
  This is the haunt of those monsters he told us of.

DIONYSUS: He'll be sorry he did.
  He is trying to fool us, the fraud, and make me afraid.
  He knows how fierce I am and he's jealous.
  He's very touchy is Heracles about his prowess.

I'd give anything to run into a dragon or something right now
and stamp a real triumph on this enterprise.

XANTHIAS: [*smirking*] So you would, boss. . . . Hey,
what's that noise?

DIONYSUS: [*nervously*] Where? Where?

XANTHIAS: Right behind you.

DIONYSUS: Get in front of me.

XANTHIAS: No, it's in front.

DIONYSUS: Get behind me.

XANTHIAS: Oh, brother, what a monster!

DIONYSUS: What s-sort of monster?

XANTHIAS: Horrible. It changes all the time . . . a
cow . . . no, a mule,
now it's a girl—quite beautiful!

DIONYSUS: Where? I'll affront her.

XANTHIAS: Wait a minute: she's no girl, she's a bitch.

DIONYSUS: [*shaking*] Must be Em . . . p-p-pusa.*

XANTHIAS: Her whole face blazes like a beacon.

DIONYSUS: Is one of her legs copper?

XANTHIAS: It is, by Poseidon! The other one cow dung,
I reckon.

DIONYSUS: W-where can I f-fly to?

XANTHIAS: Me too.

DIONYSUS: [*turning to the priest of* DIONYSUS *in the
audience, who was always honored with a front seat*]
Rescue me, reverend sir, so I can come to your
celebrations after.†

XANTHIAS: Lord Heracles, we're dished.‡

DIONYSUS: Don't use that name, boy, don't call me that.

XANTHIAS: Well then, Dionysus.

DIONYSUS: That's even worse.

*A legendary bogie.
†Aristophanes is throwing out a hint that he expects first prize.
‡Dionysus is still dressed as Heracles.

XANTHIAS: [*pretending to see something*]
   You there, Empusa, go and get pissed!
      Come over here, boss.

DIONYSUS: What is it?

XANTHIAS: Cheer up! Everything'll be all right
   and we can pronounce with Hegelochus:
"After the storm I can see the tom."*
      Empusa's hopped it.

DIONYSUS: Are you sure?

XANTHIAS: Zeus be my witness.

DIONYSUS: Swear it.

XANTHIAS: I do, by Zeus!

DIONYSUS: Once more.

XANTHIAS: By Zeus, on my heart!

DIONYSUS: You know, she made me go quite white.

XANTHIAS: [*pointing at the priest*] And him there,
   flaming red. In empathy of course.†

DIONYSUS: I wonder where these provocations come
         from,
   which of the gods is to blame: Ether, Zeus's bed-
         room,
or the Footsteps of Time?

XANTHIAS: Shh.

DIONYSUS: What now?

XANTHIAS: That sound?

DIONYSUS: What sound?

XANTHIAS: Flutes.

DIONYSUS: You're right. [*sniffing*]

---

*A play on the word γαλήνη (galēnē), meaning *calm* and γαλῆ
(galē) meaning *tom cat*. Playing the lead in Euripides' *Orestes,* the
actor Hegelochus made the famous slip.

†A line that even the splendid Loeb translation gets wrong, though
it is clear enough in the Greek if one realizes that it is a friendly
below-the-belt punch at the august priest of DIONYSUS sitting in the
front row, who, the Scholiast tells us, was noted for his (appropri-
ately) rubicund complexion.

And I can smell a hint of mystical torches in the air.
Let's listen and crouch down here.
CHORUS: [*from afar*] Iacchus! O Iacchus!*
XANTHIAS: I know what it is, guv:
the Mystery novices he told us of.
They're gamboling away happily somewhere near.
Listen; they're chanting that hymn by Diagoras.†
DIONYSUS: I think you're right.
Mum's the word until we're sure.

[*The men and women of the* CHORUS *of novices
enter. They are raggedly dressed and carry torches.*]

STROPHE

MEN: O Iacchus, wonderful one in your stately hall,
Iacchus, Iacchus!
Come to this meadow, enjoy our flutter,
Come with your pious followers, all
Who have crowned your forehead with a vigor-
ous coil
Of exuberant myrtle as they pepper
The earth with a stimulant step
Wildly ebullient
Worshipping merrily,
In the way the Graces themselves made hip,
For these our novices pure and reverent.

XANTHIAS: O wonderful daughter of Demeter,‡
what a scrumptious whiff of pork is in the air!
DIONYSUS: If you'll just keep your muzzle shut
you might just get some sausage meat.

---

*Another name for Bacchus.
†A notorious atheist who was outlawed from Athens in 416 B.C.
‡Persephone.

ANTISTROPHE

WOMEN: Light the flares and flourish them in your hands.
  Iacchus, Iacchus,
  Dazzling star of our ritual night.
  Look, the meadow—it's on fire
  And knobbly old knees frisk about
  Of men oblivious of care
  And the long leviathan of years
  As they adore.
  Let the flames and the light
  Usher our dances of the young
  Through the floodlit meads, O blessed one.

[*The dancing goes on for a while until the smell of cooking entices everyone to take their places for the feast. The two* LEADERS *then give advice to the novices.*]

MEN'S LEADER: To make it explicit we're singling out
                for dismissal the following,
  Who'll not take part in any of our dancing:
                those who ignore
  Our jurisdiction or go in for
                downright obscenity,
  Or who have never been present
                at the ritual dances
  Of the excellent Muses, nor
                ever been introduced
  To the Bacchic rites so admirably
                described by Cratinus,*
  Or are hoping to see this reduced
                to the silliest slapstick,

---

*Cratinus was an older contemporary and rival of Aristophanes. He died at the age of ninety-six. He won the prize for comedy nine times, and in 423 B.C. (the year he died) defeated Aristophanes' *Clouds* with his *The Bottle* (which incidentally he was fond of).

Or those who do nothing to ease
    some factional split
And foster attitudes of peace
    among all folk
But instead in hope of gain
    add fuel to fire;

WOMEN'S LEADER: Or a minister who's a traitor
    to his hard-pressed city,
And is willing to sell out
    a fortress or a navy;

MEN'S LEADER: Or a bloody tax collector
    like Thorycion*
Who is busy cheating Customs
    by shipping items
From Aegina such as paddles and oars,
    flax and tar
To Epidaurus; or those who are
    financing
The fleet of our enemies, or anyone
    defecating
On the offerings to Hecate
    during the
Dithyrambic songs and dances.

WOMEN'S LEADER: Or a politician who
    chews off chunks
Of a poet's profit just
    because the poet
Debunks him in a comedy
    during the holy
Dionysian rituals.

MEN'S LEADER: To these we shout,
proclaiming again and again and again,
    yes, three times:

*Thorycion was a tax collector.

Keep away from the dance and songs
of our novices.

[*turning to the* CHORUS]

So we look to you to arouse
the revel and song
Of this festival that lasts
all night long.

STROPHE

MEN: Let everyone now proceed
Into the blossomy lap of the mead
Joking away and pounding the ground
And gamboling
And making fun of everything
After a famous breakfasting.

ANTISTROPHE

WOMEN: Foot it featly and extoll
The goddess Athena all the while
With full-throated chanting, she'll
Make doubly sure
Of protecting our land for ages more
Whatever Thorycion has in store.*

MEN'S LEADER: Now let us jubilate in a song of a different manner
and celebrate the queen of the bounteous harvest,
the goddess Demeter.

STROPHE

MEN: Lady Demeter, queen of the wholesome
Rites of religion, stand beside us

*Using the island of Aegina as his base (conveniently midway be-
tween Attica and Sparta), Thorycion was plying an illicit and traitor-
ous trade with the Spartans.

And keep your choruses from harm
So we can frolic and dance regardless
Of what the day offers to come.

ANTISTROPHE

WOMEN: I hope you'll prompt us with many a jest
And many a serving of serious stuff
So we can frolic and be at our best
Throughout the duration of this feast
And finish the festival with a wreath.*

MEN'S LEADER: Hold on a sec:
  in your call to song you've got to include the
    god of youth:
he's our dancing mate and on our staff.

STROPHE

WOMEN: Illustrious Bacchus, musical genius
Of songs for the feast days, join our parade
As we march to the goddess,
And deign, we pray, to give us an inkling
Of how you cover the ground with such speed.†
Escort us, Bacchus, lover of dancers, on our way.

ANTISTROPHE

MEN: For you were the one who decreed while
    laughing
That my sandals be torn and my garb be worn‡
And money be saved.

*That is, with first prize.
†About twelve miles from Athens to the Mystery precincts of
Eleusis.
‡The wearing of old clothes by the initiates was part of the ritual
and, because of the impoverished state of Athens, most appropriate.
It had even proved impossible to find anyone who could afford
single-handedly to produce *The Frogs* at the City Dionysia, so two
producers were assigned.

And so you arranged there'd be no fee
For us to go frisking when we go dancing
As you escort us, Bacchus, lover of dancers, on
   our way.

EPODE

MEN'S LEADER: A moment ago I caught a glimpse
Of a mademoiselle ready for fun.
Her dress was torn and through a chink
The bonniest tit gave me a wink.
Escort us, Bacchus, lover of dancers, on our way.

DIONYSUS: Dedicated pilgrim that I am
She's the one I'd say
With whom I'd like to dance and play.

XANTHIAS: [gawking] I'm the same.

MEN: Say, how about us both
Getting that meathead sorted out,
Archedemus, who's still waiting for his second
   teeth?*

WOMEN: He's up there in the highest circles
Doing well among the brain-dead—
Bottoms up and first in the fraternity of rascals.†

MEN: Cleisthenes' son is also said‡
To be in the cemetery, scratching his arse,
Clawing away at his mouth.

WOMEN: In despair, all bent double,
Moaning and groaning and thwacking his noodle
All for some fucker-bating youth.

MEN: Hipponicus' son—you know what!—

---

*Archedemus prosecuted one of the admirals at Arginusae. Also
known as Bleary Eyes. A play on words in the Greek difficult to
bring over into English: *phrateras,* "members of a fraternity," and
φράτερες (*phrateres*) "second teeth."
†There is also an implied pun between Πρῶτος (*prōtos*) "first" and
Πρωκτός (*proctos*) "arse" or "bottom."
‡We have no knowledge of who Cleisthenes' son was.

    Callias, is fighting at sea
    In a lionskin made of twat.

DIONYSUS: [*cutting short the rhythmical repartee of the* CHORUSES]
  Could you tell us please where Pluto lives?
    We're strangers and have only just arrived here.
CHORUS: You haven't far to go, in fact you're there
  and needn't ask again.
DIONYSUS: [*to* XANTHIAS] Up with the baggage again,
  laddie.
XANTHIAS: [*with a groan*] The same old groove!
MEN: Onward with you now into the blessed circle
    of the goddess in her flowery grove,
    where you'll gambol and make whoopie
    in the festival dear to heaven.
    So let us go with the girls and the women,
    flourishing the sacred flares for a night of revel.

STROPHE

WOMEN: Enter the rosy flowerful meadows
    To frisk in our own peculiar way
    And dance the beautiful dances
    The blessed Fates themselves
    Have arranged for us to dance,
    Yes, dance and play.

ANTISTROPHE

MEN: For us is the sun, us alone,
    For us the holy light of day;
    For we are the sanctified ones
    Because our lifestyle is fine
    And we are always kind
    To stranger and common man.

[they have now arrived outside the portals of PLUTO's
front door]

DIONYSUS: How d'you suppose I am to knock? . . .
hm. . . . How do they do it here?
XANTHIAS: Stop dithering. You're supposed to be
Heracles.
You should copy his fire as well as his attire.
DIONYSUS: *[knocking with his cudgel]* Hey, boy! Boy!
AEACUS:* *[from within]* Who's there?
DIONYSUS: The mighty Heracles.
AEACUS: *[peering from the threshold]* So it's you,
you insolent piece of shit! Yes, shit, shittiest shit!
You beat up our dog Cerberus
and after nearly throttling him dragged him away
with you.
That hound was in my care.
Now you're well and truly in the soup.
The black-hearted rock of Styx confronts you.
The bleeding peaks of Acheron beetle above you.†
The greyhounds of Cocytus‡ and the dreaded
Echidna§
are ready to rip up your insides,
and the giant eel of Tartesia
will squeeze out your lungs. Besides,
the Terthrasian Gorgons will chew your bleeding
balls and your guts as well.

*AEACUS was a son of Zeus and the father of Peleus. He was one
of the three judges in Hades. The others were Rhadamanthus and
Mino. Like St. Peter holding the keys to heaven, AEACUS held the
keys to hell.
†Acheron: the Netherworld.
‡The Cocytus (wailing) was one of the four rivers in Hades and
became a name for Hades itself. The other rivers were: Lethe (oblivion), Phlegethon (fire), Styx (abomination). It was across the Styx
that Charon ferried the dead.
§A monster, half woman and half serpent.

I'm off splitarse to bring them here
and give you hell.

[AEACUS *hurries away as* DIONYSUS *faints*]

XANTHIAS: My my, what d'you think you're doing?
DIONYSUS: My butt runneth over. Let us pray.*
XANTHIAS: Get to your feet, you damn fool,
   before anyone sees you.
DIONYSUS: But I feel faint.
   Do get me a sponge for my . . . my heart.
XANTHIAS: [*leaves and returns with a sponge*]
   Here, use it.

[*he watches* DIONYSUS *wiping his bottom*]

   Golden gods of Olympus! Is that where you keep
      your heart?
DIONYSUS: Can't help it—it got a fright
   and skedaddled down to my behind.
XANTHIAS: You're the most abject coward, human or
      divine.
DIONYSUS: Me, a coward, just because I asked for a
      sponge?
   I'm the bravest man alive, bar none.
XANTHIAS: What would someone else have done?
DIONYSUS: A coward would have lain sprawled in his
      stinking mess,
   but I not only raised myself but sponged myself
      clean.
XANTHIAS: By Poseidon, how manly!
DIONYSUS: You can say that again!

*Jeffrey Henderson's brilliant rendering in the Loeb translation.

But weren't *you* in a funk after that stream of
   threats and abuse?
XANTHIAS: It never entered my head, by Zeus!
DIONYSUS: In that case, since you're such a manly man,
   be me and take this cudgel, oh, and the lionskin too.
   Since you're so indomitable
I'll be your errand boy—that's you.
XANTHIAS: Fine, hand them over. That's an order.

[*he drops the bags, puts on the lionskin and seizes
the cudgel*]

Now take a hard look at Heracanthias
and see if he turns out to be a wimp like you.
DIONYSUS: [*looking him over*] Ha! the spitting image
   of a whipped slave from Milite*. . . . Now let me
   pick up the baggage.

[*a* MAIDSERVANT *comes out of* PLUTO'S *palace*]

MAID: [*addressing* XANTHIAS] Heracles, darling,
   is it really you? Do come in.
      As soon as the goddess heard that you were here
she set to baking bread, bringing
two or three cauldrons of lentil soup to the simmer,
not to mention barbecuing an entire ox;
rolls and cakes are in the oven,
so do come in.
XANTHIAS: No, but thanks.
MAID: Nonsense, I'm not going to stand by and let
   you disappear . . .
   Chicken casserole is on the bill of fare,

*Milite was a deme near Athens where Heracles had a temple. It
seems that the spendthrift son of Hipponious, Gallias, had also once
rigged himself up as Heracles and was ridiculed by the playwright
Cratinus as a whipped slave.

and there are toasted pasties and a lovely sweet
  wine,
so come on in.
XANTHIAS: [*nervous of being detected as a fraud*]
  Thanks, but I'm doing fine.
MAID: Get along with you! I'm not letting you off
    so easily;
  besides, the piper girl in there is stunningly
    pretty,
and there are two or three dancing girls as well.
XANTHIAS: Dancing girls? Really?
MAID: Yes, perfect buds . . . ready for the cut,
  so come on in. . . . The cook's just taking the
    fish off the grill
and they're setting up the tables.
XANTHIAS: Great! Tell those dancing girls
  I'm not just coming but coming right in.

  [*turning to* DIONYSUS]

  Boy, hoist those bags and bring them along.
DIONYSUS: Hold on a jiffy,
  d'you mean to say you're taking literally
our little game of dressing you up as Heracles?
  Now look here, Xanthias, pick up our stuff
and stop acting daft.
XANTHIAS: Really?
  So all that jaw you gave me was just bluff?
DIONYSUS: Bluff, indeed? Just watch me.
  Take that lionskin off.

  [*he seizes the lionskin*]

XANTHIAS: Witnesses, do you see what he is doing?
  I appeal to the gods.
DIONYSUS: Gods, did you say? How theologically
    illiterate!

And how presumptuous of you to imagine
that you could be Alcmene's son!*
XANTHIAS: [*letting go the lionskin and cudgel*]
   Take the damn things. A day may come, God
      willing,
when you'll need a Heracles again.

STROPHE
CHORUSES: There's something fine about a man
      Of resource and steady aim
      Who's traveled far and voyaged the main
      But shifts to the present from where he has been.
      As he moves to the easier side of the ship
      And is not clamped to the same strip
      Like some dullard in a frame
      But knows how to roll with the roll
      As he moves to the side of greater ease.
      That's the mark of a clever soul:
      Just like Theramenes.†

ANTISTROPHE
DIONYSUS: Wouldn't it be a funny thing
      If Xanthias, who's only a slave,
      Were caught in a twirl and wallowing
      As he kissed a dancing girl
      But had to break it off to pee?
      I'd be there as voyeur, you see,
      Twiddling my willie like a stave.

*Zeus disguised himself as Amphitryon, the husband of Alcmene,
and produced Heracles by her.
†A friend of Socrates and praised by Aristotle. He was a leading
politician who acquired a reputation of always landing on his feet
in any crisis and was nicknamed "Buskin"—a boot that fits either
foot. (In 404 B.C., however, he would be forced to drink hemlock
by his rival Critias.)

But when he sees a fellow lecher,
With his fists he lets go
Landing a punch full on my jaw
And knocking out my chorus row.

[*a* BISTROKEEPER *with her maid enters shouting*]

BISTROKEEPER: Plathane! Plathane! Come at once.
That ruffian's here:
the one who came to my inn and downed sixteen loaves.
PLATHANE: [*entering with her maid and seeing* DIONY-
SUS, *still dressed as* HERACLES]
Great Zeus, it's him!
XANTHIAS: Someone's under fire.
BISTROKEEPER: But that's not the only thing: the bum
put away twenty-five orders of stew.
XANTHIAS: Somebody's in for it.
BISTROKEEPER: And garlic galore.
DIONYSUS: Tommyrot, madam!
You don't know what you're talking about, do you?
BISTROKEEPER: You didn't think I'd recognize him,
did you,
Not in that Herculean topboot attire?
And I haven't totted up the fish course yet.
PLATHANE: Nor the fresh cheeses he gobbled up—you
poor thing!—
even what they were wrapped in.
BISTROKEEPER: And when he was confronted with
the bill
he looked daggers at me and let out a yell.
XANTHIAS: But that's his character. He's like that
everywhere.
BISTROKEEPER: And he unsheathed his sword, like a
madman.
PLATHANE: You poor, poor thing!

BISTROKEEPER: We were so frightened we bounded up
    to the attic,
and he ran off taking our mattresses with him.

XANTHIAS: That's also in character.

BISTROKEEPER: But we ought to do something about
    this—something emphatic.
    [*to her maid*] Go and fetch my patron here, Cleon.*

PLATHANE: [*to her maid*] And you go and get mine,
    Hyperbolus,† if you can find him.
    We've simply got to squash this bounder.

BISTROKEEPER: [*to* DIONYSUS] You dirty swine!
    I'd like to take a boulder
and bash in those teeth of yours that gorged me out
    of house and home.

PLATHANE: I'd like to fling you into the hangman's
    pit.

BISTROKEEPER: And I'd like to carve up your gizzard
    with a cleaver.
    That would teach you to tuck in to my sausages.
    I'm all set
    to find Cleon.
    This very day he'll issue this fellow with a writ
and wind the guts out of him.

[BISTROKEEPER *and* PLATHANE *leave with their maids*]

DIONYSUS: Boiling oil's too good for me if I don't love
    you, Xanthias.

XANTHIAS: I know what you're thinking, I know,
    so don't go on, just don't.

---

*A pointed anachronism: Cleon, friend of the people and lead-
ing politician of the 420s B.C., had been dead some seven-
teen years.
†He was succeeded by Hyperbolus, who died in 411 B.C.—i.e., about
six years before the production of *The Frogs*.

I won't be Heracles again no matter what you say.

DIONYSUS: Xanthias, please, don't be that way.

XANTHIAS: Haha! "A mere mortal of course
and a slave simply can't be Alcmene's son."

DIONYSUS: I know you're cross with me, I know, and
you have good reason,
and even if you landed me a hefty blow I'd not
object; and I swear
that if ever again
I try to deprive you of all that lionskin gear
I'm ready to suffer an excruciating death and total
extinction
together with my wife, my kids, and dim-eyed Archedemus.*

XANTHIAS: All right, I accept your oath
and you can put me back in harness.

STROPHE

MEN: Since you've taken on the job
Of dressing up as Heracles
As before, you mustn't jib
At showing his martial spirit again.
Don't forget you are the god
Whose camouflage you've taken on:
You must display his fiery mien.
But if you're spotted dithering
And coming across like a sod
You'll be loading up and carrying
All that baggage once again.

---

*After the Athenian naval victory over the Spartans at Arginusae
in 406 B.C., many sailors were lost in a storm. Archedemus was
one of the demagogues who persuaded the Assembly to punish the
commanders for carelessness. Eight of them were senselessly put
to death.

ANTISTROPHE

XANTHIAS: Not a bad suggestion, men;
      The same had just occurred to me
      Just a little while ago.
      One thing's for sure: that presently,
      For what it's worth, he'll have a go
      At taking back my garb again.
      Don't you worry, I'll have you know
      I'll display a warlike front
      And in my eye a caustic glint.
      That is what I'm aiming for . . .
      But there's someone at the door.

[AEACUS *with two servants comes blustering in*]

AEACUS: [*making for* XANTHIAS]
  Quick, get hold of that dog snatcher on the double
and give him what for.
DIONYSUS: Here it comes!
XANTHIAS: [*showing his fists as the two servants
      advance*]
  Touch me if you dare and I'll see you both in hell.
AEACUS: You want knuckle games? [*he calls into the
      house*]
  Ditylas! Scebylas! Pardocas!*
    Get yourselves out here and fight this rascal.

[*three tough-looking young men appear and straitjacket* XANTHIAS]

DIONYSUS: Isn't it scandalous the way this stinker
  robs people and then beats them up?
AEACUS: Quite beyond the pale!
DIONYSUS: Shameful!

*Names typical of the Scythian archer police.

XANTHIAS: So help me heaven and I hope to die
 if I've ever been here before or ever gone off
with a single filament of your stuff.
    I'll tell you what—here's an offer:
take this slave of mine and put him through the
    third degree,
and if you find the faintest spot
besmirching my record, lead me off
and do away with me.
AEACUS: Third degree, you say?
XANTHIAS: Third degree in every way.
    String him to a ladder,
whip him with bristles, flense him, stretch him, pour
    vinegar
up his nose, but from one thing refrain:
don't beat him with a leek or a spring onion.
AEACUS: Spot on!
    But if your slave gets damaged by the third degree
will you be wanting compensation?
XANTHIAS: Oh, don't bother! Just take him away for
    torture.
AEACUS: I'd rather he stays and says
    whatever he's got to say right here
in front of your eyes.

[*turning to* DIONYSUS]

    You can dump those bags right now, fella,
but make sure that here you tell no lies.
DIONYSUS: And I advise
    you not to torture me.
    I'm an immortal deity,
you'd better not try.
AEACUS: [*to* XANTHIAS] Hear that?
XANTHIAS: I certainly do,

and all the more reason to give him a flogging:
if he's a god he'll feel nothing.

DIONYSUS: In that case, since you claim to be a god
   too
   you should be flogged along with me, stroke for
   stroke.

XANTHIAS: [*to* AEACUS] Agreed, and whichever of us
   cracks first and gives a shriek
   or the tiniest hint of being in trouble,
he's no god at all.

AEACUS: You're a sportsman, sir, no doubt of that,
   and all you ask for is fair play.
   Now both of you strip.

[*a servant hands* AEACUS *a strap*]

XANTHIAS: Fair play, but how in fact?

AEACUS: Simple: stripe for stripe.

[XANTHIAS *bends down briskly, followed gingerly
by* DIONYSUS]

XANTHIAS: All's fair, here goes. See if I wince . . .
   Have you hit me yet?

AEACUS: Not yet, by Zeus. [*he strikes* XANTHIAS]

XANTHIAS: That's what I thought.

AEACUS: Now I'll give the other one a whack. [*he
   strikes* DIONYSUS]

DIONYSUS: When are you going to start?

AEACUS: Already have.

DIONYSUS: Then why didn't I blow my top?

AEACUS: Don't know. I'll give the other one another
   thwack.

XANTHIAS: Okey-doke. . . . Wow!

AEACUS: "Wow" what? Did that hurt?

XANTHIAS: Not a bit. . . . I was just wondering
  when the festival of Heracles at Diomeia is due to begin.

AEACUS: The man's a saint—
  Let's have another swipe at the other. [*strikes*
  DIONYSUS]

DIONYSUS: Ow! Ow!

AEACUS: Anything wrong?

DIONYSUS: Cavalry in the offing!

AEACUS: Makes you cry?

DIONYSUS: Their onions do.

AEACUS: But didn't you feel a thing?

DIONYSUS: Nothing.

AEACUS: Let me try the other again. [*he takes a swipe
  at* XANTHIAS]

XANTHIAS: Wow!

AEACUS: Anything wrong?

XANTHIAS: [*holding out a foot*] No, it's only this thorn.

AEACUS: What's going on?
  Suppose I whack the other again. [*he takes a swipe
  at* DIONYSUS]

DIONYSUS: [*whining*] Apollo! . . . [*as if woolgathering*]
  who lives on
  Delos or perhaps at Pytho. . . .

XANTHIAS: That stung him, didn't you hear?

DIONYSUS: [*nonchalantly*] Not so,
  a line of Hipponax was in my mind.*

XANTHIAS: [*to* AEACUS] You're getting nowhere,
  wallop him one right in the ribs.

AEACUS: Can do better than that.
  Show us your belly, Dionysus. [*lands him a punch*]

DIONYSUS: [*reeling*] "Holy Poseidon . . . who doth
  reign . . ."

XANTHIAS: That one really got to him.

*A famous sixth-century B.C. poet from Ephesus in Asia Minor.

DIONYSUS: ". . . o'er all Aegae's cape or on the deep
blue main . . ."*
AEACUS: Holy Demeter, I cannot tell
which of you is a god at all,
so go inside, the master there,
Pluto himself, together with Persephone,
will figure it out; they're gods as well.
DIONYSUS: Be that as it may;
it would have saved me a buffeting galore
if you'd only told me that before.

[AEACUS, DIONYSUS *and* XANTHIAS, *together with
sundry servants, withdraw into* PLUTO'*s palace*]

STROPHE†

MEN AND WOMEN:‡
  Fling yourself, Muse, into this the most heav-
      enly dance
  Breathing élan and happiness into my hymn.
  See what a horde of people is here, give them
      a glance;
  Intelligent all of them,
  More notable by far even than Cleophon,
  Though he possesses the nimblest tongue,
  From which, as if from Thrace, there comes
  The bursts of the hirondelle in full throttle,
  Perching on some barbarian petal

---

*A fragment from Sophocles' lost *Laocoön*.
†For the antistrophe see p. 122.
‡Although some parts of this Chorus are difficult to unravel, the
gist of it is both a warning and a prophecy presaging the downfall
of the neodemocratic politician Cleophon, who in spite of his success was resented by many as not being a true Athenian and stem-
ming from "barbarian" Thrace. Though he was largely responsible
for the restoration of democracy in 410 B.C., he was finally brought
down on false charges by antidemocratic forces in 405 B.C. (after
the second performance of *Frogs*) and put to death.

And changing the nightingale's melancholy song
Into a wail of "What did I do wrong
  To get a jury hung?"
LEADER: It's right and proper for a dedicated chorus
      to give advice
To the city on what to do. In my opinion
      the first thing
Is for every person to be considered equal
      and reassured,
And if he's made the blunder of supporting
  Phrynichus*
      but then is cured,
"Let sleeping dogs lie," I say, and I say this:
      Let nobody
In this city ever lose his citizenship;
      it's outrageous
That those who happen to have served in a single
  battle at sea†
      be put on the same footing
As the heroes of Plataea and go from slave to master.
      No matter;
Actually, I extol it as the one rewarding
      thing you've done.
For doesn't it make sense that the sailors who've
  fought so often
      at your side,
As have their fathers, and are in fact your kith
  and kin,
      should be forgiven

*Phrynichus was a leader of the oligarchical party, which was over-
thrown in 410 B.C., and he was assassinated. Meanwhile many citizens who had supported the oligarchy lost their citizenship.
†In 427 B.C. the Plataeans, whose city had been destroyed by the
Spartans, were given Athenian citizenship. Aristophanes compares
this to the granting of freedom to the slave sailors who fought in
the victorious battle of Arginusae.

For this one misjudgment,* especially as they
  ask you?
        So let it slide.
You're a fairly intelligent lot and you ought to
  welcome
        as fellow citizens
Every man who fights in our ships no matter who.
        If we can't do this,
Because we've become inflated (though we're all
  related),
        and proud of a city
Hugged by the ocean main, one day it will be seen
        what fools we've been.

ANTISTROPHE

MEN AND WOMEN:

If I'm correct in my assessment of a character
Who without doubt is going to come a cropper
Though at the moment he's only a monkey and
  a nuisance,
The pint-sized Cleigenes†
Who runs a sham laundry and poses as a fuller
Using fake detergent and nothing
But hanky-panky to get the spots out . . .
Well, he'll get his comeuppance.
He's quite aware of this and it makes him nervous.
He's terrified that one night very soon

*I'm not sure what "misjudgment" is intended. Is it the implied
presumption of leaping from slave to freeman, or is it an echo
of the aftermath of Arginusae, when the leaders of the fleet
were charged with not doing enough to save lives following the
storm after the battle; or is it the brutal decision of the Assembly
to put those leaders to death? Finally, is it for having supported
Phrynichus?
†Little is known about him except that he served as a secretary to
the Assembly in 410/9 B.C.

Stickless and sozzled and meandering home in the
    dark
He'll be set upon.

LEADER: You know what I often think:
        we treat our best men
The way we treat our mint,
        the silver and the golden.*
We were proud to invent
        these unalloyed
Genuine coins, no less,
        ringing true and tested
Both abroad and in Greece,
        and now they're not employed,
As if we were disgusted
        and want to use instead
These shoddy coppers minted
        only yesterday
Or just the day before
        (as if that matters).
They're cheap, they really are.
        Well isn't that the way
We treat our best men,
        the ones we know are fine,
Upright men of parts,
        educated, honed
By wrestling and the arts?
        They might as well be rotters.
If the truth be told.
        We'd rather have the coppers,
The aliens, the dopes;
        rubbish born of rubbish,

---

*The traditional coinage was made of silver from the Laureium
mines, largely incapacitated since the enemy occupation of Deceleia.
New coins were issued in 407/6 B.C.

All the latest washouts.
There are no doubts
That once upon a time
the city wouldn't have used them
Even as its scapegoats.
But even now, you jerks,
It's not too late to mend.
Cultivate the cultured
Again, and when this works
and everything goes well
You'll be congratulated.
If on the other hand
It all comes to an end
and you are up a gum tree,
Discerning folk will say:
"The tree's fine anyway."

[XANTHIAS *and an old servant of* PLUTO *come out of the palace*]

SERVANT: My word, that master of yours, 'e's a real gent.

XANTHIAS: Of course he is: all he knows is jagging and shagging.

SERVANT: What I meant was,
'e never lambasted you for trying to pass yerself off as the boss.

XANTHIAS: It would have been his loss.

SERVANT: That's real cool! The spirit I love to see—
spoken like a true lackey.

XANTHIAS: You love it, eh?

SERVANT: Yeah, it gives me a real kick
to bad-mouth the guv'nor be'ind 'is back.

XANTHIAS: Like the joy of a good grouse
after a beating when you've left the house.
SERVANT: Boy oh boy!
XANTHIAS: Or snooping?
SERVANT: Tip top!
XANTHIAS: By Zeus, yes!
Or cocking the ear to overhear the boss?
SERVANT: Mad with joy!
XANTHIAS: And blabbing about what you hear?
SERVANT: Sheer ecstasy! Good as a 'and job!
XANTHIAS: Let's shake on that, by Phoebus Apollo,
give us a hug. . . . But tell me, old fellow,
by our mutual god, Zeus the Flogger,
what's going on inside the palace?
Sounds like a mob of people screaming insults at
each other.
SERVANT: That be Aeschylus and Euripides.
XANTHIAS: Aha!
SERVANT: A mighty tussle be going on 'mong the dead;
yer wouldn't believe what a tussle,
an' people are taking sides.
XANTHIAS: Tussle about what?
SERVANT: Well, there's an old custom down 'ere, see,
for the top brass in their professions, like, to 'old
a competition,
and 'oever comes out on top gets to 'ave free meals
in the Town 'all
and sit next to Pluto, see?
XANTHIAS: I get it.
SERVANT: But 'e only 'as it till
somebody comes along 'ho's better 'an 'e gets it
instead.
XANTHIAS: But why's that put Aeschylus in a tizzy?
SERVANT: Cuz 'e 'eld the Pedestal of Tragedy for being
tops in that.

XANTHIAS: And who holds it now?

SERVANT: When Euripides turned up 'ere, the bard, an' began 'is productions,

aimed at all the cutthroats, pickpockets, thieves, assassins,

(down 'ere we 'ave every kind of bastard);

an' when they 'eard all 'is clever harbee-jarbee an' funny kind of logic,

they went bonkers over 'im, said 'e was the bee's knees an' ought to 'ave the chair an' old Aeschylus kicked out.

XANTHIAS: Wasn't he squashed?

SERVANT: Not a bit of it.

The people clamored for a competition
to find out, like, 'ho was best.

XANTHIAS: All those hooligans? Well, I'm dashed!

SERVANT: Clamored to 'igh 'eaven, they did.

XANTHIAS: But wasn't there a pro-Aeschylus faction?

SERVANT: Aye, but yer know 'ow the decent folks is always a minority,

both down 'ere an' up there. [*gestures toward the audience*]

XANTHIAS: What's Pluto doing about it?

SERVANT: 'e wants a competition—like immediately— to see

which of the two is better at 'is art.

XANTHIAS: And Sophocles never put in a claim?

SERVANT: Not 'im.

When 'e arrived down 'ere*
Aeschylus went straight up to 'im, took 'is 'and and kissed 'im.

"It's all yours," 'e says, "the Chair,
I ain't going to run."

---

*Sophocles had just died the previous year (406 B.C.), in his early nineties, leaving Aristophanes with a problem (and probably a regret). It was too late to put him into *Frogs*, which was already in production.

According to the critic Cleidemedes
'e's withdrawn 'isself but says:
"If Aeschylus wins, well and done,
but if not, for the sake of art,
I myself'll take Euripides on."

XANTHIAS: Is that actually going to happen?

SERVANT: Sure is, and soon.
We're going to see something great:
poetry sold by measurement and weight.

XANTHIAS: What, tragedy on the scales like pork chops?

SERVANT: Yeah, with yardsticks and measuring tapes.
Words'll be fitted into little boxes an' . . .

XANTHIAS: You mean, like making bricks?

SERVANT: Sure thing, with rulers and setsquares,
cuz Euripides says 'e's going to analyze
poetic tragedy syllable by syllable.

XANTHIAS: Poor Aeschylus! He must have thought: What the hell?

SERVANT: Sure did; buried 'is 'ead like a charging bull.

XANTHIAS: Who's judging?

SERVANT: Ah, there's the rub,
cuz they couldn't find no one literate enough,
an' Aeschylus vetoed anyone from Athens, see?

XANTHIAS: Thinks it's too full of crooks probably.

SERVANT: Aye, but 'e didn't think much of the rest either,
not when weighing up what poets are.
So they've shoved the 'ole bloody thing onto yer master,
him being artistic like.
Eh, but let's go inside. It ain't wise
when bosses get down to business
to be in the offing for the likes of us.

[XANTHIAS *and the* SERVANT *go into* PLUTO's *palace as other servants assemble an assortment of scales and weights and every kind of measuring implement*]

MEN: I expect that his thundering heart will rage
    fiercely
    When Aeschylus sees the snarling fangs of his
        rival in art.
    Primed for the fight, his eyes will flare and dart,
    Filled with fury.

WOMEN: Words will be waving their plumes over hel-
        mets that shine
    And phrases planed into works of art are chis-
        eled apart
    As foe parries foe with words that fly fast and
        sublime,
    While all the time . . .

MEN: Aeschylus, shaking the mass of his shaggy bris-
        tling mane,
    His tremendous forehead scored with a beetling
        frown
    Will hurl a bolted thunder of riveted power that blasts
    Timbers apart.

WOMEN: Ah, but Euripides' loosening and licking and
        testing slippery tongue
    Will match this onslaught with a counterattack,
    Sniping and picking off word from word with a
        deadly knack
    In this duel of the lung.

[PLUTO, DIONYSUS, AESCHYLUS *and* EURIPIDES *arrive and chairs are put out for them.* PLUTO *is in the center,* DIONYSUS—*no longer dressed as* HERACLES—*on his left, and* AESCHYLUS *on his right, the place of honor.* EURIPIDES *marches forward and grabs his chair.*]

EURIPIDES: Don't anyone dare tell me to let go of
this chair.

With me—in the art of poetry—there's no one to
compare.

DIONYSUS: Aeschylus, you say nothing;
don't you hear what this man's claiming?

EURIPIDES: As always, he's being aloof—like his
tragedies.

DIONYSUS: That's a bit much, friend, don't exaggerate.

EURIPIDES: I've had this fellow's number for a long
time.

The most boring primitives is what he likes to create:
unlettered, unfettered, unruly, uncouth, they froth
at the mouth
in a flood of bombastical—diarrheical foam.

AESCHYLUS: Really? You son of a vegetable-selling bitch?

This coming from you, you bleeding-burst-bubble-
piece-of-bosh!

You beggar-monger with an avocation to stitch
old sacks, you'll be sorry you said that.

DIONYSUS: Hold on, Aeschylus, "Heap not the fuel on
your fiery gall."*

AESCHYLUS: No, I won't hold on. Not till I've laid bare
the impudence of this creator of spastics here.

DIONYSUS: Hey, boys, a lamb, bring on a black lamb.†
I can see what's heading our way—a storm.

AESCHYLUS: [*continuing his tirade against* EURIPIDES]
You connoisseur of dirty Cretan songs
fouling our art with incestuous intercourse.

DIONYSUS: That's enough, illustrious Aeschylus,
and you, Euripides, poor fellow, it would be wise
to move out of range of this storm of hail.

---

*Quoting probably a line of Aeschylus.
†It would seem that the sacrifice of a black lamb was a defense
against bad weather.

He's so angry he might break your skull
with a crushing retort and your *Telephus* would come
      to naught.
      And you, Aeschylus,
do try to keep calm and free your repartee
from rancor and abuse.
      It's simply not done for two well-known literary men
to wrangle like fishwives or go up in a blaze
like an oak tree on fire.

EURIPIDES: I am ready to take him on if *he* is,
   I'm not backing down.
      He can have the first go in this verbal bout
and pick away at the entire
gamut and guts of my songs and tragedies;
I don't care which: my *Peleus*, my *Aeolus*,
my *Meleager*—yes, and even my *Telephus*.

DIONYSUS: And Aeschylus, what about you? Speak out.

AESCHYLUS: I could have wished avoiding this
      altercation;
   the odds are so uneven.

DIONYSUS: How d'you mean?

AESCHYLUS: My poetry hasn't died with me,
   it's still alive up there,
whereas his is as moribund as he.
      Still, if that's what you want, I don't care.

DIONYSUS: Will someone go and get the incense and
      the fire
   and I'll begin this display of supererogation
      with a prayer
that my decisions in this contest will be fair.
      Meanwhile will the Chorus invoke the Muses with
      a hymn.

MEN AND WOMEN:
      Come you holy maidens of Zeus,

You Muses nine, who activate the decisions and
    the minds
Of men along wonderfully clear and luminous lines
When they are pitted against each other in tough
    and abstruse
Debate, we invite you to come and admire the
    vigor and prowess
Of this couple of speakers, each of which is a master
Of handling enormous slabs of verb
As well as piddling chips of syllable; look and observe
The mighty minds that are about to commence.

DIONYSUS: Both of you now offer up a prayer before
you say your piece.
AESCHYLUS: Great Demeter, who sustains my faculties,
let me be worthy of your Mysteries.
DIONYSUS: You now, Euripides.
Present your incense, make your prayer.
EURIPIDES: Thanks, but I pray to a different set of
deities.
DIONYSUS: Your own personal ones? Brand-new, of
course?
EURIPIDES: Sure.
DIONYSUS: Go on then, have recourse to those per-
sonal gods of yours.
EURIPIDES: Ether—you, my grazing pastures—
    As well as Nous and Nosey Parker
    Arm me with the words for argument.

STROPHE*
MEN: Now we're all agog to hear
    Two literary geniuses at work
    Who have decided to go to war

*For the antistrophe see p. 137.

In a duel of words.
The tongues of both will go berserk,
Their spirits are not short of valor
Nor are their minds short of vigor.
So we may safely assume that soon
One will utter something smart,
Whetted and keen,
The other score with a brilliant thrust
And reasons torn up by the roots
Scattering words in a cloud of dust.

LEADER: Very well, begin your speechifying at once.
  Don't fail to make it clever, but not pretentious
or commonplace with silly riddles.
EURIPIDES: Good, but before I tell you the kind of
    creative writer I am
  let me make clear what an imposter and sham my
      adversary is.
  What he did was set himself up to diddle
the audiences he inherited from Phrynichus,*
who were already pretty far gone in imbecility.
  His prologues always begin with some solitary soul,
an Achilles, say, or a Niobe,
all muffled up so you can't see their faces
and not uttering a syllable.
  Quite a travesty, I'd say, of dramatic tragedy.
DIONYSUS: Yes, you've got it exactly.
EURIPIDES: And while they sit there mute as dummies
    the Chorus lets go in a litany
of nonstop choral baloney.
DIONYSUS: All the same, I quite enjoyed his silences;
    they weren't as bad as today's babbling histrionics.
EURIPIDES: That's because you're easily taken in.

*A tragic writer who flourished a little before Aeschylus. Not to be
confused with Phrynicus the general and Phrynicus the flatterer.

DIONYSUS: Perhaps you're right, but how else could he have written?

EURIPIDES: Nevertheless, it's sheer chicanery.

He wants the audience to sit there interminably,
all ears cocked for the moment Niobe
utters a whimper. Meanwhile the play drags on.

DIONYSUS: The rascal, he took me in!
Aeschylus, I'll thank you to stop fidgeting.

EURIPIDES: It's because I'm showing him up. . . .
Then after he's bumbled along like this till the
play's almost done
he lets fly with a volley of words
as formidable as a beribboned bull
flaunting crests and a shaggy scowl,
which is followed by a whole string of scarecrow weirdies
designed to make your flesh crawl.

AESCHYLUS: How cruel!

EURIPIDES: And never does he utter a word that makes sense.

DIONYSUS: Aeschylus, do stop grinding your molars.

EURIPIDES: It's all river-Scamanders,
fosses and bronze-bossed bucklers
emblazoned with eagle-griffins
and great rough-hewn declarations
for which there are never explanations.

DIONYSUS: Don't I know it!
"I've lain awake all through the long leviathan of
the night, trying to tell
what is meant by a swooping hippocockerell."*

AESCHYLUS: It's the figurehead painted on our ships
at Troy, you cretin.

DIONYSUS: And I was imagining it to be Eryxis, son
of Philoxenus.†

*Parodying a line from Euripides' *Hippolytus*. The quote ends at *night*.
The rest is from Aeschylus. It is not known in what play Aeschylus
talks of a "swooping hippocockerell."
†Well known for his ugliness.

EURIPIDES: But honestly
  do we really have to have cockerells in high
    tragedy?
AESCHYLUS: All right, you god-detested,
  in what sort of themes have you invested?
EURIPIDES: Well, for start,
  no hippocockerells and not a single stag crossed
    with a goat,
the kind of freak you might expect to see
on a strip of Persian tapestry.
      None of that!
      When you passed on to me the tragic art
the poor thing was loaded to the ground with bom-
        bast and fat.
      Immediately, I put her on a diet
and got her weight down by a course of long walks
and little mouthfuls of syllables in fricassée.
      I also fed her chopped repartee
and a concoction of verbal juice pressed out of
        books.
      Then as a pick-me-up I dosed her with a tincture
of monodies from Cephisophon.*
      I never shambled along like you
with the first thing that entered my noggin,
or plunged ahead leaving the audience in a stew.
      The first character to walk on
explained the nature of the play and—
AESCHYLUS: A better nature than yours, any day!
EURIPIDES: [*ignoring the interruption*] . . . from the
    opening lines
  I got all the characters going:
wife speaking, servant speaking,

---

*A fellow poet and friend of Euripides.

and of course the boss and young girl,
not to mention the old crone.

AESCHYLUS: Such vulgarity! It calls for the death
  penalty.

EURIPIDES: Not so. It's straightforward democracy.

DIONYSUS: Be that as it may, pal,
  but that's a topic I'd keep off if I were you.

EURIPIDES: [*gesturing to the audience*] And I taught
    you people
  the art of conversation and—

AESCHYLUS: I'll say you did, and in my view
  you should have been sliced down the middle.

EURIPIDES: . . . some of the nicer subtleties
  like how to make words tell;
how to think and observe and decide;
how to be quick off the mark and shrewd;
how to expect the worst and face reality in the
  round—

AESCHYLUS: I'll say you did!

EURIPIDES: . . . by re-creating the workaday world
    we know
  and things that are part of our living,
things I couldn't sham without being shown up as a
  fraud
because they're common knowledge. So
I never tried to bamboozle them by fibbing
or by bombast and persiflage.
    I never tried to frighten them with brutes like
      your Cycnus and your Memnon*
careering about in chariots with bells clanging.
    And just look at the difference between his devo-
      tees and mine;

*Cycnus ("Swan") and Memnon ("On Cue") were Trojan warriors
slain by Achilles.

he's got Pussy-Beard Phormisius* and Sidekick Meg-
   aenetus†
rip-'em-uppers-treetrunk-twisters
and bushy-bearded-bugle-blowing lancers
whereas I've got Cleitophon‡ and the clever Theramenes.§

DIONYSUS: Theramenes? Yes, he's supersmart,
   surmounts every crisis and on the brink of disaster
always manages to land on his feet.
   Whatever the fix, he always throws a six.

EURIPIDES: That's exactly what I meant,
   Teaching people how to think,
   Putting logic into art
   And making it a rational thing
   Which enables them to grasp
   And manage almost everything
   Better than they've ever done,
   Especially matters in the home,
   Asking "Is everything all right?"
   "What happened to this?" "Oh, damn!
   Who the deuce went off with that?"

DIONYSUS: Ye gods, you're right!
   When an Athenian comes home now
   He starts to bawl the servants out:
   "What's happened to that cooking pot?"
   "Who bit the head off that sprat?"
   "The basin I bought last year is shot."

---

*A moderate democrat whose beard suggested genitalia. (Loeb)
†Megaenetus ("Big 'n' Burly"): a tough young soldier.
‡Cleitophon ("Illustrious One"), a moderate democrat and friend
of Euripides.
§Theramenes ("helpful"), known as "the boot that fits either foot,"
was a remarkable survivor in the vicissitudes and turmoil of Athenian politics of 415 B.C. onward. He was one of the loudest in urging
the condemnation of the Athenian commanders after the battle of
Arginusae.

"Where's the garlic? Do you know?"
"Who's been getting at the olives?" . . .
Whereas before Euripides
They sat like gawking dummies half alive.

ANTISTROPHE*

WOMEN: "Renowned Achilles, do you behold this?"†
How will you respond to it?
Will you lose that famous temper?
Do take care.
And not go running amok.
His gibes certainly are no joke,
So, good sir, do take care.
Do not be consumed with bile,
Furl the canvas, slacken sheets,
Shorten sail.
Slowly slowly cruise along
Till the breeze blows soft and strong
And bears you steadily along.

LEADER: [*to* AESCHYLUS] You first of Greeks to raise
pinnacles of praise
to adorn all tragic waffle, open up your throttle.
AESCHYLUS: I'm furious matters have come to this, my
stomach turns
that I have to demean myself by arguing with this
man's
pretensions, but I must because otherwise
he'll say that I'm reduced to silence. . . . So tell me this:
What are the attributes that make a poet famous?
EURIPIDES: Skill and common sense, by which we are
able to make
ordinary people better members of the State.

*Answering the strophe on p. 131.
†The opening lines of Aeschylus' *Myrmidons* (fr. 131). (Loeb)

AESCHYLUS: And say you've done the opposite, made honest folk
  into libertines, what punishment would you merit?
DIONYSUS: Don't ask him—death.
AESCHYLUS: Just give a thought to what they were like when they came from my hand:
six-foot heroes all of them who never shirked,
unlike your loafers and your useless berks,
these latter-day washouts we have now.
   Those others were men of spears, men of darts, the very breath
of white-plumed helmets waving and ox-hide hearts.
DIONYSUS: Heavens, it's helmets now! He'll wear me out.
EURIPIDES: What method did you use to make them so elite?
DIONYSUS: Come on, Aeschylus, lay off being aloof.
AESCHYLUS: I did it by shoving Ares into everything.
DIONYSUS: Exactly how?
AESCHYLUS: In my *Seven Against Thebes* . . . I contrived
  to make every male who saw it hot for war.
DIONYSUS: Not very nice to have connived
  in making Thebans braver in battle than us Athenians!*
   You ought to be chastised.
AESCHYLUS: I think not.
You Athenians could have had the same training
but you didn't think it worth it. . . .
   Then when I produced my *Persians* it sent them raving
to annihilate the enemy. So you see,

*In the Peloponnesian War Thebes sided with Sparta against Athens.

in the end I didn't come off too badly.*

DIONYSUS: I love the part when they heard that Darius was no more,

and they couldn't celebrate enough, clapping their hands and shouting,

"Hurrah! Hurrah!"

AESCHYLUS: This is the sort of thing that poets should celebrate,

and this, you may remember, is what one finds
among the best of poets from earliest times.

Orpheus revealed to us the mysteries,
and also taught us to abhor murder as a crime.

Museus made us aware of things like clairvoyance
and also how to cure diseases.

Hesiod taught us how to work the land, when to plough,

when to sow; and as to Homer, the divine,
did he not earn his fame and undying renown
by giving us lessons on how to esteem
military training, armory, and the discipline of men?

DIONYSUS: That may be so but all the same

he did pretty dismally with that airhead Pantacles†
who only yesterday made a fool of himself on parade
trying to fix the plumes of his helmet while he had it on his head.

AESCHYLUS: I know, but surely he did inspire other brave men,

for instance, the indomitable Lamachus,‡
who was for me the role model in courage, like Patroclus§

---

*The Athenians defeated the invading Persians at the naval battle of Salamis in 480 B.C., and at Plataea in 479 B.C.
†Unknown except that the joke is repeated by the playwright Eupolis in the 420s B.C.
‡An illustrious commander who died in action at Syracuse in 414 B.C.
§Bosom friend of Achilles in the Trojan War and slain by Hector.

and the lion-hearted Teucer*—the role model for
all of us,
inspiring valor and giving us courage to emulate
them whenever
the bugle for battle blew. . . . I never did create
strumpets like Phaedra or Stheneboea, like you,†
    You'll never find anywhere in anything I wrote
a lascivious bitch.

EURIPIDES: Don't I know it! You left poor Aphrodite out.

AESCHYLUS: I should think so, whereas you
have let her squash you and your whole household flat.

DIONYSUS: He's got you there, Euripides, for you've
been hit by the same fate
you invented for other people's wives.‡

EURIPIDES: [*ignoring the insult*] You tiresome man,
what harm to the community was ever done
by my *Stheneboea*?

AESCHYLUS: You put decent women married to
decent men
in a situation like that with Bellerephon
that drives them to suicide.

EURIPIDES: All right, but I didn't invent the plot of
Phaedra.

AESCHYLUS: Worse luck, no! But the poet shouldn't
side

---

*Teucer, the half brother of Ajax, was the greatest archer among
the Greeks at Troy.
†Phaedra tried to seduce her stepson Hippolytus; Stheneboea, her
stepson Bellerephon. Both women accused these young men of rape
when they rejected their advances. Euripides tells the story in his
Hippolytus and his *Stheneboea* (lost).
‡There seems to have been some scandal in Euripides' home, with
his wife having an affair with one of the servants.

with what is evil and display it on the stage like a
   demonstration.

   Children may have teachers but adults have the
      poet

and the poet ought to keep things on a higher plane.

EURIPIDES: [*sarcastically*] As high as Mount Lycabet-
   tus, no doubt, or lofty

   Parnassus, and they're to be our instructors in the
      good?

      My word! Can't you do your teaching in the lan-
         guage of men?

AESCHYLUS: Listen, you miserable heel, the lofty
   thought and the high ideal

   call for a language to match,

and if the deities are clothed in rare attire

their language too should be out of the ordinary.

   This is where I blazed a trail

which you've managed to undermine.

EURIPIDES: How have I?

AESCHYLUS: For a start, by the way you dress your
   royalty.

   They're all in rags like any pitiful wretch.

EURIPIDES: But whom do I hurt by that?

AESCHYLUS: Well, to begin with,

   it tempts the rich to shirk their responsibility:

a wealthy tycoon evades the funding of a warship

by dressing up in rags and whimpering about his
   poverty.*

DIONYSUS: Yes, underneath the rags, by Demeter,
   he's in lovely fleecy underwear

and you see him splashing out on fish in the market
   square.

---

*It was the duty of the wealthier citizens to pay for and equip
a trireme.

AESCHYLUS: What's more, you've taught people to
    prattle and gab,
  emptying the wrestling schools and turning the
young men's bottoms into flab
as they prattle away—and you've encouraged the crew
of the *Paralus* to answer their officers back.*
        But in the old days when I was alive all they knew
was how to clamor for their grub
and shout "Ship ahoy" and "Heave-to."
DIONYSUS: That's exactly it, by Apollo.
  Now they fart in the bottom bencher's face,
shit on their messmates and go off with people's
    clothes when on shore.
      What's more,
they give lip to their commanders and refuse to row,
so the ship goes drifting to and fro.
AESCHYLUS: What bad behavior is he not responsible for?
      Showing us a woman acting as a pander,†
      Or producing a baby in the very temple,‡
      And others even coupling with their brothers§
      And saying that "something living's not alive,"‖
      The consequences naturally are simple:
      A society swamped by lawyers' clerks
      And buffoons lying their heads off to the people,
      And, because nobody takes any exercise,
      When it comes to running with a torch, no one tries.

*One of the two State galleys used for official missions.
†The nurse of Phaedra in *Hippolytus* (Euripides).
‡The heroine in *Auge* (Euripides, lost).
§Canace with her brother Macareus, in *Aeolus* (Euripides, lost).
‖The significance of this quotation is doubtful. Jeffrey Henderson
suggests that it may refer to Pasiphae in *Polybus* but *Polybus* is
another lost play of Euripides and we can only guess the possible
connection of "coupling with their brothers" with saying that
"something living's not alive." Pasiphae coupled with a bull (Minos)
and produced a monster (the Minotaur). Is Aeschylus hinting that
Euripides supports abortion? Possibly.

DIONYSUS: You couldn't be righter; I almost doubled
   up
   At the Panathenaea laughing when
   A slow coach of a booby thumped along,
   Stooped, white as a sheet, fat;
   And when he got to the Gates by the Potters' field
   People whacked him on his belly and butt
   And ribs and sides and all his miserable hide.
   As he scurried along he began to fart
   With gas enough to keep his torch alight.

STROPHE

MEN: Great is the struggle, grand the tussle,
   The war's now under way.
   One of them lands a hefty biff,
   The other ducks with a swing
   In counterattack. It's hard to say
   Which of them will win. . . .
   Hey, you two, you've not fought enough,
   Many more buffetings are due
   And plenty of cerebral stuff.
   Whatever it is you're fighting about
   Go at it hard and argue it out.
   Flense the old and strip for the new.
   Get down to the nitty-gritty
   And something erudite.

ANTISTROPHE

WOMEN: And if you're afraid that people won't know
   What it is all about
   And have no inkling, are unable to follow
   The twists of an argument,
   Don't give it a thought; as a matter of fact
   Things are different today:

Everyone's an expert now
And knows his book of rules by heart
And every nicety;
Is fully briefed and clever as well,
And sharply honed, as we all know,
So that's not something to worry about.
Don't be afraid, enjoy it all;
People are primed to the hilt.

EURIPIDES: Very well then, we'll look at his prologues first
and see how this famous poet begins his tragedies,
because their plots are far from clear.

DIONYSUS: Which of his prologues do you mean to
criticize?

EURIPIDES: A whole pile of them; for starters, something from his Oresteia.

DIONYSUS: Quiet, everyone, let Aeschylus begin.

AESCHYLUS: [*reciting*]*

"Thou who visiteth the nether realms, O Hermes,
And also watcheth o'er my sire's domain,
I have returned to this land and am back again."

DIONYSUS: [*to* EURIPIDES] Do you have anything to
criticize?

EURIPIDES: Plenty: at least a dozen things.

DIONYSUS: Even in only three lines?

EURIPIDES: Each of which contains a score of sins.

DIONYSUS: Keep quiet, Aeschylus, otherwise
you'll have to deal with more than three iambic lines.

AESCHYLUS: Keep quiet for him?

DIONYSUS: That's what I advise.

EURIPIDES: It's my opinion that he's made a gargantuan blunder.

---

*The opening lines of the second play of the Oresteia (*The Libation
Bearers*), Orestes speaking. The version differs from our extant version.

AESCHYLUS: Don't be dim.

DIONYSUS: Proceed as you will. . . . What do I care!

AESCHYLUS: All right, show me the blunder that I made, Euripides.

EURIPIDES: Recite those lines again.

AESCHYLUS: "Thou who visiteth the nether realms, O Hermes,
And also watcheth o'er my sire's domain . . ."

EURIPIDES: Hold on. Aren't these lines said by Orestes at the tomb of his dead father?

AESCHYLUS: Correct.

EURIPIDES: I see. So what he's saying is that when his father
was brutally murdered by his wife in a neatly arranged plot
Hermes was a conniver?

AESCHYLUS: He is not. The Hermes he addresses is not Hermes the Trickster
but the Hermes of Hades, because it was over Hades that he had jurisdiction
by Zeus his father's dispensation.

EURIPIDES: That makes it an even bigger blunder than I thought,
because this jurisdiction granted by his father . . .

DIONYSUS: Suggests a grave-robbing's in the offing condoned by his father.*

AESCHYLUS: Dionysus, have you been drinking sour wine?

DIONYSUS: Recite some more, Aeschylus.
Euripides, keep your ears cocked for a bloomer.

AESCHYLUS: [*reciting*]
"I ask you now to be my helper and preserver,
For I've returned to this land and am back again."

---

*Gifts of milk, honey, and other edibles were laid on graves as symbols of support for the dead.

EURIPIDES: The sapient Aeschylus has said the same thing twice.

AESCHYLUS: How, the same thing twice?

EURIPIDES: It's obvious. Listen.
"I've returned to this land," he says,
then, "and am back again."
    Aren't they the same?

DIONYSUS: Of course they are.
    It's like saying "Give me a kneading bowl,
but a bowl for kneading will do."

AESCHYLUS: You're missing the point, you birdbrain,
    the line couldn't be better.

DIONYSUS: Really? Please explain.

AESCHYLUS: Anyone can "come" into his native land
    but if he's coming back from exile he's "returning."

[*there is a burst of applause*]

DIONYSUS: Bravo, by Apollo! What d'you say to that, Euripides?

EURIPIDES: I'd say that Orestes wasn't simply "coming home,"
    he slunk back secretly without telling the authorities.

DIONYSUS: Sounds smart, by Hermes! I wonder what the difference is.

EURIPIDES: Fine! Let's have another line.

DIONYSUS: Off you go, Aeschylus. And you, Euripides, keep your ears skinned for blunders.

AESCHYLUS: [*reciting*]
    "So by my father's burial mound
    I call on him to hearken and to listen."

EURIPIDES: There, he's done it again:
    "hearken" and "listen" are indubitably the same.

DIONYSUS: But he's speaking to the dead, you poor sap,
    I doubt that even three times would get to *them*.

    How do *your* prologues begin?

EURIPIDES: Let me tell you, and if you catch me saying
    anything twice
  or filling up the gaps with pap,
you can jolly well spit in my face.

DIONYSUS: Off with you, then. Recite a line.
  I can hardly wait to hear how you make your pro-
    logues precise.

EURIPIDES: [*reciting*] "Oedipus, once upon a time,
    Was a happy man . . ."

AESCHYLUS: Tommyrot!
  He was unhappy the moment he was born,
no, even before he was born:
Apollo had predicted that he'd kill his father.
    He wasn't even conceived yet,
so how could he be "once upon a time a happy man"?

EURIPIDES: [*ignoring the interruption*]
    ". . . but of all mortals he became
    The most unhappy later on."

AESCHYLUS: Not "became," for heaven's sake, he al-
    ways was.
  Take a look at the story line.
    As a newborn baby, in the dead of winter,
he's put in an earthenware pot and exposed
to keep him from murdering his father when he grows
up to be a man; but he does grow up and off he goes
limping along on swollen feet to Polybus
who he thinks is his father.
    He's a young man and meets a woman who is
    older,
and who does she turn out to be but his own mother.
    At which he blinds himself because he no more wants
    to see.

DIONYSUS: [*sarcastically*] Sublimely happy!

He might as well have been Erasinides.*

EURIPIDES: Balls! . . . Anyway, I insist my prologues are a marvel.

AESCHYLUS: Look, I'm not going to go nitpicking through your phrases
syllable by syllable;

all I need to wipe out your prologues, the gods willing, is a cruet of oil.

EURIPIDES: Wipe out my prologues with a cruet of oil?

AESCHYLUS: Sure, one will do. . . . The way your metrics go is: dumdi-dumdiddi-dum.

You can tag any old thing on to your iambs, like
"and a tuffet of wool," "and a cruet of oil,"
"and a diminutive sack . . ." Look, I'll show you.

EURIPIDES: You'll show me, will you?

AESCHYLUS: That's what I said.

EURIPIDES: All right, here's a quote.

"Aegyptus as the story goes
Put to sea with his fifty sons
Making for Argos,"†

AESCHYLUS: And lost his cruet of oil.

DIONYSUS: Cruet of oil, my hat! . . . Another prologue, please,
so's we can have another shot.

EURIPIDES: "Dionysus, clad in fawnskins‡
Midst the pine trees of Parnassus,
Was waving his wand and prancing about . . ."

AESCHYLUS: And lost his cruet of oil.

DIONYSUS: That cruet of oil will be the end of us.

---

*One of the admirals executed after the naval engagement off Arginusae in which the Athenians defeated the Spartans.
†From Euripides' lost play *Archelaus*, one of his last plays, written while he was a guest of Archelaus, King of Macedon.
‡From Euripides' lost *Hypsipyle*.

EURIPIDES: No matter. Here's a prologue that's non-
    cruet-of-oil-able.
    "No man is fortunate in all.*
    One is highborn but bereft,
    Another lowborn and he's lost . . ."
AESCHYLUS: His cruet of oil.
DIONYSUS: Euripides.
EURIPIDES: What?
DIONYSUS: Better shorten sail,
    we're in for a cruet-of-oil squall.
EURIPIDES: Not a bit of it, I'm not worried;
    just watch me knock that cruet right out of his
        hand.
DIONYSUS: Let's have another quote,
    and we'll dodge that cruet with a feint.
EURIPIDES: "Cadmus, Agenor's son,
    Left the citadel of Sidon . . ."†
AESCHYLUS: And lost his cruet of oil.
DIONYSUS: For heaven's sake, mate, buy that cruet
    of oil
    or we'll have nothing left but wrecked prologues.
EURIPIDES: You're kidding—me buy from him?
DIONYSUS: That's right.
EURIPIDES: Never. And when it comes to prologues
    I've got bags
    more I can recite,
and they're all proof against cruets of oil.
    "Pelops son of Tantalus came
    To Pisa on swift chargers . . ."
AESCHYLUS: And lost his cruet of oil.
DIONYSUS: Listen, buddy, we're stuck with that cruet
    of oil,

---

*From Euripides' lost *Stheneboea*.
†All the quotations are from plays of Euripides.

do make an offer for it. It's virgin and won't cost
   more than an obol.
EURIPIDES: I certainly won't, and I've got heaps more
      to come.
   "Oeneus once upon a time
   From his land was offering up . . ."
AESCHYLUS: A cruet of oil.
EURIPIDES: Oh, do let me finish a verse!
   "Oeneus once upon a time
   From his land was offering up
   The firstfruits of the harvest when . . ."
AESCHYLUS: He lost his cruet of oil.
DIONYSUS: While the sacrifice was going on?
   Who went off with it, anyway?
EURIPIDES: No matter, pal. Let him get on with this:
   "Zeus, if the truth be told . . ."*
DIONYSUS: I can't stand it. He's going to say:
   "Lost his cruet of oil." That cruet of oil
fixes on your prologues like cold
sores on the eyes. For goodness' sake, let's switch to
   his choral lyrics.
EURIPIDES: Very well, I'll show that his lyrics are no
      good at all;
he keeps saying the same thing twice.
MEN AND WOMEN: How is this turmoil going to unravel?
   I have to confess I don't have a clue
   To the kind of stricture he will level
   Against this man—to my mind—who
   Composed more lyrics that were a marvel
   Than anyone else to this very day.
   So naturally I'm dying to know
   What kind of strategy he'll display
   Against Aeschylus, a virtuoso who

*Fragment from Euripides' lost *Meleager*.

Is master of the Bacchic form,
And naturally I fear for him.

EURIPIDES: "Lyrics that were a marvel," eh?
We'll soon see. . . . Watch me prune them to a
single stem.

DIONYSUS: And I'll pick up some pebbles to number
them.

[*There follows a roll of drums, the clash of cymbals
and the bleat of a flute.* EURIPIDES *breaks into a kind
of pibroch—half challenge, half triumph—as he prepares to tear* AESCHYLUS's *lyrics to pieces.*]

EURIPIDES: "Are you not heeding the slaughter of
heroes,*
Achilles of Thrace?"

[*clash of cymbals*]

"Are you not coming our way to help us
Who live by the lake and honor our forebear,
Hermes?"†

[*clash*]

"Are you not coming our way to help us?"‡

[*clash*]

DIONYSUS: He's ahead of you, Aeschylus, by a couple
of clashes.

*Fragment from Aeschylus' lost *Wise Melanippe*.
†Fragment from Aeschylus' lost *Myrmidons*.
‡Fragment from Aeschylus' lost *Ghost Raisers*.

EURIPIDES: "Most famous of Greeks, Agamemnon,
      Atreus' offspring,
   are you not listening?"

   [clash]

   "to me who am calling on you to help us?"*
DIONYSUS: Clash number three, Aeschylus!
EURIPIDES:
   "Pray hush! A holy hush.
   The priestesses are coming
   to open the temple of Artemis."†

   [clash]

   "Is nobody coming our way to help us?
   It's still within my hope to declare the triumph of
      heroes."‡

   [clash]

   "Are you not coming to help us?"
DIONYSUS: Zeus, O king, what a fusillade of clashing.
   I've got to get to the bathroom quick, my bowels
      are churning.
EURIPIDES: Hold on till you've heard the next batch
      of choral lyrics,
   especially composed for the lyre whose tunes it
      mimics.
DIONYSUS: On with them then, but no more clashes.

---

*Source unidentified.
†Fragment from lost *Priestesses*.
‡Fragment from *Agamemnon* (extant).

EURIPIDES:

> "See how the twin-throned might of Achaea*
> Full-blown in Hellas . . . phlattothratto-
>   phlattothrat†
> Dispatches that bitch of a Sphinx with a spear
>   phlattothrattophlattothrat
> And armed to the teeth like a bellicose bird
> Drops her into the claws of curs
> Which wheel in the sky, that is why
>   Phlattothrattophlattothrat
> Ajax finds himself beset
>   Phlattothrattophlattothrat."

DIONYSUS: Wherever did you get all that Phlatto-
  thratto?

A spot of Persian from Marathon, rope-twisters'
  ditties?‡

AESCHYLUS:

> Be that as it may, my sources
>   are impeccable,
> Impeccable too my use of them;
>   they do not stem
> Like blessed flowers of the Muses culled
>   from the same
> Meadow of Phrynichus, whereas
>   this man here

---

*The nonsensical outpouring of these verses is a jumbled echo of several mythical tales: Agamemnon and Meneláus in the Trojan War, Oedipus and the Sphinx, the Women of Thrace, and probably Memnon: all plays of Aeschylus of which we have only fragments except for his *Agamemnon* (Oresteia).

†Aristophanes has φλαττοθραττοφλαττοθρατ, which means "sound without sense."

‡Marathon: a plain in Attica where the Athenians defeated the Persians in 490 B.C. Before the battle, Pheidippides ran 150 miles in two days (from Athens to Sparta) to get help. The Athenians raised a temple to his memory.

Pinches stuff from everywhere:
    the songs of tarts,
Erotic drinking madrigals
    from, say, Miletus,*
Chantings from Caria played on flutes,
    dirges and dances . . .
Will somebody go and fetch my lyre?
    On second thoughts
No, one doesn't require a lyre.
    So let's go
And get that girl who uses shards
    for castanets.
Come out, you Muse of Euripides,
    it's you we'll use
For these musical bits and interludes.

[*the Muse of* EURIPIDES, *a pretty and nearly naked
dancing girl, appears as* AESCHYLUS *prepares to sing
his parody of* EURIPIDES]

DIONYSUS: My word, I bet this Muse never gave
    tongue to a Lesbian lay!†
AESCHYLUS: You twittering halcyons over the waving surf
    Splashed by droplets of spume
    Bedizened on the wing
    And wet with rain of foam;
    You spiders in crannies under the roof
    Whose nimble fingers twiddle and fiddle and spin
    Flexible threads for a loom
    As strong as a minstrel's song;
    And you flute-loving dolphins that run
    In the wake of the dark blue slicing prows;
    And the blossoms that shine into grapes on the vine

*An erotic poet of the sixth and early fifth century B.C.
†In other words, this girl is good for fellatio and not for cunnilingus,
and of course for a good heterosexual lay.

In clusters that are a solace to man . . .
Fling out your arms, my girl, to me,
Muse of Euripides [*addressing* EURIPIDES],
Look at that foot—make it scan?

EURIPIDES: I can.
AESCHYLUS: And the other too.
EURIPIDES: I do.
AESCHYLUS: And you the writer of such tripe
    Have the gall to damn my songs
    When your own are such a flop
    And worthy of a common tart.

So much for your choral lyrics—
now let's have a look at your longer monologues.

[*with the flute player playing and perhaps someone
else thumping a drum,* AESCHYLUS *opens his scroll
again and launches into another parody of* EURIPI-
DES, *echoing many of his plays and not expected
always to make sense*]

AESCHYLUS: O glistening black and somber Night,
    What horrible dreams do you send?
    Is it from hell these nightmares come?
    Things alive that have no life
    Yet black as the night they spawn a brat,
    A terribly disconcerting sight,
    Swaddled in necrophilic black
    And glaring murder with a murderous gleam,
    Baring enormous claws to attack.

    I'll thank you maids to light a light
    And fetch a pail of dew from the stream
    And heat the water till it is hot.
    I want to scrub away the blight
    Of that demonical dream.

Hey there, you god of foam,
Hey there, all in my home,
Extraordinary things are happening here:
Glyce's grabbed the cock and gone.*
Nymphs of the mountainside and you,
Mania, come to my help, for I,
Wretched I, as I was busy
Twiddling a spindle of flax in my fingers
To make me some cloth and sell it early,
As early as dawn, in the marketplace,
Up he soared into the sky
On pinions as light as lace
Abandoning me. My soul malingers,
Tears are streaming down my face.

Cry, cry, do I not cry
To you Artemis and you children of Ida†
To seize your bows and come to my succor.
So get to your feet, besiege her house,
Go with the exquisite Dictynna,‡
Run with her bitches through her land.
And Hecate, daughter of Zeus,
Brandishing the double torch
Wildly flaring in each hand,
Light my way to Glyce's house,
I'll enter and begin my search.

DIONYSUS: Both of you can stop your songs.
AESCHYLUS: I certainly have had enough.
    The next best step to test our art
is to weigh it on scales. It's the ultimate proof.
    We will now submit to that.

*Glyce and Mania are typical servants' names.
†Ida was the Cretan Artemis.
‡A Cretan goddess equivalent to Artemis.

[*a pair of exaggeratedly large scales is brought out and* DIONYSUS *walks over to it*]

DIONYSUS: Over here, please, the two of you. It belongs
to me to weigh the art of poetry like so much cheese.
MEN AND WOMEN: How thorough these experts seem
   to be!
   What an extraordinary thing to see,
   So novel and original
   Whoever could have thought of it?
   If someone off the street had told me
   Of such a curiosity
   There's not the faintest chance in hell
   I'd have believed him. I'd have thought
   Him to be incurably beyond the pale.

DIONYSUS: Ready, both of you? Over to your scales.

[AESCHYLUS *and* EURIPIDES *step to their scales*]

AESCHYLUS: Ready.
EURIPIDES: Ready.
DIONYSUS: Now pick up your scales ready to speak
   a line.
   Keep hold of your scale until I give the cuckoo call.
AESCHYLUS: Right.
EURIPIDES: Right.
DIONYSUS: Now each speak a line into the dish of
   your scale.
EURIPIDES: "Would that the good ship *Argo* had never
   winged in vain."*
AESCHYLUS: "O river Sperchius and vale where graze
   the kine."†

*From Euripides' *Medea*, the Nurse's speech.
†From Aeschylus' lost *Philoctetes* (fr. 249). We have Sophocles'
Philoctetes.

DIONYSUS: Cuckoo.

AESCHYLUS and EURIPIDES: [*as if at a race*] We're off.

DIONYSUS: Look, the scale of Aeschylus has dropped
down.

EURIPIDES: Good grief!

DIONYSUS: That's because he put a river in his line,
which made it wet, like a wool merchant wetting
his wool,*

whereas you endowed your line with wings.

EURIPIDES: All right, let him speak another line
and weigh it against mine.

DIONYSUS: Take hold of your scales again.

AESCHYLUS: Ready.

EURIPIDES: Ready.

DIONYSUS: Speak.

EURIPIDES: "A building made of words is Persuasion's
only shrine."†

AESCHYLUS: "Alone of the gods Death doth never
take a bribe."‡

DIONYSUS: Hands off scales.

AESCHYLUS and EURIPIDES: They're off.

DIONYSUS: Look, Aeschylus' scale has dropped again.
It's because he weighted down his line with Death.

EURIPIDES: But I put in Persuasion, a word to conjure with.

DIONYSUS: I know, but Persuasion is a featherweight.
It doesn't have the tonnage of its own conviction.
What you want now is a real heavyweight
to make your scales go down: something with heft
and brawn.

*To make it heavier.
†Fragment from Euripides' lost *Antigone*. The *Antigone* we have
is Sophocles'.
‡Fragment from Aeschylus' lost *Niobe*.

EURIPIDES: Where, I wonder, can I find that? I wonder where?

DIONYSUS: Perhaps in "Achilles threw two singles and a four."*

Get ready to speak your lines for the last weigh-in.

EURIPIDES: "In his right hand he took the handle heavy with iron."†

AESCHYLUS: "Chariot piled on chariot and corpse on corpse."‡

DIONYSUS: I'm afraid Aeschylus has licked you once again.

EURIPIDES: I don't see how.

DIONYSUS: The words "chariot" and "corpse" each put in twice.

To lift that lot even a hundred Egyptians wouldn't suffice.§

AESCHYLUS: Let's stop this line-by-line stuff now, I've had enough.

Even if he put himself on the scales complete with wife, brats, Cephisophon, as well as all his books, two lines of mine would outweigh the lot.

DIONYSUS: [to PLUTO]

They're friends of mine, these men, and I certainly don't want

to decide between them or make an enemy of either.

One amuses me, the other is a master.

PLUTO: So it looks as if you won't achieve what you came to do here.

DIONYSUS: Unless, of course, I do decide to take one of them.

---

*From an unknown play of Euripides. A bad throw, therefore heavy.
†From Euripides' lost *Meleager*.
‡From Aeschylus' lost *Glaucus of Potniae*.
§After the reconquest of Egypt by the Persians many Egyptians took refuge in Athens and earned a living as masons and artificers.

PLUTO: Whichever it is, him
 you may take back with you, and you won't have
  come down here in vain.
DIONYSUS: That's generous of you. [*turning to* AESCHY-
 LUS *and* EURIPIDES]
 May I remind you both that I came here
to save our city and ensure
the choral festivals of drama would endure.
 So whichever of you is ready and willing
to come to the aid of the State with sound thinking
he's the one I'll take upstairs with me.
 So, first things first, which of you, if either,
is able to make head or tail of Alcibiades?*
 The city's in a turmoil because of him.
AESCHYLUS: What's the general opinion of him,
 please?
DIONYSUS: They pine for him, they hate him,
 dismiss him and want him back. . . .
 But what do you two think of him?
EURIPIDES: I despise any citizen
 who shows himself slow to help his own

---

*The "enfant terrible" of fifth-century B.C. Greece: beautiful, noble,
brilliant, but also arrogant, unscrupulous, dissolute. He was one of
the young men who hung around Socrates and figures in Plato's
Symposium as well as in the dialogue that bears his name. He entered politics and was soon in the forefront of events. He was chosen
as one of the three leaders of the disastrous Sicilian expedition of
415 B.C. but on the eve of departure disgraced himself by a prank
that the authorities did not think funny. One morning the Athenians
awoke to find all the sacred herms of the city smeared with pitch.
He was allowed to sail, his punishment being deferred. The rest of
his life was a mixture of political intrigue (with Sparta and Persia),
acceptance and reversals at Athens, naval exploits, and final dis-
missal. He betook himself to his refuge on the Hellespont, where
he was assassinated on Persian orders in 404 B.C. at the age of forty-
six. As to the prank, there's no proof that Alcibiades was responsible.

but quick to do his country harm;
who's out for himself and a dead loss to the State.

DIONYSUS: Holy Poseidon, that's neat!

[*turning to* AESCHYLUS] But what do you think?

AESCHYLUS: It's not a good idea in a town
to rear a lion cub, but if you do,
make sure he's happy when he grows up
and not liable to run amok.

DIONYSUS: By Zeus the Preserver, I can't make up my
mind which to take.

One was clever, one was clear.

So once again I ask you both: have you any idea
of how best to serve our State?

EURIPIDES: Couldn't Cleocritus and Cinesias be
winged together*
and sent soaring into the air?

DIONYSUS: A hilarious sight, no doubt, but off the
point.

EURIPIDES: You see, if a battle at sea were going on
they could be armed with cruets of vinegar
and squirt these into the enemy's eyes.

DIONYSUS: [*sarcastically*] Brilliant, my dear Palimedes,†
what a genius you are!

Did you think of that yourself or was it
Cephisophon?‡

EURIPIDES: Entirely mine . . . though Cephisophon
thought of the vinegar.

---

*Cleocritus was a notably fat man parodied in *Birds* as having an
ostrich for a mother. Cinesias was a ridiculously thin man, a dithyrambic poet and musician noted for his irreligion. Plato blames him
in *Gorgias* for producing poetry that aims at giving pleasure rather
than telling the truth.

†Engineer, inventor, and the cleverest Greek hero at Troy. Euripides wrote a play about him that Aristophanes parodies in *Women
of the Thesmophoria*.

‡The chief actor in Euripides' tragedies.

Here's another brainwave of mine I'd like you
to hear.

DIONYSUS: Shoot.

EURIPIDES: If we put faith in the faithful and stopped
having
faith in the faithless . . .

DIONYSUS: Eh? You've lost me. Can't you be less
clever
and try to be more clear?

EURIPIDES: If we stopped trusting the citizens we're
trusting
and began to trust the citizens we don't . . .

DIONYSUS: We'd be saved?

EURIPIDES: Well, we're getting nowhere with the present lot
so at least we might have a chance with their opposite.

DIONYSUS: [to AESCHYLUS] What's your opinion?

AESCHYLUS: First tell me the kind of people the city
is using,
is it the useful?

DIONYSUS: Certainly not, the city damns them as useless.

AESCHYLUS: But the useless the city thinks are fine?

DIONYSUS: Not exactly, the city's forced to use them.

AESCHYLUS: How can anyone save a city like that?
A city that'll eat neither lean nor fat?*

DIONYSUS: Damn it, man! If you really want to go upstairs again
you'd better think of something.

AESCHYLUS: I can't down here, I'd rather wait till I
get up there.

DIONYSUS: Oh no, you won't, you'll ruddy well do your
good right here!

---

*The Greek proverb runs "One that will wear neither jacket nor
shirt," for which the English equivalent perhaps is "Jack sprat
would eat no fat, his wife would eat no lean."

AESCHYLUS: All right: this for one thing,
   treat the enemy's domain as yours, and yours the
      enemy's,
and treat the fleet as everything and everything else
   as nothing.
DIONYSUS: All very well, but that "everything"
   gets gobbled up by the jurymen.*
PLUTO: Make your choice then.
DIONGSUS: My decision between you two
   will be to choose the one my intuition tells me to.
EURIPIDES: Remember the gods you swore by
   when you promised to take me home.
      You've got to stick to your friends.
DIONYSUS: It was my tongue that swore. . . .† I've
   chosen Aeschylus.
EURIPIDES: What's that? You scum!
DIONYSUS: I've just declared that Aeschylus has won.
   Why shouldn't I?
EURIPIDES: How can you look me in the eyes?
   Swine!
DIONYSUS: What's swinish if the audience don't think
   it is?‡
EURIPIDES: Shithead, d'you really mean to leave me dead?
DIONYSUS: Who knows if life be death and death be
   really breath,§
   with supper, sleep, and a cozy bed?

[EURIPIDES *departs in a huff*]

PLUTO: You two can go inside now.

*A gibe at the way money for public services is apt to get subverted
into the pockets of shysters.
†This is the second time that these famous lines from Euripides'
Hippolytus are quoted: "It was my tongue that swore, my heart
remained aloof."
‡Adapted from a line of Euripides' lost *Aeolus*.
§Adapted from a line of Euripides' lost *Polybus*.

DIONYSUS: Whatever for?
PLUTO: So we can prepare
    a little celebration before you go.
DIONYSUS: I won't say nay to that—a splendid idea!

[PLUTO *leads* DIONYSUS *and* AESCHYLUS *into the
palace*]

STROPHE

WOMEN: Happy the man who is endowed
    With the blessing of a clever brain;
    A fact that's being verified,
    For here we have an intelligent man
    About to return to his home again:
    A godsend to his fellow men,
    A godsend to his closest friends
    And of course to his family
    Because of his perspicacity.

ANTISTROPHE

MEN: This means not hanging about
    Blabbing away with Socrates
    And not caring a fig for art
    Or giving a damn for the very best
    Productions of the Tragedies,
    But fiddling around and killing time
    With never-ending futile chatter
    In a niggling senseless game.
    That is the mind of a downright nutter.

[PLUTO *returns escorting* AESCHYLUS, DIONYSUS *and*
XANTHIAS. *He puts into the hands of* AESCHYLUS (*or*
XANTHIAS) *various "gifts" to mete out to sundry po-
litical scoundrels whom the world would do better*

*without. Fifes, cymbals, and tambourines accompany
the valedictory chants that follow*]

PLUTO: Aeschylus, now we must say good-bye.
    You have to go and save your city,
    Injecting sense into a senseless race
    Who seem forever to multiply.
    Offer this hemlock to Cleophon;*
    And here's a noose for the tax collector
    Which Myrmex would like to share
    With Nichomachus, as well as this
    Dagger for Archenomus, and
    Tell him to hurry on down here
    Without delay. If they're remiss
    I'll clap them in irons and I'll brand
    Them when they arrive here below.
    I'll do the same to that nasty fellow
    Adeimantus, son of Leucolophos.
AESCHYLUS: All this I'll do, and meanwhile you
    Must bequeath my chair to Sophocles
    For him to care for and preserve
    Until such time as I return
    Here again, and this because
    I count him second only to me.
    But remember this: on no account
    Allow that liar, that miscreant,

---

*The identity of most of the names mentioned here is either un-
known or obscure. Adeimantus was a cousin of Alcibiades and became mixed up in various scandals before serving as a general in
the Athenian army. He was captured by the Spartans at the Battle
of Aegospotami in 405 B.C. but his life was spared.

That clown to sit himself down
In my chair—even by accident.*

PLUTO: [*to the* CHORUS]

With a flourish of your hallowed flares
Honor this man as he wends his way,
And go with him as he goes upstairs,
And sing him his hymns and songs today.

MEN AND WOMEN: First we ask you gods below
To deign to bestow
A favorable journey for our poet
As he ascends
Into the daylight;
And we beg you to inspire
Him with many a great idea
As he departs, so he may shower
Our city with many a blessing to make amends
For all our sufferings in war
And bring them to an end.
And if Cleophon wants to fight†—
This goes for his friends—
Let them do it in their own lands.

[*the* CHORUS *of* MEN AND WOMEN—*the Mystery nov-*

---

*Is Aeschylus speaking here or is this harsh assessment of Euripides
Aristophanes' own opinion? Probably a bit of both. Euripides was not
popular in his lifetime. His outlook was too new and his portrayal of
humanity too real not to shock the Athenians of his day. It is not
surprising that he left Athens and ended his days at the court of King
Archelaus of Macedon. It may have been a consolation had he known
that in the next century and onward he was more popular than Aeschylus and Sophocles combined. When Marcus Licinius Crassus, the
Roman general and multimillionaire, was defeated by the Parthians in
53 B.C., Euripides' *The Bacchae* was being played in the local theater.
It is said that for the gruesome scene of Agave gloating over the head
of her son (whom she murdered while possessed by the Bacchic spirit)
the head of Crassus was rushed to the theater.

†Cleophon, a hawkish demagogue, was not regarded by Aristophanes as a proper Athenian because he came from Thrace.

ices—is joined by the CHORUS OF FROGS—*which has been in the background throughout quietly dancing and miming—and together with* AESCHYLUS *and* PLUTO *they begin a slow march off the stage*]

A PARLIAMENT
OF WOMEN

(Ecclesiazusae)

A Parliament of Women was probably produced in 392 B.C., but we do not know by whom or how it fared in competition.

THEME

This comedy is about the establishment of a utopia along communist lines managed by women, in which the assessment of worth would derive from a new set of values, based not on wealth and worldly success but on usefulness to the new State. Men would be released from the burdens of administration (which they habitually bungled) and be allowed to parade like peacocks, with no other role than to enjoy themselves and to be at the disposal of women. There would be free meals for all. The young and the beautiful of both sexes could copulate at will but only after they had offered their services to the old and the ugly.

CHARACTERS

PRAXAGORA*, an Athenian housewife
MADAM A, neighbor of Praxagaora
MADAM B, ditto
BLEPYRUS, husband of Praxagora
NEIGHBOR, of Blepyrus
CHREMES, citizen of Athens
MEAN MAN, devoid of public spirit
FEMALE REPORTER, a girl employed by Praxagora
CRONE A, old woman of Athens

*The name means "public spirited."

GIRL, living next door
PIPER (silent)
EPIGENES, a young man in love
CRONE B, old woman of Athens
CRONE C, ditto
MAID, of Praxagora
SICON AND PARMENON, servants of Neighbor (silent)
TWO GIRLS (silent)
CHORUS, women of Athens

THE STORY

A group of determined women convened by Praxagora
dress up as men with the intention of packing the Parliament and by a coup d'état saving Athens from the blunders of their men. Blepyrus wakes up and wonders what
has happened to his wife, his cloak, and his boots, so
early in the morning. Neighbor spots him from a balcony
wandering among the bushes. Then Chremes returns
from Parliament and recounts what is going on there.
Meanwhile, Praxagora, mission accomplished, returns
home, where she, Blepyrus, and Neighbor have a long
conversation about the pros and cons of the new order.
Mean Man appears and vows that he's not going to let
go of any of his property in the interests of common
ownership, at the same time expecting to be fed at the
communal dinner that is in the offing. A young man
coming from the dinner and hoping to meet his girlfriend is met and dragged off by the three crones, who
insist that they now have a legal right to him. In the
final scene, Blepyrus appears on his way to the dinner
with his arms around two young girls. It is evident that
he is full of sap and already transformed by the new
regime. A boozy maid grabs him and amid dance and
song everyone, including the Chorus, heads for the feast.

OBSERVATIONS

It is not the intention of Praxagora and the women to usurp or take on the obligations of men but simply to implement their own. They are, after all, the managers of their households and are merely extending the scope of their competence. It is a time when Athens is at the lowest ebb of her history: without money, without a fleet, without an empire, and in· her dealings with the rest of Greece playing second fiddle to Sparta. Whatever has been tried before no longer works, and in a mood of unacknowledged despair Praxagora and her women are saying: "We may as well try communism." What follows is a kind of parody of what Plato was later to expand on in his *Republic*.

As to my translation, let me—at the risk of being tedious—return once again to the problem and fascinating challenge of translating Greek into English. People in general have no idea what it entails. Once long ago when I told a friend that I was translating *Antigone*, the friend came out with: "Oh, I thought that had already been translated."

So what is required? Fidelity to the original, of course, but even fidelity can be a stumbling block. I think of the village in Mexico called Santo Tomas de los Platanos, near which I once lived. How romantic! What if I rendered this, quite accurately, as Saint Thomas of the Bananas! Then there's the Latin tag *Laudator temporis acti* to describe someone who lives in the past. One could just say *A lover of times gone by*, and that's not bad, but it gets nowhere near the piquancy of *Those were the days*.

What's in a· word? Just about everything. Even among the synonyms of one's own tongue we cannot ignore the emotive charge of words without being ridiculous. You might for instance decline an invitation to dinner when the bill of fare is dead calf with fungus in heated dough, scorched ground tubers and cabbage stalks, all swilled down with rotten German grape juice and topped off with the powder of burned berries in scalding water diluted with drops squeezed out of a cow's udder. You might well be excused from attending such a dinner, but you would have missed an excellent meal of veal-and-mushroom pie, roast potatoes and spring greens, chased by a bottle of hock, and finished off with a steaming cup of coffee and cream.

TIME AND SETTING

It is a little before dawn on a street in Athens not far from the Assembly (Parliament). From a house flanked by two others a young woman emerges dressed as a man and carrying a staff. She swings a lantern from time to time as if signaling and looks around anxiously. Now she holds the lantern up and addresses it in the mock accents of High Tragedy.

PRAXAGORA: "Luminous eye in the wheeling axis of
    light,"*
  brilliant evolution of the craftsman's skill on the
    potter's wheel,
I make no excuse for saluting you as you peep
    through
your eyeholes like an imprisoned sun, the way you do.
    Beam out the signal we arranged and do your part,
for to you, and you alone, we confide our plot;
not least because in our bedrooms every night
when our bodies in the acrobatic spell

---

*Parodying a quotation from an unknown source.

of Aphrodite writhe and merge and you are there,
    voyeur,
Licking into the ecstatic niches between our thighs,
searing the bristling thickets while standing near.
    And when we sneakily open a larder door
to raid the shelves of food and wine, you're there,
a conniver who does not go off prattling to a
        neighbor.
    That is why we're trusting you with our present
        plans as well:
the plans my friends and I have hatched at the
    Scira festival.*
    But no one's yet arrived. I cannot understand.
    It's almost daybreak and the Assembly'll soon
        begin . . .
time we women-men set our bottoms down
and quietly took our seats . . . but why have they
        not come?
    Are they trying still to get themselves false beards
or are they funking snaffling hubby's clothes? The
    cowards!

[*a woman dressed as a man and carrying a lamp
comes into view*]

    But I see a light coming this way . . .
better dodge out of sight in case it is a man.

[PRAXAGORA *hides behind a pillar as women dressed
as men appear in twos and threes until there is a full
muster that will constitute the* CHORUS]

LEADER: Get moving, ladies. I've heard the cock
    crow twice.
PRAXAGORA: [*stepping forward*] I should think so:

*A women's festival in honor of Demeter.

I've been waiting for you all night.
My friend next door ought to be here. I'll stroke
her door.
Her husband mustn't hear.

[*she does so and* MADAM A *comes out*]

MADAM A: I was just dressing when I heard your fingers scratching.
I wasn't asleep, and you know how my man, darling,
is from Salamis and all night long he was plying his oar*
under the sheets and it wasn't till now that I got the chance
of swiping his cloak.
PRAXAGORA: Look,
I see Cleinarete and Sostrate arriving,
and there's Philainete.†
LEADER: About time too! Glyce swore that the last
woman here
would be fined four liters of wine and a sack of chickpeas.
PRAXAGORA: And I see Smicythion's wife Melistiche
trying to run in his boots. She was the only one,
I expect, who had no problem getting away from
her man.‡
MADAM A: And there's the barkeeper's wife,
Geusistrate,
look, she's got a flare in her hand!
PRAXAGORA: There's Philodoretus' wife and the wife
of Chaeretades,
and a whole pile of women—
a regular "Who's Who" in town.

---

*The natives of the island of Salamis were noted for their
oarsmanship.
†These and the other names were typical.
‡A suggestion that her husband was impotent.

[MADAM B *enters running*]

MADAM B: I had the darnedest time getting away, dar-
    ling,
  my husband hiccuped all through the night from
    guzzling
sardines at dinner.

PRAXAGORA: Now that I've got you all here, please
    seat yourselves
  while I ask you if you've done all we agreed on at
    the Scira.

MADAM A: Sure! My armpits are now thicker than
    groves,
  as we agreed; next, when my man left for the agora
I covered myself in oil and stood in the sun all day
to get a tan.

MADAM B: Me, the same. I immediately threw my
    razor away
  and let myself get hairy all over—the ultimate
    nonfeminine.

PRAXAGORA: And you've brought the beards we
    agreed upon?

MADAM A: By Hecate we have! Take a look at mine.

MADAM B: And mine beats even the beard of
    Epicrates.*

PRAXAGORA: What about the rest of you?

MADAM A: They've all got their beards: nodding "yes"
    to a man.

PRAXAGORA: And I see you have the rest of the
    paraphernalia:
  Spartan boots, staves, cloaks and men's attire—
all that we agreed to.

*A politician with a great square beard nicknamed "the Shield-
Bearer."

MADAM A: I've also got Lamias' cudgel. I nipped it
    during his nap.*

MADAM B: That must be the cudgel he uses when he
    wants to fart.

PRAXAGORA: By Zeus the Savior, if he wore the
    leather jacket

of the giant Argos with a hundred eyes he'd be ripe†

for summary execution. . . . But we've still got quite
    a packet

to get through while the stars are shining, so let's start.
    Parliament is due to meet at dawn.

MADAM A: Ye gods, you're right!

    We'd better make sure of our seats under the
        Speaker's Platform

facing the Chairman.

MADAM B: [producing a basket of wool]

    I'm jolly glad I brought my carder with me:

I'll get some wool carded while the Assembly's coming in.

PRAXAGORA: While they're coming in? Don't be silly.

MADAM B: Not at all silly. Carding doesn't stop my
    listening.

    My children can't exactly go about naked.

PRAXAGORA: Well, I never! What good is dressing
    up as a man

    if you're going to sit there carding wool?

        Not to mention the fact that it would be pretty
            awkward

if in full view of everybody from town

some female has to go clambering over them,

pulling her skirts up and revealing her you-know-what.

*This Lamias is unknown but his name brings to mind the ogre
Lamia, who carried a cudgel and farted when captured.
†Argos was the giant with eyes all over his body whom Hera sent
to spy on Io, with whom Zeus was having an affair and whom she
had turned into a cow. When Argos died, Hera placed his hundred
eyes in the peacock's tail.

So we'd better make sure of being in our seats
    on time
and no one will twig the reason we're swaddled tight.*
    And when they see the beards we've managed to
    fix on
whoever's going to know that we're not men?
    A good example is Agyrrhius, who's really a
    woman†
but gets away with being a man by dint of wearing
the beard of Pronomos,‡ and now, if you please, is
    strutting
up there in the highest echelons of the city.
    If he can do it, I swear by this dawning day
that we too can carry out a coup and essay
something for our city, but as things are
we lie stuck in the doldrums
with power of neither sail nor oar.

MADAM A: And how, pray, can a congregation of
    women
    hope to address an audience of men?

PRAXAGORA: Famously, if you want to know.
    It's said that the young men who've been most thor-
    oughly squashed
are the ones that express themselves with the greatest
    juice;
and that, because of our natures, is exactly the case
    with us.

MADAM A: About that, I have qualms. It's inexperience
    that numbs.

PRAXAGORA: That's precisely why we're here. This is
    a rehearsal

---

*The women's disguise, apparently, was chiefly in wearing beards.
They kept their own clothes on under their cloaks.
†Agyrrhius was a rich politician and, it seems, a homosexual.
‡Nothing is known of Pronomos.

of what we're going to say when we're there.

But it's time for you to get your beard on, the others too.

I expect they've been practicing on how to waffle.

MADAM A: Waffle? There isn't a woman here who can't do that.

PRAXAGORA: Then fix your beard on and be a male.

I'll set these wreaths aside for myself in case I speak.

MADAM B: [*putting on her beard and holding up a mirror*]

Praxagora, sweetie, how silly I look.

PRAXAGORA: Silly? I don't see why.

MADAM A: Well, isn't my dial like a plateful of calamaries?

PRAXAGORA: [*marshaling the women*]

Let the celebrant circulate with the sacrificial cat.*

The rest of you move into the sanctuary . . . Ariphrades,†

stop jabbering . . . and take your places . . .

who wants to say her bit?

MADAM A: I do.

PRAXAGORA: Then put on the wreath, and good luck to you.

MADAM A: Ready?

PRAXAGORA: Start.

MADAM A: What, without a drink first?

PRAXAGORA: A drink?

MADAM A: Why else, dearie, do I have a wreath on?

---

*Actually the Assembly was purified with a piglet; the women, normally confined to the house, think of a house pet.
†Not known, but obviously one of the women.

PRAXAGORA: Get off the rostrum. You'd shame us at the Parliament proper.

MADAM A: You mean they don't drink in the Parliament proper?

PRAXAGORA: Just listen to you: "don't they drink?"

MADAM A: They drink all right, swill it down, and when you think
of the wacky decrees they promulgate, they really must be
sozzled to the brim. How d'you suppose they don't drink
when the wine's flowing and they're making toasts
and bawling at each other in their cups, till the police arrive
and cart away the sodden blokes?

PRAXAGORA: Please go and sit down. You're simply too naive.

MADAM A: But it's true. Meanwhile this beard's reducing me to nought
and I'm suffering from drought.

PRAXAGORA: Would anyone else like to spout?

MADAM B: I would.

PRAXAGORA: Put on the wreath then, things are going fine.
Be forceful, bang your stick and rant away like a man.

MADAM B: Oh dear, I'd much rather that speechifying
was left to one of the experts and I be left alone.
However, I don't mind saying
that my vote is for abolishing barrels of water
in the bars; it's a damn bad idea, I swear
by Persephone and Demeter.

PRAXAGORA: By Persephone and Demeter?
You nincompoop, where's your brain?

MADAM B: What's the matter? I wasn't asking for wine.

PRAXAGORA: I know, but you swore by Perse-
   phone and Demeter*
when you're supposed to be a man.
   The rest of what you said was nonsense too.
MADAM B: Honestly, by Apollo ...!
PRAXAGORA: You've said enough. Give me the wreath.
   I'm finished with being a woman in Parliament
if we don't do things right.
MADAM B: Give me the wreath back. I want to speak
   again.
   The whole thing's clear to me now, good ladies as-
      sembled here. . . .
PRAXAGORA: Another blooper! You're supposed to be
   speaking to men.
MADAM B: It's because I caught a glimpse of Epigonus
   over there†
and naturally thought I was talking to women.

[PRAXAGORA *seizes the Speaker's wreath and mounts
the rostrum*]

PRAXAGORA: You buzz off and get back to your chair.
   It's obvious from your performance, my poor dear,
that I must assume the wreath and make a speech.
   So let me beg the gods to bring to fruition
whatever we may decide in today's resolution.
   My concern for the welfare of this State
is no less than your own; and I'm upset
and not a little peeved by what is going on
in our city, because without the slightest doubt
she elects for her leaders the worst of men,

*To swear by the twin goddesses was a female oath.
†Unknown except for the fact that he had got himself enrolled in
a women's cult and was notoriously womanish.

and if any of them manage to be honest for a sin-
    gle day
he'll prove himself the worst of scoundrels for ten.
    Then the search begins for someone who is better
and he turns out to be an even greater rotter.
    It isn't easy, of course, to reason with men
as unreasonable as you Athenians, who shun
those who want to help them and go after
those who don't. Once upon a time we women never
convened assemblies but at least we always knew
that Agyrrhius was a rascal, and now we do*
convene them, and the people who draw a salary
    think he's marvelous,
while those who don't think those who do are fit for
    the noose.

MADAM A: [*to the sound of clapping*] Bravo, by
    Aphrodite!
PRAXAGORA: Pathetic! Swearing by Aphrodite!
    Wouldn't that go down well in Parliament!
MADAM A: I'd not have said it there.
PRAXAGORA: Then don't get used to saying it
        here. . . . As for the alliance,†
when it was mooted the people were vociferous
claiming that if we didn't confirm it the city
would come to a stop but when we did confirm it finally
the people were glum, and those who had enthusiastically
supported it had to flee.
    Meanwhile, we really ought to have a fleet.‡

---

*Agyrrhius was a rich politician who had recently persuaded the
government to grant a salary to members of Parliament.
†With Argos and Corinth against Sparta.
‡The Athenian fleet had recently been destroyed by the Spartans
at the Battle of Aegospotami in 405 B.C., when the Spartan navy
was under the command of Alcibiades.

> The rich man and the farmer vote No, the pauper
>   votes Yes,
and everyone's furious with the Corinthians and
    they with us.
> They're really decent people, so we should be too.
> The Argives are idiots though Hieronymus is shrewd,
and every now and then a light comes into view
only to be scotched by Thrasybulus, who's in a rage
because no one ever asked him to take charge.*
[*after another burst of clapping*]
> Thanks, thanks for your approval, but you the
>   people
have landed us in this muddle,
because though drawing your salaries from the tax-
    payer's purse
every one of you is out for himself, and of course,
all semblance of public spirit dwindles,
just as you see poor old General Aesimus dwindle.†
> But if you pay attention to me you'll soon see
a solution to your puzzle.
> My proposal is that the management of the city
be handed over to us women. After all,
it's we women who already
look after our households and finances.

MADAM B: Hear hear! Spot on!

MADAM A: Please continue, my good man.

PRAXAGORA: You see, they're absolutely better than
    us men.

> To begin with, they dye their wool in boiling water,
every one of them, just as they've always done,

---

*Hieronymus was probably the admiral of that name. Thrasybulus
was a veteran general who had argued against the Spartan peace
terms.
†A general who had commanded the democratic forces in the civil
war of 403 B.C.

which the Athenian government's disallowed—the
dunces—
though this worked really fine, in favor
of some newfangled innovation, and all the while
the women go on with their cooking just as usual,
and just as usual carry burdens on their heads,
and celebrate the Thesmophoria festival
just as they've always done, and bake breads
just as they've always done, and drive their men
up the pole just as they've always done,
and hide away their lovers just as they've always
done,
and treat themselves to tidbits just as they've always done,
and drink their wine as usual just as they've always done,
and enjoy their fucking just as they've always done.
    Wherefore, my good fellows, let us let the women
take control of the government of our city;
and don't let's hargee-bargee about the way they
do it
but let them just get on with it, provided only
that their first concern is to shield our soldiers,
just as our second is—wouldn't you agree?—
to send them generous food parcels because you
      love them.
    Nobody compares with women as money raisers
and once in power no one will ever get away
with cheating them—not a bit of it—for they
themselves are masters of the art. . . . I won't go on
with details; if you'll just accept my proposition
you'll live a life of blissfullest abandon.
MADAM B: Praxagora, you sweetie-pie, what you say

is so impressive; wherever did you learn to speak
that way?

PRAXAGORA: From listening to the speakers on the
Pnyx when
I lived there with my husband during the Spartan
invasion.

MADAM A: Then I'm not surprised my dear,
that you've learnt to be so formidable and so
shrewd;
What's more, we fellow women will appoint you
our commander in chief
in this enterprise of yours if we succeed.
But what if that clever speaker Cephalus*
makes mincemeat of you in Parliament and you
come to grief?
How will you deal with his abuse?

PRAXAGORA: I'll inform him that he's bonkers and
obtuse.

MADAM A: Yes, we all know that as well as you.

PRAXAGORA: I'll tell him he's a manic-depressive.

MADAM A: We know that too.

PRAXAGORA: Then I'll tell him that one who's such
a massive
flop at making pottery will make a shoddy city.

MADAM A: There's cross-eyed Neocleides too,†
what if he disapproves of you?

PRAXAGORA: Pray direct your gaze, I'll say, up a
dog's behind.

MADAM A: But what if they attempt to screw you?

PRAXAGORA: In screwing I know a thing or two—I'll
screw.

---

*A formidable orator who also sold pottery.
†A politician known for his aggressiveness.

MADAM A: But there's something you must bear in
    mind:
  what will you do if the police pin you down?
PRAXAGORA: I'll jab them with my elbow, so,
  they won't get near enough for a clinch.
LEADER: And if they carry you off I have a hunch
  we'll just tell them to set you down again.
MADAM A: So we've got it all well arranged
    except for one thing: when we vote how can we
    be certain
to raise our hands when we're so used to raising our
    legs?
PRAXAGORA: That's a stiff one! But remember this
    at least,
  free your arm when you vote and raise your fist.
    Now let's get on with things.
    Hitch up your skirts right away and put on your
      boots—
the way you see your husband do when he goes off
to Parliament or some mission. And when that's done
fix on your beards—making sure that your beard fits—
put on the manly cloaks you filched, pick up your staff,
and start to sing a good old farmers' song.
LEADER: Excellent advice.
PRAXAGORA: Other women'll be arriving from the
    country, so hurry on
  and get ahead of them.* It would be nice
to reach the Pnyx before them; otherwise at dawn
when this whole show is over and done,
you'll go home with not so much as a clothes-peg to
    your name.

*Only the first six thousand assemblymen in attendance were
paid. (Loeb)

[PRAXAGORA *leaves together with* MADAM A *and* MADAM B]

LEADER: It's time for us, you fellows, to press on
  and never let us forget that that is what we are.
     The risk of getting caught is not a trifling danger,
togged up as we are for a bold and dark affair.

STROPHE

CHORUS: Come on, you fellows, it's time we were off,
     the magistrate
  Just now has sounded the summons
  And if you arrive too late
  Though you be covered in dust
  And garlic and soup were your breakfast,
  And your eyes are sharp as lemons,
  You'll miss your three obols a day.
  Hullo, Charímedes! Hey,
  Smithycus and Draces!*
  Hurry yourselves along
  Taking care that no
  Discord comes among you
  And undermines our mission
  And the part we're taking on.
  When we reach our stands
  We'll stick together like glue
  Ready to raise our hands
  Supporting every issue
  We are pushing as women.
  Whoops! What am I saying?
  I should have said "as men."

*Typical men's names.

ANTISTROPHE

Let's give the Parliament men from town a rough-
   ish time.
They never bothered before today
To show up here and come
When an obol was the pay.
They sat in the shops that sell wreaths
Passing the hour of the day.
But now they're fighting for seats.
Not once in the time
Of Myronides the Great*
(A golden age) would they
Have had the face to take
On the affairs of State
For a stash of paltry cash.
Everyone would come
With his little bag of lunch:
Bread and something to drink,
Two onions and three olives.
Today they'd make a stink
If they didn't get three obols
For ministering to the people
And doing what is noble.

[*The* CHORUS *retires and the old man* BLEPYRUS *enters. He is wearing slippers and a woman's slip.*]

BLEPYRUS: Where's my wife? What's going on? It's
   .   nearly dawn
   and of her there isn't a sign.
      I've been lying awake and wanting to poop for
         an aeon.
      Where are my shoes? Where is my cloak?
      It's devilish difficult to see in the dark;

*A triumphant general at the time of the Persian wars.

meanwhile the man who cleans out the chamber pots
   has been*
hammering at my back door and making such a din
that I've grabbed my wife's slip and put her slippers on
and been forced to let him in.
> But to poop, to poop, where can I poop without
>   being seen?†

Anywhere, I suppose, will do in the dark:
my pooping will be difficult to spot.
> Lord, what a fool I've been

letting myself get married at my age—what a dunce!
> I deserve to be whipped. . . . Oh, where has she
>   slipped?

> Anyway, I've got to do my wants.

[*he squats by some bushes but is spotted from* MADAM
B's *balcony by* NEIGHBOR, *who holds up a lantern*]

NEIGHBOR: Who's down there? . . . Surely not Blepyrus my neighbor?
> My God, it is. . . . Hey, what are you wearing yel-
>   low for?

> It looks like Cinesias' diarrhea.‡

BLEPYRUS: Not so. It's the little crocus-colored slip
   my wife likes to wear.
NEIGHBOR: Don't you have a cloak?
BLEPYRUS: Seems not . . . I couldn't find it on the bed.

---

*The procedure must have been much the same as it was in my boy-
hood in India. In those days, there were no flush loos. Once a day,
the Ramussi (the lowest caste) would clean out the chamber pots.
†Why is BLEPYRUS having difficulty? Presumably because his urgency coincides with the fact that there *are* no chamber pots avail-
able. They are being cleaned out.
‡A contemporary dithyrambic poet, teased elsewhere for some de-
fecatory incident, cf. *Frogs* 36b, with Scholiast. (Loeb)

NEIGHBOR: Couldn't you have asked your wife to help you look?

BLEPYRUS: No, I couldn't. . . . As a matter of fact she isn't here.

She's eluded me and is probably up to something bad.

NEIGHBOR: Surprise surprise! I've run into the same thing.

My paramour's gone off with the cloak I wear,

and my boots are missing, which is even more exasperating.

There's no sign of them anywhere.

BLEPYRUS: Surprise surprise! I couldn't find my boots either

and when I suddenly had to shit I bolted in these slippers

and managed to avoid doing it on the comforter,

which has just come back from the cleaners.

NEIGHBOR: And your wife? I expect she's gone breakfasting

with one of her cronies.

BLEPYRUS: You're probably right. I don't think she's depressed or anything.

NEIGHBOR: [scrutinizing the bushes]

Seems to me you must be shitting a length of hawser.

Anyway, I'm off to the Parliament sitting

once I get hold of my cloak again—my one and only.

BLEPYRUS: Me too, as soon as I've done my business here.

Trouble is, I'm blocked up by a sort of prickly pear.

NEIGHBOR: [as he leaves the balcony]

Blocked up like the way Thrasybulus made sure the Spartans were.*

BLEPYRUS: Begad you're right! . . . But I'm in a spot.

[continuing to himself]

*When the Spartans offered peace in 405 B.C. Thrasybulus, the veteran and much-respected Athenian general, was largely responsible for blocking the measure.

What do I do? Even after this I'm not
in the clear. What's going to happen when I eat?
　　There'll be more crap with nowhere to go:
all bottled up and the backdoor shut.
　　I need a doctor. Fetch one somebody, please.
　　But the right kind, an arsehole specialist, no less.
　　Does that fellow Amynon know? He'll probably
　　　say no.
　　Then get hold of Antisthenes, oh, please!*
　　He's a master of diagnosis when it comes to
blocked and grunting bottoms. . . . Oh, Madam
　　Hileithya,
mistress of childbirth, I'm in labor, come and deliver
me—all blocked up inside though ready to shatter.
　　Say "not" to a comedy of the pot.

[CHREMES *enters*]

CHREMES: What are you doing? Don't tell me you're
　　having a shit?
BLEPYRUS: Thank heavens, no more! I'm upright
　　once again.
CHREMES: But why are you wearing your wife's
　　slip?
BLEPYRUS: Well, it was dark inside the house when I
　　got the grippe.
But where on earth have you been?
CHREMES: The Parliament assembly.
BLEPYRUS: You mean it's over already?
CHREMES: Certainly is . . . Even before sunup.
　　There was much merriment, dear God,
when they started branding us with red.†
BLEPYRUS: And you got your three obols?

---

*Amynon and Antisthenes were probably not real doctors but
Machiavelli types and adepts at political abortions.
†Red dye was used to mark the latecomers.

CHREMES: Balls! I arrived too late, and I'm not ex-
    actly proud
of coming away empty-handed.

BLEPYRUS: You mean with nothing at all?

CHREMES: Nothing but my empty wallet.

BLEPYRUS: But why were you late?

CHREMES: Too much human traffic round the Pnyx.
    Something terrific.
One couldn't help thinking of a crush of cobblers:
a pasty-faced lot the Assembly seemed.
    So I and a bunch of others got nothing.

BLEPYRUS: And if I went now I too would get no-
    thing?

CHREMES: Nothing. Even if the rooster has stopped
    crowing.

BLEPYRUS: That makes me prince of losers.
    "Antilochus, for those three obols wail thee not
but for me who have lost all though am living yet."*
      What could possibly have been the reward for
        such a crowd
and at such an early hour?

CHREMES: What else could it have been but some idea
    among the members of the committee for the saving
        of the city?
    And of course the first thing to transpire
was old cross-eyed Neocleides groping toward the Chair
and trying to be the first to speak; which made
    the people
cry foul, shouting; "Isn't it outrageous
that in the crucial business of our salvation this

---

*Parodying Achilles' lament for Patroclus in Aeschylus' *Myrmidons*
(fr. 138), substituting "those three obols" for "the deceased."
(Loeb)

scumbag has the nerve to harangue us
when he can't even save himself from being cross-
      eyed?"
    And he retorted with a yell, squinting like hell:
"How can I help it?"
BLEPYRUS: "Pound up garlic, figs and Spartan spurge,
      you nit,"
I'd have told him had I been there, "and smear
the paste on your eyelids when you go to bed."
CHREMES: [*sarcastically*] Next on the scene came that
      great achiever Euaeon,*
almost naked everyone present would have said,
though he would have it that he had a cloak on,
and he aimed his speechifying at the hoi polloi; "Let
      me mention,"
he said, "that I myself could do with some salvation—
a fourpenny bit would do it—I'll tell you nonetheless
how to save the city and every citizen.
    Let the garment-makers when midwinter comes
      around
give everyone in need a cape, and then
we wouldn't all be catching pneumonia. It would be nice
as well if everybody without blanket or bed were allowed
to sleep in the tanneries when they'd cleaned them up,
and any tanner in winter refusing to open
should be made to pay three sheepskin rugs."
BLEPYRUS: By Dionysus, what a good suggestion!
    But he would have got universal support if he'd added
that the grain merchants should open up their bags
and donate three measures for midday consumption
or face a stiff penalty. A fine collection

---

*Unknown but obviously a pauper.

would have been got from Nausicylides—he's padded.*

CHREMES: After that, a fair handsome young man
    looking like Nicias†

leapt to his feet to address the people and suggested
it wouldn't be a bad idea to let the female class
take charge of the state, which everyone thought
    was great
and made this horde of cobblers cheer "Hear hear!"
    But else-
where the country folk growlingly protested.

BLEPYRUS: Of course, they were using a little com-
    mon sense.

CHREMES: But there were less of them and the
    young man
bawled them out of court. In his opinion
women were the source of good and you of bad.

BLEPYRUS: What exactly did he say?

CHREMES: That you were a blackguard for a start.

BLEPYRUS: And you?

CHREMES: I'll come to that. . . . And a crook to boot.

BLEPYRUS: Just me?

CHREMES: I'll say so . . .
    and pretty well everyone here.

BLEPYRUS: Who can say no?

CHREMES: Then he went on to say
    that woman is a creature bursting with brains‡
and a moneymaker too, and that they never give away
the secrets of the Thesmophoria, unlike you and me
who after Council meetings always spill the beans . . .

---

*A rich grain magnate.
†A lad hardly twenty years old and the grandson of Nicias, the
commander in chief of the Athenian Sicilian expedition of 415 B.C.
‡I could not resist stealing Jeffrey Henderson's rendering of this
line in the Loeb translation.

    Such is our behavior.

BLEPYRUS: Strike me, Hermes, that's no untruth.

CHREMES: Then he pointed out how women lend
    each other
  dresses, jewelry, money, goblets, one to one
without the need of witnesses and never loath
to give back everything or try to slip one over
like we men do and have done.

BLEPYRUS: Even when there are witnesses, holy
    Poseidon,
  we men try to slip one over.

CHREMES: And he continued to heap praises on
    womenfolk:
  they're not traitors, don't issue writs, don't undermine
our democracy, have other commendable traits—a
  whole stack.

BLEPYRUS: So what was the plan?

CHREMES: To turn the city over to women:
  something that seems never to have been tried before.

BLEPYRUS: And this went through?

CHREMES: Yes, I tell you.

BLEPYRUS: So now they're going to look after every-
    thing that before
  was the province of men?

CHREMES: That's how it is.

BLEPYRUS: So my wife will be going to court, not me
    anymore?

CHREMES: And your wife will be looking after your
    dependents, not you as before.

BLEPYRUS: And I won't have to wake up with a gasp
    every morn at dawn?

CHREMES: God no, that'll be your wife's business;
  you can fart away all day at home quite gaspless.

BLEPYRUS: But men of our age run an awful risk:
  the women, once they've seized power, can force us.
CHREMES: To do what?
BLEPYRUS: To fuck,
  and if we can't get it up they'll refuse to make us
    breakfast.
CHREMES: Then you'll jolly well have to learn to jog-
    gle, like this,*
  if you're going to fuck and have breakfast at the
    same time.
BLEPYRUS: But fucking by force is pure torture.
CHREMES: Nevertheless, if that's the policy of the
    city
  every red-blooded male will have to conform.
BLEPYRUS: Ah well, there's an old saying that no
    matter
  how senseless and idiotic is a program
everything'll turn out for the best.
CHREMES: Yes, ye gods and Mistress Pallas,
  for the best. . . . But farewell, my friend, go I must.
BLEPYRUS: And farewell to you, good Chremes.

[CHREMES *and* BLEPYRUS *go off in different directions and the* CHORUS *reappears*]

LEADER: Forward march,
    and turn to take a look to see if any man
    is following us. Be careful, a suspicious batch
    of men are loitering near. It could be one of them
    is following us and watching every move.

*Taking out his stage phallus and wagging it.

STROPHE

CHORUS: Proceed, as you march, with a bold step and
  stamp with verve.
  It would be awful if our husbands came to know
  And something blew the top off of our show.
  If that happened, whatever would we do?
  So make sure your cloaking is secure
  And you're looking around with both eyes,
  Here, there, and everywhere,
  Left and right, for otherwise
  Disaster'll overtake our enterprise.

LEADER: Now then get a move on, we're almost at
  the spot
  near Parliament for which we set out.
    Look, there's the building where our general
    dwells,
she who's engineered this plot involving ourselves.

ANTISTROPHE

CHORUS: Yes, there isn't the slightest need for us to
  dally.
  These beards of ours are barely hanging on.
  We could be seen in the daylight easily
  And then someone surely would turn us in.
  So make a move now toward the shadows;
  That means moving to the wall,
  Keep your eyes skinned as well.
  Wait a while and see what follows
  Then change back to the place you were in.

LEADER: There's no time to waste, for I can see our
  general
  heading in our direction from the Parliament,
so speed it up all of you and peel

those awful appendages off your jowl,
we've put up with them for longer than we meant.

[PRAXAGORA *arrives*]

PRAXAGORA: Ladies, our design's gone surprisingly well,
    and now before some man catches sight of us
dump those capes as fast as you can; unlace
those Spartan boots, off with them, meanwhile
fling away your sticks [*turning to* LEADER] and you, miss, make sure
the women are properly organized. I must steal
back to the house before hubby sees me, and restore
his cape and all the other paraphernalia.
LEADER: Everything's been done according to your plans
    and now it's for you to give us further commands.
        We so want to acquit ourselves well in your eyes.
        I've never known a woman of such formidable enterprise.
PRAXAGORA: You'll all be needed, so be at hand
    ready for the job I've taken on; I realize
how manly you were during all that risk and noise.

[BLEPYRUS *emerges from his house*]

BLEPYRUS: It's you, Praxagora, what have you been doing?
PRAXAGORA: What is that to you, boss?
BLEPYRUS: What's that to me, indeed? . . . Oh, so ingenuous!

PRAXAGORA: I suppose you'll tell me I've been with
  a lover fucking.

BLEPYRUS: More than one, is my guess.

PRAXAGORA: Go ahead and find the evidence.

BLEPYRUS: How would it show?

PRAXAGORA: Smell any scent on my brow?

BLEPYRUS: Come on! A woman doesn't need scent
  to fuck.

PRAXAGORA: No, worse luck.

BLEPYRUS: But why did you leave the house so early
    without a word
  and go off with my cape?

PRAXAGORA: A friend of mine was in the throes of
  delivering a child.

BLEPYRUS: Even so, couldn't you have said you were
    leaving?

PRAXAGORA: I was too distraught, hubby, thinking of
  her plight.

BLEPYRUS: You could have said a word.
  Something shady's in the offing.

PRAXAGORA: By the twain goddesses, there is not.
  I simply dashed off as I was. The maid
who came for me said I mustn't lose a minute.

BLEPYRUS: But what stopped you wearing your own slip?
  Did you have to fling it over me, swipe my cape,
and leave me lying like a corpse in the morgue
complete with wreath and funeral urn?

PRAXAGORA: Well, it was cold outside and I'm delicate
    and thin,
  so I put your cape on to keep warm
and left you lying in bed as snug as a bug.

BLEPYRUS: And my Spartan boots walked off with
    you. Why?
  And my stick as well.

PRAXAGORA: With me your cape was perfectly safe,
  and I wore the boots to sound like you with your staff,
stamping around and smiting the wall.

BLEPYRUS: I'll have you know you cost me eight bags
    of rye
  which would have been mine from Parliament.*

PRAXAGORA: Don't worry, she had a boy.†

BLEPYRUS: Who? Parliament?

PRAXAGORA: Of course not. The woman I
  delivered. . . . So Parliament sat?

BLEPYRUS: God yes, I told you all about it yesterday.

PRAXAGORA: You're right. I remember now.

BLEPYRUS: But you've no idea what they sought to
  settle?

PRAXAGORA: No way.

BLEPYRUS: Then sit you down with some cuttlefish
  and nibble.
  They say the State's been handed over to you
    women.

PRAXAGORA: For the sake of what? Sewing?

BLEPYRUS: Heavens no, for governing.

PRAXAGORA: Governing whom?

BLEPYRUS: Something that covers the whole urban
  span.

PRAXAGORA: By Aphrodite, the city's in for a lovely
  time.

BLEPYRUS: How d'you mean?

PRAXAGORA: For every kind of reason:
  it stops bullies from bullying all round the town,
and informers from false-witnessing, and . . .

BLEPYRUS: For the gods' sakes don't go on,

---

*The Assembly pay was three obols.
†A remark that can be taken either as a feminine non sequitur to
change the subject, or very much to the point. Praxagora would
have earned more than three obols as a midwife.

you're taking the words out of my mouth—I'll
starve.

[NEIGHBOR *emerges from his house and stands
listening*]

NEIGHBOR: My good sir, do let your wife go on.
PRAXAGORA: . . . there'll be no more thuggery, no
    more envying
the man next door, no more having to live
dressed in shreds, no more paupers in the land,
no more quarreling, no more squeezing
some poor wretch who's owing.
NEIGHBOR: All very nice, by Poseidon,
    if it's not just wishful thinking.
PRAXAGORA: Let me make it all clear to you and
    you're bound to agree,
    and even my husband here won't contradict me.

CHORUS: Now's the time to chivvy the brain
        And wake up your intelligence,
        Make it do some thinking again
        And come to your desperate defense.
        The happiness of all depends
        On the brainwave your tongue commends,
        Brightening the lives of citizens
        With untold benefits and blessings
        It's time to bring it to the fore,
        They need your inspired guessings
        Pointing in the right direction
        Tell it in detail but make sure
        That none of it's been aired before

Or ever been brought to completion.
No one wants the same old hoary
Endlessly repeated story.

LEADER: No more lingering, act on your scheme at
    once.
What our audience wants is speed—so advance.
PRAXAGORA: I'm confident my scheme is sound,
    nevertheless
I've got a gnawing fear about the audience:
is it ready to mine an undiscovered vein
and not just cling to some old-fashioned boring thing?
NEIGHBOR: Don't be anxious about mining a new vein;
    to act differently from what's been always done
makes all the difference to the way we govern.
PRAXAGORA: Let no one, then, presume to contradict
    or criticize
until he's heard me speak and knows the whole design.
    Very well, this is what I now propose:
let everyone have everything there is and share
in common. Let everyone enjoy an equal living;
no more rich men here, poor men there;
no more farmer with a huge extensive farm
and some impoverished farmer with absolutely
    nothing,
not even a patch to bury his body in;
no more someone with a regiment of servants
while another has not a soul to serve his wants.
    You see, I'll make one level of life for everyone.
BLEPYRUS: How exactly would you make all in
    common?
PRAXAGORA: You won't get your serving of turds be-
    fore mine.

BLEPYRUS: So even dung's going to be shared in
   common?
PRAXAGORA: Don't be silly. I was just about to explain
   what I meant, when you came butting in.
      The very first thing I'll do is make all land,
valuables and money, public property:
all of which is now retained severally.
      We women will undertake to manage money
with thrift and shrewdness, and take you men in hand.
NEIGHBOR: How would you deal with someone who
      doesn't own any land
   but has invisible assets like silver-edged stocks and
      bonds?
PRAXAGORA: He'd add whatever they were worth to
   the common funds.
BLEPYRUS: Otherwise he's going to find himself in
   trouble, eh?
   Not to mention that he got it by embezzlement.
PRAXAGORA: In any case, it won't be any use to him.
BLEPYRUS: In what way, pray tell?
PRAXAGORA: Because there'll be no motive or vestige
   of inducement:
   poverty will have lost every ounce of vim
because everyone will have all that's necessary:
bread, salt, fish, buns of barley,
coats, wine, wreaths, chickpeas. Tell me, please,
what good would it do him not to be contributing?
BLEPYRUS: Meanwhile, those who already have all these
   will be seen, surely, as the bigger thieves.
NEIGHBOR: That was different, pal, from what it's
      going to be
   now that life'll be lived from a common capital,
so what will he gain by donating nothing?
BLEPYRUS: Say a fella comes on hard when he spots
    a girl

whom he'd like to sap, he'll find the required fee
from the common purse and enjoy what's on offer
and go to bed with her.

PRAXAGORA: But he's not going to have to pay a fee:
  these girls too I'm making common property
for men to sleep with as they will and make a baby.

BLEPYRUS: Yes, but everyone's going to pounce on
  the prettiest girl
  and she's the one they'll all try to ball.

PRAXAGORA: Ah, but the ugly and the pug-nosed will
  be sitting cheek by jowl with the desirable,
and if a man wants to hump one of these
he'll first have to service one of the ugly ones.

BLEPYRUS: What about us older men, if we plug
  the plain ones first, our pricks won't have stuff enough
to screw along the lines that you propose?

PRAXAGORA: Cheer up! They're not going to squabble over *you,*
  there'll be no squabbling, I assure you.

BLEPYRUS: Squabble over what?

PRAXAGORA: About not going to bed with you.
  As it is, your problem is exactly that.

BLEPYRUS: Your arrangement on the whole is not entirely wrong:
  there'll be no female socket without a manly prong;
but what do you propose to do for us poor men?
Surely the ugly are the ones the women are going to shun
and make a beeline for the handsome ones.

PRAXAGORA: Well, the ugly ones will tag along behind
  the good-looking ones after dinner parties
and make quite sure in all the public places
that the tall and handsome don't go off to bed
with any female unless first he's done
something for the puny and the gruesome.

BLEPYRUS: So Lysicrates will go about with his nose
     in the air*
  among the beauties!
NEIGHBOR: God yes, and this gives a chance to the
     mediocre.
  It'll be a laugh when some oaf wearing clogs
sidles up to Mr. Big wearing rings
and blurts out: "Have to wait till I am done,
then I'll let you have your whack for seconds."
BLEPYRUS: That's all very well but how's a man to tell
     which are his own brats?
PRAXAGORA: Why should he need to? The children
     will take for granted
  that older men of maturer age are their dads.
BLEPYRUS: Yes, but won't this lead to sons all over
     the place
  throttling every older man they come across?
     Even now the throttling of fathers by sons is gross,
and these are recognized fathers, what happens when
     they're not?
     Won't they make it complete and top them up
       with shit?
PRAXAGORA: No, the people around are not going to
     allow it.
  They used not to mind who was beating up
someone else's father, but now if there's a racket
and someone's being whacked, they'll wonder if it's not
their own dad that's being attacked, and they'll fight.
BLEPYRUS: There's a lot of sense in your conclusion, but
     if someone, say, like Epicurus or Leucolophos†
starts to follow me around bleating "Daddy,"
I hate to think how awful that will be.

---

*Unknown, but obviously one of the "puny and gruesome."
†Epicurus is unknown. Leucolophos is probably the commander
prosecuted for being a traitor at the Battle of Aegospotami.

NEIGHBOR: I can think of something infinitely worse.

BLEPYRUS: Such as?

NEIGHBOR: Being kissed by Aristyllus,* saying he's my father.

BLEPYRUS: If he ever does that he'll be mighty sorry.

NEIGHBOR: And *you* won't exactly smell of eau de cologne.

PRAXAGORA: But he was born long before the date of our decree,

so worrying about his kissing you's a nonstarter.

BLEPYRUS: All the same, he'd still be sorry. . . . But on the question of cultivating the land, who'll there be?

PRAXAGORA: Servants. Your only job'll be sprucing up for dinner

when the shadow on the sundial points to ten.†

BLEPYRUS: Here's another question that needs to be asked:

when it comes to cloaks, who's to be the supplier?

This is a serious question, so don't be aghast.

PRAXAGORA: You'll have to make do with what you've got, for now,

eventually a cloak will be woven and given to you later.

BLEPYRUS: One thing more: suppose in a suit before the archon

a fellow loses his case and has to pay—how?

It wouldn't be right to take it from the communal chest.

PRAXAGORA: There won't be any lawsuits for a start.

BLEPYRUS: That remark will spell your downfall.

NEIGHBOR: I'm inclined to think so too.

---

*Apparently a coprophiliac, cf. *Wealth* 313–14, fr. 551. (Loeb)
†The time of day is ambiguous in the Greek, but even if the dinner were at 10 A.M., that would not be entirely unusual. The main meal of the day was seldom in the evening.

PRAXAGORA: What'll there be for them to sue for, dumbo?

BLEPYRUS: A lot, in my opinion, by Apollo;
especially when a debtor won't pay anything at all.

PRAXAGORA: But where would the creditor get the money to lend the debtor?
Funds are held in common. He'd obviously be a robber.

NEIGHBOR: You're right, Praxagora!

BLEPYRUS: Then let her answer this: after a dinner party
when people become rambunctious and get themselves into fisticuffs
how will someone pay the fines for assault and battery?
That's a tough one for you to rebuff.

PRAXAGORA: He'll pay out of his bread allowance—his loaf.
That'll hit him hard in the belly
and he won't get uppity again in much of a hurry.

BLEPYRUS: And you mean no one's going to be a thief?

PRAXAGORA: How can you thieve what you already have?

BLEPYRUS: And no more cutthroats at night?

NEIGHBOR: Not if you're asleep at home.

PRAXAGORA: Not even if you do wander out as usual, because every person'll be content.
If someone wants to pinch a coat
the owner will simply give it to him;
what would make him want to fight?
He'll go to the communal store and get another—
a better one to boot.

BLEPYRUS: And there'll be no gambling at dice?

PRAXAGORA: What would be the point when there are no stakes?

BLEPYRUS: What standard of living would you set?

PRAXAGORA: The same for everyone; I'm going to make the town
　into a single home: all barriers would be down.
　　It'll be like one sole edifice
and people can wander in and out of one another's space.

BLEPYRUS: For dinners where will you set your site?

PRAXAGORA: I'll turn the halls and courts of law into clubs.

BLEPYRUS: What will you use the Speaker's rostrum for?

PRAXAGORA: I'll make it into a locker for basins and mugs,
　and youngsters can declaim poetry from it
about heroes in battle, about cowards as well;
which will make any coward around
ashamed to share the meal.

BLEPYRUS: By Apollo, how absolutely sweet!
　But what will you do with those urns in which one casts a vote?

PRAXAGORA: I'll set them up in the marketplace a little beyond
　Harmodius' statue, and people will dip their hands inside
and pull out the dining club to which they are assigned.
　　The usher, for instance, will tell someone who's drawn a Beta
to make his way to the Royal Porticoe for his dinner;
another will go to the one next to it with a Theta,
and someone else to the Barley Market with a Gamma.*

BLEPYRUS: Gamma as in gobble?

PRAXAGORA: No, as in greedy.

---

*Beta, Theta, and Gamma—that is, B, TH, and G.

BLEPYRUS: But say someone doesn't draw a ticket, will
   he be driven by others from the table?
PRAXAGORA: [*in a change of meter and a mocklike
      chant*]
   That's not the sort of thing we do,
   We lavish everything on everyone.
   Every man will leave as drunk as hell
   With torch in hand and garlanded as well.
   The women will say as they come from dinner, "You
   Really ought to go along with us.
   We've got a pretty girl waiting to be done."
   From a second-story window someone else
   Will call: "Oh, do step inside,
   I've got a lovely lass, as fair as fair,
   She really is my pride;
   But you'll have to sleep with me before
   You sleep with her."
   Meanwhile, among the wanking men,
   Out chasing every handsome lad,
   With catcalls like: "Where are you off to, my
      young man?
   It's not going to do you any good.
   The weasely and the pug-nosed, says the law,
   Take precedence of you to screw.
   You might as well grab your flower and your
      twin balls
   And jerk off in the hallway near the door."

   Tell me, do you like the plan I've set before you?
BLEPYRUS and NEIGHBOR: Tremendously!
PRAXAGORA: Now I'm off to the marketplace to
      organize
   the reception of the goodies arriving presently,
and I'll have to find a girl with a carrying voice
to act as herald. Such is the kind of duty

of an elected official. I must also regularize
the dinners in common, for yes,
today's the day you're going to enjoy your first spread.

BLEPYRUS: You mean today's the day we're going to
be fed?

PRAXAGORA: I'm telling you so,
and then I want you to banish every whore.

BLEPYRUS: Whatever for?

NEIGHBOR: Don't you know? [*pointing to* PRAXAGORA
and the CHORUS]
It's so that these women can have their prick of the
young men.*

PRAXAGORA: And no more cosmetics for the slave
women
to undermine the hearts of freemen.
Let slaves sleep with slaves, their pussies shaved
like cropped fleece or a scraped porker.

BLEPYRUS: You know what, I want to be seen as your
supporter
with people yelling: "Fancy that,
he's the major-Generaless's partner."

[PRAXAGORA *and* BLEPYRUS *go off hand in hand*]

NEIGHBOR: Meantime, I've to take my gear to the
agora,
and had better make a list of all I've got.

[NEIGHBOR *goes into his house and there follows an
interlude—no longer extant—of song and dance, at
the end of which* NEIGHBOR *reappears with two servants,* SICON *and* PARMENON, *and stands staring at a
collection of household utilities that he and his servants have assembled outside*]

*Jeffrey Henderson's clever rendering of this line in Loeb.

NEIGHBOR: Hey there, you pretty Winnower of Bran,
  favorite of all my kitchen gadgets, run
to me here outside and be my basket carrier,
so delicately spattered by the powder
from many a pannier of flour.
        Where's Camp-stool, and Saucepan, come here.
        My, but you're black as if you'd been used
for boiling the dye for Lysicrates' hair . . .*
        Better stand next to her.
        And you, my lady Jug Tray, I'd be pleased
if you brought that pitcher over here.
        Coffee-grinder, you can be our music master:†
How many times have you roused me for Parliament
with your dawn aubade at an unearthly hour
in the middle of the night. Will someone bring out Salver
and also the candles.‡ And put the sprigs of olive
alongside, and set the Trivets out and leave
space for Oil Flask. And now it's time
for that bunch of little pots to follow on in line.

[*Enter* MEAN MAN. *He stares at* NEIGHBOR'*s collection
of pots and pans with disgust.*]

MEAN MAN: Would anyone expect me to do such a
        thing?
        I'd not be a man but someone without a brain.
        No, that's certainly not me. I'd scrutinize
        methodically
the whole bloody thing from A to Z; I'd not fling

*A well-known fop.
†The ancients, so far as we know, did not have coffee, but they
used burnt millet and other grains with boiling water.
‡The word used is κηεια, which can also be translated "honey-
comb." I have opted for something else waxen because the word is
in the plural and because it is not comestibles that are being num-
bered but household items.

away all that I'd earned with such sweat in this
    senseless way.
    The whole layout is something I'd have to exam-
      ine and survey.
    Hey, you, what is the big idea with all this litter?
    Are you moving? Going to pawn it?
NEIGHBOR: Of course not.
MEAN MAN: But they're all lined up in a row
    as if you were marching them off to the auctioneer.
NEIGHBOR: God no, they're on their way to the agora,
    destined for the city according to the law.
MEAN MAN: You mean you're getting rid of them all?
NEIGHBOR: Completely.
MEAN MAN: Zeus save us, you're a fiasco.
NEIGHBOR: Really?
MEAN MAN: I'd say so.
NEIGHBOR: And ignore the law?
MEAN MAN: What law, you poor ass?
NEIGHBOR: The law that's just been passed.
MEAN MAN: Just been passed? How brainless can you
    be?
NEIGHBOR: Brainless?
MEAN MAN: Well, aren't you? Not only utterly
    without a brain but totally clueless.
NEIGHBOR: Because I follow instructions?
MEAN MAN: So it's sensible to follow instructions?
NEIGHBOR: Absolutely.
MEAN MAN: Like a frigging wimp?
NEIGHBOR: So you're not going to surrender your
    stuff?
MEAN MAN: I'll wait and see what most people do,
    I'm not going to jump.
NEIGHBOR: Why wait? They're already turning in
    their stuff.
MEAN MAN: I'll believe it when I see it.

NEIGHBOR: It's already happening in the town, they say.

MEAN MAN: They say? Of course they would.

NEIGHBOR: They say they're going to bring it all in personally.

MEAN MAN: They say, they say? Naturally!

NEIGHBOR: You're killing me; you think nobody's any good.

MEAN MAN: Nobody? That's not odd.

NEIGHBOR: Damn you, it is, by God!

MEAN MAN: Do you imagine that anyone in his right mind
is going to give everything up? That's not our national style.

NEIGHBOR: You mean we should just take?

MEAN MAN: God yes! Do as the deities do.
Isn't it obvious when we pray before their effigies
that they're on the make?
They just stand there, hands extended, palms up,
not to give but to receive.

NEIGHBOR: See here, stinker, let me get on with the job.
All this stuff's got to be packed. . . . Where's my strap?

MEAN MAN: So you really believe
you've got to give all this up?

NEIGHBOR: I really do. I'm tying these two trivets together right now.

MEAN MAN: You ought to wait a tab:
see what everyone else is doing. Only then in my view . . .

NEIGHBOR: What?

MEAN MAN: Wait some more, then postpone.

NEIGHBOR: For what reason?

MEAN MAN: Well, there could be an earthquake or ominous stroke
of lightning, or a black cat crossing,

which could change everything, you dummy!

NEIGHBOR: Meanwhile, I'll be damned if I can't find anywhere to dump all this lot.

MEAN MAN: Can't find anywhere, eh? Think positive, you may have to wait a jot

but they *will* take all this stuff you've left behind.

NEIGHBOR: What's that prove?

MEAN MAN: Just that these people like to jump to a conclusion,

then do a somersault and reverse their decision.

NEIGHBOR: I think, buddy, they'll hand it all in.

MEAN MAN: Say they don't?

NEIGHBOR: They will. It's not worth a thought.

MEAN MAN: But say they won't?

NEIGHBOR: We'll fight.

MEAN MAN: What if there're more of them than you?

NEIGHBOR: I'll turn my back and leave them to it.

MEAN MAN: Leave them to sell your things?

NEIGHBOR: Damn you, man . . . scatter!

MEAN MAN: And if I do scatter?

NEIGHBOR: It would be a blessing.

MEAN MAN: Are you sure you want to surrender everything?

NEIGHBOR: I am. And I see that that's exactly what my neighbors are doing.

MEAN MAN: Of course, someone like Antisthenes— he'd add his bit,*

though a month of enemas would do him more good.

NEIGHBOR: Oh, come off it!

MEAN MAN: And Callimachus the chorus master, would he contribute?†

---

*One of a group of Cynic philosophers. He sold all he possessed, keeping only a ragged old coat. Socrates teased him, saying: "Antisthenes, I see how vain you are through the holes in your coat."
†Unknown.

NEIGHBOR: More than Callias could.*

MEAN MAN: The silly fellow's gone and lost all he had.

NEIGHBOR: Isn't that being a little hard?

MEAN MAN: What's so hard? Wacky decisions are the
        order of the day,
    think of that tax on salt.

NEIGHBOR: You're right. .

MEAN MAN: Or when we voted for copper coins,
    remember?

NEIGHBOR: That got me into a mint of trouble,
    for after selling my grapes I hightailed it to the agora,
chockful of coppers, to buy some barley meal,
but when I produced my lolly
the superintendent called out: "Sorry,
we're into silver now, not copper."†

MEAN MAN: And not long ago didn't we all swear
    that the two-and-a-half-percent tax proposed by
        Heurippides‡
would yield the state five hundred talents? And
    immediately
wasn't Heurippides our darling golden boy,
till we looked into the matter more closely
and saw that the whole thing was a damn fantasy
impossible to realize? And then, if you please,
poor Heurippides became everybody's whipping boy.

NEIGHBOR: I know, my friend, but we were in con-
        trol then,
    now it's the women.

---

*A young man who squandered the fortune his father left him and
reduced himself to poverty.
†Although copper had been put into circulation following the deba-
cle of the Sicilian campaign, Athens never debased her silver
currency.
‡A young man brought to the fore by Conon, the admiral who
was defeated at Aegospotami in 405 B.C., but who subsequently
commanded the Persian fleet and defeated the Spartans in 397 B.C.

MEAN MAN: I mean to keep them well in focus
and not let them piss all over me.

NEIGHBOR: I don't know why you're making such a
fuss . . .
Hey, boy, up with the bags.

[*a female* REPORTER *enters*]

REPORTER: Citizens, all of you, aye, there ain't no ex-
ceptions now,
make yer way at once to our Commanderess
for the comin' dinner. Each man must find 'is place.
The tables is groanin' under every kind
of delicacy. Them pallets is strewn with cushions
and quilts.
The booze is being mixed in the kitchens,
the scent girls 'overing around.
The fish filets is sizzling, the 'ares is on the spits.
The buns is in the ovens,
the garlands is plaited and ready.
Them tidbits are grilling, and the daintiest little lasses
is simmering lentil soup. And Simoeus is nearby*
in 'is cavalry duds, polishing with 'is tongue
all the women's dishes.
Geron is there as well, all spruced up an' shod†
in the nattiest of pumps,
laughing with another lad as if 'e 'ad
dumped 'is cheap loafers an' 'is tattered jacket.
So come along. Yer all invited: that's the ticket . . .
Barley loaves is being offered. Just open yer
mouths.

[REPORTER *leaves*]

*Simoeus was known for cunnilingus.
†Though *Geron* means "old man," this Geron seems to be a young
man because the text says that he is laughing with another lad.

MEAN MAN: Right, I'm off. Why hang about
when the city has extended an invitation?

NEIGHBOR: Hey, where are you off to? You've not
handed in your stuff.

MEAN MAN: To dinner.

NEIGHBOR: No, you're not: not till you've made that
contribution.
The women won't feed you anyway—unless they're
completely daft.

MEAN MAN: Not to worry. I'll do it later.

NEIGHBOR: When?

MEAN MAN: Look, chum, it won't be me that holds
things up.

NEIGHBOR: What d'you mean?

MEAN MAN: There'll be lots of others even later than me.

NEIGHBOR: So you're going to go to the dinner willy-nilly?

MEAN MAN: Naturally. I've got to go.
All sensible people have to support the city
as far as they can.

NEIGHBOR: Say they don't let you in?

MEAN MAN: I'll butt my way through.

NEIGHBOR: What if they beat you?

MEAN MAN: I'll issue a writ.

NEIGHBOR: And if they laugh at that?

MEAN MAN: I'll stand in the threshold and . . . and . . .

NEIGHBOR: And what?

MEAN MAN: . . . grab the grub as it passes by.

NEIGHBOR: Then better go in behind me.
You there, Sicon and Parmenon, up with my
belongings.

MEAN MAN: Let me carry them for you.

NEIGHBOR: I'd rather not:
I don't want you presenting my chattels to the
lady boss
as if they're yours.

[NEIGHBOR *leaves with his two servants*]

MEAN MAN: I've got to find a way of keeping my gear
and at the same time being eligible for dinner.

[*he pauses and thinks*]

   Ha ha, I've got it. And it's immediate.
   Let's call it "bon appétit."

[MEAN MAN *hurries off and there is a short interlude
of dance and song, of which the words are not re-
corded. There is also a girl piper who will accompany
much of the conversations that follow. Meanwhile,
CRONE A loiters in the doorway of her house closely
watched from a window by the GIRL next door.*]

CRONE A: Why aren't the men here? They should have
       arrived ages ago.
   I'm all painted and tarted up,
humming and waiting in my party array,
all to snare some fellow on his way.
       Come, holy Muse, put spice on my lips
for a juicy and loose Ionian lay.*
GIRL: So, you old spot of mildew,
   you stole a march on me for once, did you?
       You thought you'd strip a vineyard bare
when there was no one there
and lure some strapping stud your way
with the urgency of your song,

*Ionia constituted a group of islands off the west coast of Asia
Minor, the foremost of which was Lesbos, the home of Sappho. It
became a symbol of sexual prowess—in both directions.

Just you try. I can outsing you any day
and prove you're wrong.

The audience may think this boring
but perhaps it'll get them laughing.

CRONE A: [*wagging her rear at* GIRL] Up yours!

[*turning to the* PIPER] And you, my sweet little piper,
pick up your pipes and pipe some airs.

[CRONE A *breaks into sprightly song*]

    If anyone wants to have some fun,
    It's best to get into bed with me.
    You won't find savoir faire with a young
    Girl as you would with a ripe old one
    Like me, who's itching to be nice
    To the boy she has and no one else.

GIRL: Don't belittle the charm of girls,
    Smooth and tender are their thighs
    And there the softest glory lies,
    While from their bosoms flowers rise.
    But you're a hag all pinched and furled:
    A body that beds with Death and dies.

CRONE A: I hope one day you come unstuck
    When your pussy wants to fuck
    And your couch falls on the flags.
    Or when one day you want to shag
    And feel the lovely inside ache
    But find you're shagging with a snake.

GIRL: What am I to do; I'm sad.
    My young fellow hasn't come
    And all alone here I am,
    For Mum's gone out, she's not at home.
    The next best thing that can be had
    (Oh Nanny dear, it's not so bad):

    Call Mr. Fixit* in, he can
    Put one at ease. Oh Nanny, please!
CRONE A: Too bad! Is there a hitch.
    And does your twat acquire an itch
    For the Ionian tool,† but want as well
    The real thing—as in L—
    The thing that makes those Lesbians drool?‡
GIRL: In any case, you'll never grab
    My boy's balls or ever have
    An opportunity to despoil
    Me of my youth with your gall.

CRONE A: You can sing your guts out and peer through
    the dark
  just like a cat but no red-blooded male
is going to get to you before he gets to me.
GIRL: No doubt at your funeral
  when he comes to *lay* you out . . . I say,
I think that was rather smart.
CRONE A: What a remark!
GIRL: Can anyone say something fresh to an old frump?
CRONE A: It isn't my age that'll get you unstuck.
GIRL: What then? Your white lead and rouge?
CRONE A: Why bother to enlarge?
GIRL: Why bother to peer and poke?
CRONE A: Me? I'm just humming a ditty for my be-
loved Epigenes.
GIRL: So you have a beloved? He must be decrepit.
CRONE A: You'll see for yourself. He's on his way.
GIRL: Not to see you, you cracked old shard.
CRONE A: Of course to see me, you bloodless wisp.
GIRL: He'll soon put paid to that. . . . But I must go.

---

*A dildo.
†Also a dildo.
‡Meaning cunnilingus.

CRONE A: I'm off too,
  and soon you'll see how much nearer the truth I
    am than you.

[GIRL *leaves the window, and* CRONE A *goes into the
house as* EPIGENES *enters singing. He is garlanded,
flourishes a torch, and is a bit drunk.*]

EPIGENES: Damn it, I'm pining, how much I wish
       To sleep with that girl
       Without having first to jab a hag
       That's not the style
       Of a lusty lad.

[CRONE A *reappears*]

CRONE A: Ah, my boy, you'll soon discover
       The time is over for a carte blanche lover.
       We're living in a democracy
       And must do our loving legally.

[*she goes back into the house*]

EPIGENES: Gods above, would that I could catch
       This adorable peach for which I itch,
       Catch her alone, for sozzled though I am
       She's the one for me and she's my aim.

GIRL: [*at her window*] I've hoodwinked that accursed
    old crone,
  who thinks I'm safely stuffed away inside the house,
and here's the boy we wrangled about.

                    STROPHE
       Come to me, come to me,
       Come to me, come to me, darling;
       Come to my bed and be

My stallion for the night.
An ineluctable passion has me whirling
For the curls of your head, you darling.
I'm clamped in a vise
To some inescapable yearning.
Eros, oh, why don't you let me go,
Or make this boy come to my bed tonight?
Please, oh please!

ANTISTROPHE

EPIGENES: [*looking up at the window*]
Come to me, come to me,
You too, my darling.
Run and open the door for me
As wide, as wide as you can,
Or I'll fall flat on my face on the step.
I'd rather fall flat on your lap
Exchanging caresses and fun.
Aphrodite, why
Must I go bonkers over this girl, yes, I?
Free me, Eros, and make this girl abide
Tonight in my bed.

STROPHE

How far my words lag behind
The passion that I would express,
It is a force beyond recourse.
So now I beg you, dearest one,
Open to me and let me in.
This aching for you is a wound.

ANTISTROPHE

Golden bud of Aphrodite,
So exquisitely designed:
You Muses' honeybee, you child
Of the Graces, you supreme delight,

Open . . . Let your joy be wild;
This aching for you is a wound.

[CRONE A *emerges from her front door*]

CRONE A: You there, why are you knocking on my door?
   Are you sure it's me you want?
EPIGENES: You're joking.
CRONE A: Well, you were battering on *my* door.
EPIGENES: I'd rather be dead.
CRONE A: With that torch and everything? Isn't that
   odd?
EPIGENES: I'm looking for Mr. Fuck You.
CRONE A: There are two.
EPIGENES: I don't want Mr. Screw Yourself. He's for
   you.
CRONE A: [*grabbing him*] And by Aphrodite,
   whether you like it or not, you're for me.
EPIGENES: [*shaking her off*] Hang on a minute,
   affairs with the over sixties are out of court
and won't be entered for the present.
   We have to enter the under twenties first.
CRONE A: That used to be the rule, sweetie pie,
   under the old regime, but now I've got to be en-
   tered first.
EPIGENES: It's a question of appetite, not of law.
CRONE A: And weren't you ruled by your appetite
   for dinner?
EPIGENES: I don't know what you are getting at . . .
   I simply have to knock on this door.
CRONE A: I'm the door you have to knock on first.
EPIGENES: I don't think so. I'm not a knocker.
CRONE A: [*coming close and wheedling*]
   I know you love me. It was just a bit of a shocker

your finding me here outside. . . . Give me your
lips—come.

EPIGENES: I'm scared of your lover, ma'am.

CRONE A: Who may he be?

EPIGENES: The universal artist.

CRONE A: Who's that?

EPIGENES: The one who paints the funeral urns.*
You'd better beat it before he sees you by the door.

CRONE A: I'm well aware what you're after—well
aware.

EPIGENES: And by God, so am I of you in turn.

CRONE A: Aphrodite gave me you as prize,
so you're hardly something I would readily lose.

EPIGENES: You're out of your head, you old bag.

CRONE A: Far from it. I'm taking you to bed.

EPIGENES: We waste money buying hooks for buckets,
when we could use a hag.
We could let one down the well to use as a hook
to haul things up.

CRONE A: Now, now, young man, enough's enough,
just come along chez moi.

EPIGENES: I don't have to,
not unless you've paid the city's tax on me at five
percent.

CRONE A: By Aphrodite, I'm afraid you do . . .
Oh, I so love sleeping with young boys like you!

EPIGENES: And I so hate sleeping with old hags like
you.
I'll never consent.

CRONE A: [*unrolling a scroll*] By God, this will make
you.

EPIGENES: What's that?

*Namely, Death.

CRONE A: An order compelling you to come to my house.

EPIGENES: Read what it says.

CRONE A: Very well, I shall. [*she reads*]

"We women have decreed that if a young man
becomes enamored with a young woman,
he may not hump her until first he's humped an old
    'un;
and if in his urge to screw the young woman
he refuses the preliminary screwing of the not-so-
    young,
she has every right to drag the young man away by
    his prong.

EPIGENES: Shit! This first-fucking
makes me a Procrustes—a stretcher case.*

CRONE A: Our laws have to be obeyed, nonetheless.

EPIGENES: But say one of my friends or neighbors offers bail?

CRONE A: A man's? Men's credit today is not worth
a bushel.

EPIGENES: Can't I get out of it by an oath?

CRONE A: No, you can't wriggle out of this by bluff.

EPIGENES: Surely I can as a businessman.

CRONE A: You'll be sorry.

EPIGENES: So what shall I do?

CRONE A: Just pop along with me.

EPIGENES: Is that really necessary?

CRONE A: A Diomedian necessity.†

---

*Procrustes was a robber whose curious whim was to put his victims on a bed and dock their legs if they were too long, but stretch them if they were too short. Here there is a play on words in the Greek: the verb Προκρούειν (*prokrouein*) means not only to stretch but "to have first fuck."

†Diomedes fed his horses human flesh, but he in turn was fed to them when he was killed. CRONE A seems to mean: "if you feed on her you've first got to feed on me."

EPIGENES: [*with bitter sarcasm*]
Then sprinkle dittany on the bed,
upholster it with sprigs of vine;
embellish it with ribbons and
place the pitchers by the side,
and by the doorstep have water in a can.
CRONE A: And in the end I wouldn't be surprised
if you even bought me a wedding garland.
EPIGENES: Of course, and I'll try to find one made
of wax*
because I don't think you're going to last very long.

[GIRL *enters*]

GIRL: Where are you trying to drag him?
CRONE A: He's mine and I'm taking him home.
GIRL: It doesn't make sense, it sucks
to sleep with you, he's far too young:
you're more like his mother than his lover,
and if you women enforce this law
you'll fill the land with Oedipus Wrecks.
CRONE A: You vicious little whore,
sheer envy made you come out with that.
Be sure of this, I'll pay you back.

[CRONE A *hurries inside*]

EPIGENES: By Zeus the Savior,
what a colossal blessing you've just done me,
oh, you sweet sweet thing,
saving me from that awful hag!
Just wait till evening
and I'll slip you a thick and whopping
testimony of my thanks.

[CRONE B *enters and accosts the* GIRL]

*Waxen garlands were used for the dead.

CRONE B: You there, where are you taking him? It's
   illegal.
   The law says clearly he's got to sleep first with me.
EPIGENES: Holy mackerel!
   Where did you emerge from, you abysmal
emanation, even more disgusting than the last?
CRONE B: Get yourself over here.
EPIGENES: [*to* GIRL] Sweetheart, keep her off me, don't
   let this be.

[GIRL *dashes off, presumably to get help, but we
don't see her again*]*

CRONE B: It's not me but the law that's tugging you
   away.
EPIGENES: A monstrous succubus is what I see, I'm
   aghast . . .
   a blister of pus and blood.
CRONE B: Get along with you, cut the cackle
   and don't be such a dud.
EPIGENES: Just a sec, I need to go to the WC
   to relieve myself, and if you don't allow me
I'll do it here in a gush of yellow fear.
CRONE B: Move. You can do your flood inside.
EPIGENES: But it'll be a deluge:
   Look, you can have my two testicles as bail.
CRONE B: Balls!

   [CRONE C *arrives*]

CRONE C: Hey, fella, where are you off to with her?
EPIGENES: Off to, my foot. I'm an object of pillage.
   But bless you, whoever you are
and don't just stand there watching me suffer.

*This seems to me a loose end that the playwright shouldn't have
left lying around.

[*the full impact of her ugliness suddenly hits him*]

    O Heracles, O Pan, O Corybantes* and the Heavenly Twins!†
    This one's even topped the last in horror.
    What is it? Can anyone tell?
    A plastered and painted ape? A harridan from hell?

CRONE C: Follow me and cut the drivel.

CRONE B: Not so fast! . . . This way, please.

CRONE C: I'm not letting him go.

CRONE B: Nor am I.

EPIGENES: Hey, you're tearing me apart, you hideous bogies.

CRONE B: The law says you follow me.

CRONE C: Not so. . . . Not if another hag is uglier.

EPIGENES: Meanwhile, if the two of you finish me off, please tell
    me what will be left of me for that gorgeous girl?

CRONE C: That's your worry,
    but as to your duty—watch me.

[*she makes a lunge for his phallus*]

EPIGENES: [*hopelessly*]
    All right, which of you do I bang first to get free?

CRONE C: Don't you know! . . . This way, sweetie.

EPIGENES: Then make this one let go.

CRONE B: That I will not.

CRONE C: And I won't either.

EPIGENES: You two would do a terrible job if either was a ferry skipper.

CRONE B: What?

---

*Priests of the goddess Cybele (Rhea), who followed her with wild dances and music. They had a great knowledge of all the arts.
†The twin sons of Zeus and Leda: Castor and Polydeuces (Pollux).

EPIGENES: You'd tear your passengers asunder.

CRONE C: Hold your tongue and come along.

CRONE B: Not that way, this.

EPIGENES: If I'm not wrong,
here we have the Commonus Law in operation.*
     I am held in a vise
and expected to fuck vice-versa;
it's like handling two dinghies with only one oar.

CRONE B: You'll be just fine,
an onion stew will do the cure.

EPIGENES: A sodding tragedy, I'd say: dragged to the
very verge.

CRONE C: Can't be helped, and I'm just behind.

EPIGENES: Curb that urge.
     I'd rather wrestle with one than two.

CRONE C: The choice, by Hecate, is not for you.

EPIGENES: [to the audience]
     I'm under a terrible load,
damned for one whole night and one whole day
to shag a rotting hag.
          And when I've serviced that old toad
I've got to do it all again
to yet another, whose false teeth
are by the urn that stands there for her funeral.
          Tell me please, wouldn't you say
I'm clamped to Death?
          Surely so, completely wrecked
and stuck with freaks like these.
          In the worst of these damnations
when I've actually breached the harbor mouth
and am tupping these two harridans,
drown me in the very funnel of the channel.

*Commonus Law, datable to the era of the Persian wars, ordered
that those accused of injuring the Athenian people be bound and
face (not fuck!) the charge before the people. (Loeb)

As to the third crone's turn,
bury her alive in tar and her feet in molten lead,
then prop her up over my tomb instead
of a funeral urn.

[CRONE B *and* CRONE C *drag* EPIGENES *into the house
and slam the front door. A* MAID *in her cups enters
and begins a speech, which should be delivered with
slurs and hiccups*]

MAID: You blessed people, you happy land,
    and most of all my most happy mistress;
you women too who throng our threshold,
and all you neighbors and parishioners, and me of
    course,
a maid drenched in fragrances, yes, Zeus,
but not to be compared with the fragrance
that comes off amphorettes of wine from Thrace,
whose bouquet hums around the head and stays
much longer than those other fragrances
which disappear in thin air.
    These, praised be the gods, are far superior.
    Pour it neat and it will last the night.
    But choose with care. . . . Tell me, good ladies,
        where
the boss is . . . I mean our mistress' sire?
LEADER: You'll see him soon enough if you wait here.
    In fact he's coming now, on his way to dinner.

[BLEPYRUS *enters, garlanded and looking twenty
years younger with his arms around two* GIRLS]

MAID: Dear guv'nor, you lucky, you thrice-blessed
    wight!
BLEPYRUS: Me?

MAID: Yes, you, by Zeus,
   what other man on earth could be so fortunate?
      Out of thirty thousand citizens you've not had
         dinner yet.*
LEADER: That certainly makes him out a lucky fella.
BLEPYRUS: Naturally, I'm off to dinner.
MAID: By Aphrodite, so you are, and the last to go.
   I have instructions from your wife to take you there,
   and these girls along with you.
      There's still some Chian wine and appetizing fare,
   so don't hold back.
      And you spectators too, if we're in your good
         grace,
   and any judge who's not gazing into space,
   must join us as well. We've got enough for all.
BLEPYRUS: [to MAID] Be a grande dame—what the
   heck!—
   include this whole lot, leave no one out.
      Be all-expansive and invite
   dotard, boy, and wee mite;
   there's dinner enough for the human race,
   so hurry and make yourselves at home.
      As for me, I'm off to a dinner of my own,
   and have a little flare here to light me on my way.

   [*he indicates one of the* GIRLS]

LEADER: Don't stand on ceremony, pray,
   but take these girls and while you're on your way
   I'll sing you a little dinner grace.

   [BLEPYRUS, *the* MAID *and the two* GIRLS *move into
   the* CHORUS *for the exodus dance*]

*Meaning it is still a pleasure to come.

LEADER:* Let me first deliver some wise words to
   the wise.
   Besides the jokes, remember, there's a lot of seri-
      ous stuff.
      Vote for me for that, and if you have a sense
         of fun
vote for me too for the jokes; your votes will be
      enough.
      Don't be put off by the handicap I've drawn
of having to present my play first in line.
      So, keeping this in mind,
keep faith with me and do justice to my piece.
      Don't be like those disingenuous tarts
who can only think of the bloke who screwed them
   last.
CHORUS: Whoopie! Whoopie! Dear women,
   the time has come to complete this thing
and dance away to dinner on a Cretan tune.†
BLEPYRUS: Which is what I'm doing.
CHORUS: And these young girls as well
   with limbs so lithe and limber will
move to the rhythm. Soon
they'll be fed every prodigious dish:‡
limpets-oysters-rocksalmon-salted fish,§
sharksteaks-mullets-pickled herring,
blackbirds-thrushes-pigeons-capons,
larks-and-wagtails roasted in the pan,
jugged hare stewed in wine,

---

*Speaking for Aristophanes.
†The Cretans were renowned for their dances.
‡For the list of foods that follow, Aristophanes compounds a six port-
manteau word of up to fifteen syllables, for instance: σιλφιολιπαρο-
μελιτοκατακεχυμενο *silphioliparomelitokatakexumeno*
§Rocksalmon is the fishmonger's fancy name for dogfish.

with honey and silphium capping every blessed thing,*
not forgetting oil-and-vinegar and every blessed
   dressing.
   Now you know what you're getting,
so come on the run and grab a plate for dinner.
   You could begin with pulse.
BLEPYRUS: They're already guzzling—what else!
CHORUS: Up with those legs, away, away!
   Off to dinner, iai euai!
   Off to dinner as the winner,
   Iai euai hooray hooray!

[*the whole company, actors and chorus, dances out
of the theater*]

*Silphium was the ancient wonder drug said to be worth its weight in
gold. It was an umbelliferous plant, often represented on Greek and
Roman coins and looking a little like celery. It was used not only as
food but for every possible ailment and, it seems, as an abortifacient.
It grew in Libya and Cyrene and became extinct (probably through
overuse) in the reign of Nero (A.D. 54–68). The plant was also called
laserpitium and later confused with asafetida. If by any chance Silphium still exists anywhere, my guess would be India.

PLUTUS
(WEALTH)

Plutus was produced in 388 B.C. by Aristophanes in competition with four other playwrights but we have no record of the prize results.

THEME

Perhaps it would be unwise to pin down the theme of *Plutus* to a declaration of how unevenly wealth is distributed in human society. Certainly it is that, but by making Plutus a sickly old man instead of the robust and gleaming child of Demeter, as he had always been for the Greeks, Aristophanes is pointedly saying that the disparity between rich and poor is as old as the human race. As Jesus one day would say when rebuked for letting Mary Magdalene "waste" a whole jar of precious spikenard by pouring it over his feet when the money could have been given to the poor: "The poor you have always with you." But why, one may ask, does God allow this discrepancy to exist? Well, because Zeus long ago blinded Plutus so that he couldn't tell the good from the undeserving; thus, mortals would realize that being rich has nothing to do with being good.

CHARACTERS

CARIO, servant of Chremylus
CHREMYLUS, elderly Athenian householder
PLUTUS, god of wealth
BLEPSIDEMUS, friend of Chremylus
POVERTY, hanger-on of Plutus
WIFE, of Chremylus
HONEST MAN, Athenian citizen
INFORMER
OLD WOMAN, Athenian citizen, with
    attendant
YOUNG MAN, Athenian citizen
HERMES, messenger of the gods
PRIEST, of Zeus the Savior

CHORUS, of depressed farm laborers

SILENT PARTS

CHILD, of Honest Man
WITNESS
SERVANTS, of Chremylus and others

THE STORY

Chremylus is depressed by the lack of honesty in the world and cynically wonders if it wouldn't be better to bring his son up as a crook. He goes to the oracle at Delphi with his servant Cario to consult Apollo and receives the answer: "When you leave the sanctuary take home the first person you meet." He does so, and that first person is no less than Plutus, the god of wealth. But Plutus is in a bad way. He is old and decrepit and tells Chremylus that long ago Zeus blinded him so that he couldn't tell the difference between good people and bad. Chremylus decides to take him to Aesclepius, the god of healing, and get him back his sight, but before he and Cario set out they are accosted by Poverty, a grim old hag, who tells them they are making a mistake, for without the fear of poverty what motive would there be for mortals to bestir themselves? Chremylus and Cario nevertheless proceed to Aesclepius' temple, where Plutus gets back his sight. On their return home they receive a series of visitors illustrating the good and bad consequences of Plutus' cure.

OBSERVATIONS

It is always useful to take a look at the names that Aristophanes gives his characters. They nearly always conceal an acronym of each character's characteristics. *Chremylus*, for instance, is based on a word that means "querulousness," but in this case the name would be more aptly translated as Mr. No-nonsense. Cario, which became the stock appellation in New Comedy for a servant or slave, stems from the word *karis*, which means "shrimp"; and there is something sprightly and alert about a shrimp or prawn, which well fits Cario and could translate into Smarty. *Blepsidemus* means "people-seer," so he could be called Mr. Observer.

As to the play itself, it represents a departure in form and intent from all Aristophanes' other works and is the harbinger of the New Comedy to come: that which was exploited by Menander and others and then in Rome by Plautus and was to become the bedrock of comedy right to our own day. What differentiates New Comedy from what came to be called Old Comedy is that it is not topical: individuals give way to types—the old man, the young man, the crone, the honest householder, the clever servant; wit gives way to humor; the quasi-Shakespearian richness of vocabulary is pared down to something simpler; there is less satire; the morality is urbane and politically correct; and bawdiness—if it exists at all—is less robust; the somewhat elitist take-it-or-leave-it stance is replaced by something more plebeian; the self-evolving story gives way to the contrived plot; lastly, the Chorus virtually disappears, though indications are given of where there should be interludes of song and dance.

The result of all these changes was a tremendous popular success and for generations *Plutus* became the most widely acted of all Aristophanes' comedies. One last and perhaps trifling observation: in all my translations of Greek drama I try to avoid using the word "slave" because to the Anglo-Saxon ear this has the wrong connotation. I prefer the word "servant" or "domestic." A slave could be a queen or a princess (as Hecuba and Cassandra were in *The Trojan Women*) or a highly educated ex-ambassador. There is a passage somewhere in Xenophon where the question is asked: "How can you tell a slave from his master?" The answer: "The slave is better dressed."

In *Plutus* Aristophanes does not in fact use the word "slave." Cario is an "oikades," that is, a house servant. It remains true of course that even if a slave happened to be a royal personage he or she became the property, the chattel, of the owner.

It is also worth remembering that it was the army

of slaves in Athens during the fifth century B.C. that
made possible one of the triumphs of civilization in
the arts, literature, philosophy, and even in science.
How else did men like Socrates have the leisure to
wander about the agora asking deep provocative ques-
tions, or Plato and Aristotle to give their lectures in
the Stoa and the Academy, or indeed the playwrights
to write and produce their plays?

TIME AND SETTING

A street in Athens early in the day outside the house
of CHREMYLUS. A blind and ragged old man, PLUTUS,
is seen doddering along followed by CHREMYLUS and
his servant, CARIO, both of whom are wearing chaplets
of bay because they are returning from the oracle of
Apollo at Delphi. CARIO carries a piece of meat retrieved from the sacrifice they made there. He appears
to be worked up about something.

CARIO: Zeus in heaven and all ye gods,
   what nonsense it is to work for a boss who's off his
      rocker.
     What's so unfair   •
is that when the boss decides to ignore
some utterly sensible suggestion of his servant
the wretched servant has to bear the brunt of it.
     It's so unfair
that he can't follow his own bent
simply because he's owned body and soul by the
      man who bought him.
     Well, that's the way things are,
but my next complaint is against Apollo, "who

from a tripod of beaten gold gives vent
to his oracular drone."*
    My grouse is this:
he's supposed to be a healer and the all-knowing one
yet he sends my master off in the blackest mood
traipsing after a man who's blind—the last thing he
        should do.
    It's for us who see to lead the blind, not follow,
especially with me tagging along behind.
    Meanwhile, not so much as a grunt does he deign
        to award
my questioning mind.

  [*turning to* CHREMYLUS]

    Hey, boss, I'll not shut up until you tell
me why we're following this fellow.
    I'm going to give you hell until you do,
and you won't dare beat me with my holy garlands
    on and all.
CHREMYLUS: If you keep pestering me I'll rip them
    off you
    and give you the hiding of your life.
CARIO: Bullshit! I won't stop unless you tell me
    who that geezer is. I only ask for your sake.
CHREMYLUS: All right, I'll not leave you in the dark:
    you're the most trustworthy and accomplished . . .
    thief
in all my household.
    I'm a god-fearing honest mortal,
but I'm poor and have never done well.
CARIO: Don't I know it!
CHREMYLUS: Others have grown fat:
    bank robbers, politicians, snoopers, and every sort
    of scoundrel.

*Quoted from a lost play of Euripides.

CARIO: Quite!

CHREMYLUS: That's why I went to consult the god:
  not for my own wretched sake—

at this stage of my life I've shot all my bolts—

but for my son, the only son I've got. I want to ask

if he should change his direction and take to
  crime . . . become

a rotter, a total dropout,

since that seems to be the road to success in life.

CARIO: And what did Phoebus in his holy wreaths
  let out?

CHREMYLUS: I'll tell you. This is what the god plainly
    said: I must

  stick to the first person I meet coming out

from the shrine and invite him home.

CARIO: And whom did you meet first?

CHREMYLUS: Him.

CARIO: Well, don't you twig the god's obvious brief,
  you absolute prince of dolts?

    It's to raise your son in today's way.

CHREMYLUS: What makes you think that?

CARIO: It's plain as a pikestaff!

  Even the blind could see that in our day

the secret of success is to make sure you're rotten
  to the core.

CHREMYLUS: That can't be what the oracle is getting at.
  It's something much bigger than that.

    If this stinker will just tell us who he is

and what he's here for

we'll soon find out what the oracle is trying to tell us.

CARIO: [*catching up with* PLUTUS] Look here,
  are you going to let us know who you are

or must I use a little artificial stimulus?

    Be quick about it.

PLUTUS: Go fuck yourself!

CARIO: [to CHREMYLUS] Did you gather who he said
  he is?

CHREMYLUS: He said it to you, not me,
  and the way you approached him was rather rude
    and extremely gauche.

[sidling up to PLUTUS all smiles]

    Good sir,
if straightforwardness and manners matter to you,
please tell us who you are.

PLUTUS: Fuck yourself—you too!

CARIO: Ha ha, you can have the man!
  He and the god's message are both trash.

CHREMYLUS: [to PLUTUS] Holy Demeter, you'll be
  sorry you said what you did.

CARIO: And if you don't start spouting you'll be dead.

PLUTUS: Mister, will the two of you just leave me alone!

CARIO: Boss, may I suggest the perfect solution—
  that I just terminate this terminator, this wreck,
sit him on the edge of a ravine
and let him fall off and break his neck?

CHREMYLUS: OK, do it now.

PLUTUS: Please, no!

CHREMYLUS: [as he and CARIO advance on him] We'll
  make you talk.

PLUTUS: But once you discover who I am you'll do
    something nasty
  and never let me go.

CHREMYLUS: Gods in heaven! That we will if that's
  your wish.

[they grab him]

PLUTUS: [with immense dignity] I'll thank you to un-
  hand me.

CHREMYLUS: There you are, you're unhanded.

PLUTUS: Then hear this—
   something I wasn't going to tell you—
I am Plutus, god of Wealth, no less.

CARIO: You cesspot, you weren't going to tell us that
   you're Plutus?

CHREMYLUS: You, Wealth, Plutus? So down at heel!
   Phoebus Apollo and Zeus
   and all the gods and spirits, you can't mean it!
   Are you really he? I can't believe it.

PLUTUS: I am, yes.

CHREMYLUS: The god in person?

PLUTUS: None else.

CHREMYLUS: How come you're in such a mess?

PLUTUS: I've been staying with Patrocles,*
   and he hasn't had a bath since he was born.

CHREMYLUS: But tell me, how did you manage to fall
   so low?

PLUTUS: The work of Zeus. He's envious of mankind.
   When I was a kid I swore I'd only visit the homes
of respectable, intelligent, honorable people.
      Zeus responded by making me blind, so I never
         could tell
which were which. It just goes to show
how much he resents decent folk.

CHREMYLUS: When they're the very ones who pay
   him homage!

PLUTUS: Exactly.

CHREMYLUS: Well, suppose you got your vision back—
   as pristine as it once was—would you immediately
      follow the urge
to cut yourself off from the reprehensible?

PLUTUS: I certainly would.

CHREMYLUS: And you'd visit only the good?

*Identity uncertain.

PLUTUS: Of course!

But it's been quite a time since I've come across a
specimen.

CARIO: That's no surprise.

I haven't either and I've got eyes.

PLUTUS: Now may I go? You've heard my story.

CHREMYLUS: Far from it: we're not yet done.

PLUTUS: So I was right in thinking you wouldn't make
things easy.

CHREMYLUS: Wait, don't go,

you'll never find a better sort of man than me.

CARIO: That's right,

there *is* no one better—except for me.

PLUTUS: Everyone says so,

but the moment they have me in their grips—nice
and tight—

there's no limit to their wickedness.

CHREMYLUS: That's the way of it, yes,

all the same, not all are rips.

PLUTUS: Oh but they are, every man jack of them.

CARIO: [*aside*] You'll be sorry you said that.

CHREMYLUS: You've no idea of all the things you'd get
if you stayed with us. Just listen.

I think, yes I really think, that with the help of heaven
I could heal your eyes and you could see again.

PLUTUS: Please, not that! I don't want to see again.

CHREMYLUS: What?

CARIO: This blighter's a born nonstarter.

PLUTUS: No, not that

but I know only too well how silly people are
and if he found out that I saw
he'd take it out of me.

CHREMYLUS: Isn't he doing that already,

letting you go doddering around?

PLUTUS: Don't I know it! But I'm scared stiff.

CHREMYLUS: What a coward you are! No god could
    compare.
  Do you really think almighty Zeus
with all his thunderbolts and stuff
would care a tinker's cuss
if for a little tick you saw?
PLUTUS: You mischief-maker, please, don't say such
    things.
CHREMYLUS: Compose yourself, and I'll prove to you
    that you're far mightier than Zeus.
PLUTUS: What, me you say?
CHREMYLUS: Heavens yes!
  For a start, how comes it that Zeus rules over all
    the deities?
CARIO: [*pointing to* PLUTUS] Hard cash—him.
CHREMYLUS: And what makes people sacrifice to Zeus?
  Again, isn't it hard cash—him?
CARIO: I'd say so: wealth is the first prayer on their list.
CHREMYLUS: So isn't he the cause of it?
  And couldn't he easily stop it if he wished?
PLUTUS: How do you mean?
CHREMYLUS: Nobody'd have the dough to sacrifice an ox
    or a barley cake if you didn't make a loan:
    So, if Zeus bothers you, you yourself can put him
      in a fix.
PLUTUS: Are you saying it's because of me that people
    sacrifice to him?
CHREMYLUS: That's exactly what I'm saying, and besides,
    it's because of you that anybody possesses
anything radiant or beautiful or pleasing to mankind.
    It's all from wealth that these things stem.
CARIO: And for lack of wealth that I became a slave.*

*That is, he couldn't pay a debt and must have been a metic (resi-
dent alien without full citizenship); a citizen couldn't be sold into
slavery.

CHREMYLUS: And because of you the Corinthian tarts
  ignore the advance of someone poor
but bend over with alacrity for someone rich.
CARIO: It's for you also, they say, that boys crave:
though it's not for love but love of money that they
  itch.
CHREMYLUS: Surely not the decent ones? It's not for
  money that the craving starts.
CARIO: For what, then?
CHREMYLUS: For a handsome stallion, for a pack of
  hounds . . .
CARIO: It seems they're ashamed to ask for money
  so they mask their whorishness and get their ends
by asking for things instead.
CHREMYLUS: [turning to PLUTUS]
  Because of you
every art and skill known to man was invented:
the cobbler sitting with his last,
the bronze-worker and the carpenter,
the smelter of gold—the gold he gets from *you* . . .
CARIO: And by no means least,
  the housebreaker and the mugger.
CHREMYLUS: And the tailor.
CARIO: And dry cleaner.
CHREMYLUS: And the tanner.
CARIO: And the onion seller.
CHREMYLUS: And the adulterer,
  who gets his head shaved when caught at last.
PLUTUS: My word, I had no idea!
CARIO: Then there's the Great King, who preens him-
  self with you,*
  and our own Assembly too, that meets because of you.
CHREMYLUS: And filling the triremes with a crew.

*The king of Persia.

CARIO: And paying that garrison of Corinthian mercenaries,*
and Pamphilus the embezzler who came a cropper—
all because of you.

CHREMYLUS: And the needle seller, that sidekick of
Pamphilus.†

CARIO: Isn't he at the bottom too
of those hearty farts from Agyrrhius?

CHREMYLUS: And Philopsius with his lies . . .
And isn't the treaty with Egypt because of you?
And for you that Lais loves Philonides?‡

CARIO: There's that tower of Timotheus too . . .§

CHREMYLUS: [to PLUTUS] I hope it falls on your head
because you're responsible for every enterprise.
Yes, you're behind everything, you and you alone,
good or bad.
There's no doubt about it.

CARIO: And when it comes to war
you're always on the winning side.

PLUTUS: What, all by myself I do the lot?

CHREMYLUS: Sure you do, and much more.
You're insatiable. . . . We can have too much of
anything . . .

CARIO: Of food.

CHREMYLUS: Of arts and literature.

CARIO: Of spreads and snacks.

CHREMYLUS: Of a high position.

CARIO: Cakes.

---

*Installed in Gulf of Corinth after a Spartan attack in 390 B.C.
†Pamphilus, Agyrrhius, and Philopsius were politicians.
‡Lais was a celebrated courtesan born in 422/1 B.C. and now resident
in Corinth. Philonides of Melite is ridiculed elsewhere as rich, corpu-
lent, and foolish. (Loeb)
§The reference is obscure, but Timotheus was the son of a famous
general called Conon, and was later to enjoy a distinguished career
in both the army and politics.

CHREMYLUS: Macho posturing.

CARIO: Figs.

CHREMYLUS: Ambition.

CARIO: Barley bread.

CHREMYLUS: Commanders in chief.

CARIO: Pea soup.

CHREMYLUS: All these, but of you yourself no one
    ever fags.
  If someone lays his hands on thirteen talents he
      wants sixteen.
      He gets that and he hankers after forty. That goes
        to his head
and he wants umpteen,
otherwise he might as well be dead.

PLUTUS: I'd say you've both hit the nail on the head,
  but there's one thing that bothers me.

CHREMYLUS: Pray, what is that?

PLUTUS: You say I've got all the power,
  but how the deuce am I going to use it?

CHREMYLUS: Yes, that's the nub of it:
  Wealth is such a coward, they say.

PLUTUS: Not so, that's a burglar's slur.
  He broke into my house one day
but couldn't steal a thing because it was all locked away,
so he called my prudence cowardice.

CHREMYLUS: Don't give it further thought.
  Just take on this project like a man
and I'll give you keener eyesight than even Lyn-
    caeus can.*

PLUTUS: You're only a mortal, how can you do that?

CHREMYLUS: Mortal, yes, nonetheless I have high hopes
  because of what Apollo told me
shaking the Pythian bay tree as he spoke.

PLUTUS: Is he involved in this as well?

*One of the Argonauts famous for his keen vision.

CHREMYLUS: Certainly.

PLUTUS: Take care.

CHREMYLUS: Don't worry, my friend, you can be sure
  I've got the matter well in hand
and will see it through even if I have to die for it.

CARIO: Me too, if needs be.

CHREMYLUS: And there'll be a host of others, honest
    people
  who've gone without their daily bread.

PLUTUS: Seems to me they're a pretty useless lot.

CHREMYLUS: Not really, once they're rich again. . . .
  Cario, off you go on the double.

CARIO: For what, may I ask?

CHREMYLUS: To muster my fellow farmers here.
  You'll probably find them sweating in the fields.
  I want every one of them to have a share.

CARIO: I'll be brisk.
  Meanwhile one of the houseboys can take this steak
into the house.

CHREMYLUS: I'll see to that. You get going.

[CARIO *runs off*]

  Now, Wealth, you deity who wields
the greatest power of all, will you please
come inside with me because this is the house
that by fair means or foul you're going
to fill with riches this very morning.

PLUTUS: God, how I hate entering someone else's house!
  It's never done me any good.
    If I happen on a miser's house, the first thing
      he does
is dig a hole and pop me underground,
and if a pal of his comes round
and touches him for a paltry loan,
he swears I'm someone he has never seen.

And if it's the house of some young sot,
I'm wasted on his tarts and dice
and end up outside in my birthday suit.

CHREMYLUS: That's because
   you've never met anyone really nice:
someone for instance a little like me.
   I'm careful with money but will spend it if need be.
   Now let's go inside. I'd
like you to meet my wife and only son,
who, after you, I love more than anyone.

PLUTUS: I believe that's so.

CHREMYLUS: And who in the world would lie to *you*?

[PLUTUS *and* CHREMYLUS *go into the house. There is
a musical interlude while* CARIO, *who has returned,
leads in the* CHORUS *of old farmhands.*]

CARIO: Come, my neighbors, fellow workers, and
      dearest friends,
   Who like my master often dine on leaves of thyme,
   Get a move on, come on out and shake a limb.
   This is the critical hour and we need all hands.

LEADER: [*petulantly*]
   Can't you see that that's exactly what we're doing?
   Tearing our guts out just to get here, we old men!
   Perhaps you think we should have come here on
      the run
   Without an inkling of what that master of yours
      is thinking.

CARIO: I told you from the beginning what it was,
      it's you
   Who isn't listening: how my master made it plain
   You're going to have a lovely life, no longer frozen
   And disagreeable in every possible way.

LEADER: Really? I wonder how it will happen, what
      you say.

CARIO: [*to* LEADER]

> All right, my master's brought an old man home:
> Grimy, huddled, shabby, wizened, toothless, maimed.
> And, good heavens, I do believe his prick is tamed!*

LEADER: [*with supreme sarcasm*]

> You angel of golden news, tell me once again.
> You surely mean he's brought with him a heap
> of lolly?

CARIO: No, I mean he's brought with him a heap of
> banes.

LEADER: If you think you're going to diddle us you're
> very silly.

> I've got a nice thick walking stick in my hands.

CARIO: Do you really think I'm that kind of character?

> Do you really think I can't say anything true?

LEADER: Glib, isn't he, this jerk! . . . Methinks your
> pins

> Are aching for the stocks and you'll be scream-
> ing "Ow!"

CARIO: You've cast your lot, you've fixed the number
> of your coffin.

> Charon has your ticket and he's waiting.

> Be off with you!

LEADER: Blast yourself to hell, you impertinent piece
> of crap,

> Trying to bamboozle us and not explaining a thing
> When we've taken so much trouble to gather here
> And have wasted all this time and gone without
> our dinner.

CARIO: All right, fellows, I'll not keep you unawares.

> I'll tell you everything: my master's decided to bring
> Wealth home with him, so there's nothing you
> will lack.

---

*The Greeks regarded circumcision as a barbarity.

LEADER: D'you think there's the slightest chance of us
　　　being wealthy?

CARIO: Heavens yes, like Midas, if you can find some
　　　ass's ears.*

LEADER: If what you say is true I could dance and sing.

[*At this point a lively gavotte with drum and fife starts
up and everyone on the stage begins to dance mimicking a scene from Euripides' satyr play* The Cyclops,
*in which Polyphemus the Cyclops† is tricked out of
eating any more of Odysseus' crew in the cave full of
sheep and goats. He is made drunk by Odysseus and
rammed by a stake through his one eye. The* CHORUS
play the part of Odysseus' men and CARIO *the Cyclops. In the second strophe and antistrophe the cha-
rade changes to the story of Circe, the beautiful witch
who lived on the island of Aeaea and who captured
the crew of Odysseus and changed them into swine.*]

STROPHE

CARIO: Here goes, I'm off—flittery-flicks—
　　　To give you the Cyclops and play some tricks
　　　Dancing and prancing; watch my feet.
　　　Hark to my songs and hear the bleat
　　　Of Lambikins and the stinking goat.
　　　So goats come along and break your fast
　　　And follow me now with rampant pricks.

ANTISTROPHE

CHORUS: It's our turn now—pickety-pie—
　　　We'll give you more of the Cyclops, aye!

*Midas, King of Phrygia, made a fool of himself twice: when he
asked the gods to turn everything he touched into gold, and when
he judged that Pan was a better musician than Apollo, whereat
Apollo gave him the ears of an ass.
†The Cyclopes were one-eyed giants who lived in caves and kept
herds of sheep and goats. They were cannibals.

He's Cario still, bleating away,
Hungry it seems, with a bag of greens
Over a shoulder and leading his lambs,
And when you flop to sleep I'll ram
A burning stake right through your eye.

STROPHE

CARIO: Now I'll do Circe, who was devilishly clever
In concocting drugs; so one day in Corinth
She doped Philomedes'* pals to behave like pigs
And guzzle on cakes of shit which she
Had kneaded herself. I'll act it out, see!
Your job is to grunt with glee
And hurry after your piggy mother.

ANTISTROPHE

CHORUS: Now that you're Circe busily mixing venom,
Casting spells, besmirching Odysseus' pals,
We'll enjoy doing what Laertes' son†
Did: like a goat letting you hang
By the balls and rubbing your nose in dung.
Then like Aristyllus‡ you'll exclaim:
"Piggies, hurry after your mum."
CARIO: Now that's enough of the joke for once.
It's time to do a different dance,
But as for me, I'm slipping away
To swipe from my boss something to eat:
A chunk of bread and a hunk of meat.
It's guzzle guzzle for me the rest of the day.

[CARIO *goes inside and there follows a musical interlude, after which* CHREMYLUS *enters from the house*]

*Philomedes (the name means "laughter-loving") was one of Odys-
seus' companions in *The Odyssey*.
†Odysseus.
‡An obscure poet.

CHREMYLUS: Ah! my dear friends, no need to stand
    on ceremony,
so I'll say no more than "thank you" for coming along,
taking all that trouble and being so prompt about it.
    I do hope you'll give me your support
in whatever needs to be done
to protect our deity.
LEADER: Don't doubt it!
    In us you see the face of Ares himself.
    It would make no sense to fight and lobby
at every Assembly to get our three obols a day
just to see Wealth himself hustled away.
CHREMYLUS: Look, here's Blepsidemus coming.
    My, what giant strides! What impressive speed!
    He must have heard a rumor of what is pending.

[BLEPSIDEMUS *wanders in, muttering to himself*]

BLEPSIDEMUS: Chremylus suddenly becoming a
    millionaire?
It's very odd. I can't believe it, and yet the word
is going around among the loafers and at the barbers'
that he has indeed struck it rich.
    What beats me is why he should send for us here.
    It's most unusual for a man who's made a catch
to call in his friends. . . . At least it is here. Why
    should he care?
CHREMYLUS: [*to himself*] I shan't keep anything back.
    Look here, Blepsidemus,
we're damn well better off than we were yesterday,
and because you're my friend you'll have a share.
BLEPSIDEMUS: Are you really as rich as they say?
CHREMYLUS: Well, I'm going to be, that's
    if God wills. . . . You see, there's a slight . . .
er . . . a slight snag about the business.

BLEPSIDEMUS: What kind of snag?

CHREMYLUS: The kind that . . . er . . .

BLEPSIDEMUS: Come on, out with it.

CHREMYLUS: . . . if we win, we'll be rich forever,
  If we lose we're down the drain.

BLEPSIDEMUS: There's something not quite right about
      the deal
  which I don't like: the sudden access
of wealth and at the same time apprehension make
  me feel
that somewhere in the offing is a confidence trickster.

CHREMYLUS: A trickster—how?

BLEPSIDEMUS: What if you've snitched a spot of gold
      or silver
  from the god out there*
and now your conscience is pricking?

CHREMYLUS: Absolutely not—I swear by Apollo!

BLEPSIDEMUS: Oh yes?
  I think, my friend, thou protesteth too much.

CHREMYLUS: How dare you suggest any such thing!

BLEPSIDEMUS: Sad, sad! All health in everyone has
      gone.
  Nothing remains but the itch to be rich.

CHREMYLUS: Holy Demeter, I think you're bats!

BLEPSIDEMUS: [speaking of CHREMYLUS] So gone down
  since his beginning!

CHREMYLUS: By heaven, you're bonkers, man!

BLEPSIDEMUS: There's even a shifty look in his eye,
      and that's
  a sure sign he's done something bad.

CHREMYLUS: I know what you're getting at:
  you think I've stolen something and you want a cut.

BLEPSIDEMUS: A cut of what?

CHREMYLUS: It's not that at all. It's something else.

*Apollo's sanctuary at Delphi from which they are returning.

BLEPSIDEMUS: You mean you don't just cheat, you rob
   outright?

CHREMYLUS: You're possessed!

BLEPSIDEMUS: So you're not out to rob anybody?

CHREMYLUS: Certainly not.

BLEPSIDEMUS: Great Heracles! What next?
   He won't come out with the truth.

CHREMYLUS: And you condemn before you know the
   facts.

BLEPSIDEMUS: All right, my friend, for a trifling tip
   I'm prepared to hush things up before the whole
      town forsooth
knows about it. I'll stopper up the gossips' mouths
   with cash.

CHREMYLUS: By the gods you will and oh so friendly,
   spending three minas and charging me twelve!

BLEPSIDEMUS: I see a man before me huddled in the
      dock,
   holding up the plaintiff's bough of olive
surrounded by his wife and kids exactly like
"The Children of Heracles" in Pamphilus's tragedy.*

CHREMYLUS: Not a bit of it, you jerk,
   my sole aim is to make good, honest, sober folk
rich—and them alone.

BLEPSIDEMUS: What are you saying?
   You've stolen enough for that?

CHREMYLUS: Stop it, you're doing me in!

BLEPSIDEMUS: Doing yourself in's more apt.

CHREMYLUS: No way, you creep, because I've got Wealth.

BLEPSIDEMUS: Wealth, what d'you mean by Wealth?

CHREMYLUS: I mean the god himself.

BLEPSIDEMUS: Really! Where is he?

---

*Heracles and Eurystheus were lifelong rivals. Eurystheus made life as
difficult as possible for Heracles and continued to persecute his family
after his death. Nothing is known about Pamphilus or his tragedy.

CHREMYLUS: Inside.

BLEPSIDEMUS: Where?

CHREMYLUS: My house.

BLEPSIDEMUS: In your house?

CHREMYLUS: Right!

BLEPSIDEMUS: Wealth in your house—ha ha! Tell that to the crows.

CHREMYLUS: The gods my witness.

BLEPSIDEMUS: Is that so?

CHREMYLUS: Yes.

BLEPSIDEMUS: Swear by Hestia.*

CHREMYLUS: And by Poseidon too.

BLEPSIDEMUS: The sea god, right?

CHREMYLUS: If there's another, he'll do.

BLEPSIDEMUS: And you haven't introduced Wealth to the rest of us?

CHREMYLUS: Things haven't reached that stage—not yet.

BLEPSIDEMUS: You mean the sharing stage?

CHREMYLUS: Precisely. First we've got to . . .

BLEPSIDEMUS: Got to what?

CHREMYLUS: Get him back his eyes.

BLEPSIDEMUS: Whose eyes?

CHREMYLUS: Wealth's . . . in whatever way we can.

BLEPSIDEMUS: D'you mean he really can't see?

CHREMYLUS: I certainly do.

BLEPSIDEMUS: I'm not surprised he never visited my house.

CHREMYLUS: Of course! But, the gods willing, now he can.

BLEPSIDEMUS: Oughtn't we to call in a physician?

CHREMYLUS: I doubt there's a physician in this town. There's no pay in it and so no practice.

BLEPSIDEMUS: [gazing out over the audience] Let's see.

CHREMYLUS: Not one.

*The goddess of the hearth.

BLEPSIDEMUS: I can't see one either.

CHREMYLUS: We'll do what I originally intended:
get him a bed at the clinic of Aesclepius.*

BLEPSIDEMUS: Good, an excellent idea.
We must follow it up at once. Get moving.

CHREMYLUS: I've started.

BLEPSIDEMUS: Hurry.

CHREMYLUS: What d'you think I'm doing?

[POVERTY *enters, a bedraggled repulsive old crone*]

POVERTY: Hey there, where are you off to, you brace
of benighted pygmies?
Where are you rushing?
Just stay right where you are. How dare
you do what you have done? You brash, rash, scurvy
creatures!

CHREMYLUS: Great Heracles!

POVERTY: You nasty couple, I'll fix you with a nasty
demise.
You had the nerve to perpetrate a crime
no one's ever done, human or divine.
Get ready to die.

CHREMYLUS: But who may you be?
You don't look good.

BLEPSIDEMUS: Perhaps she's a Fury from some Tragedy.
Such a crazy tragic pallor on her features!

CHREMYLUS: But she has no torches, which she should.†

BLEPSIDEMUS: She'll be sorry.

POVERTY: Who do you think I am?

CHREMYLUS: A barmaid or a cook, otherwise
you wouldn't have raised such a hullabaloo
when we've done nothing to upset you.

POVERTY: Nothing to upset me?

*The god of healing.
†Perhaps a gibe at the inevitable torches in Greek tragedy.

What about your abominable behavior
trying to get me chucked out of the country?

CHREMYLUS: Oh that? But you'll always have the
corpse pit to use.

Meanwhile, just tell us who you are.

POVERTY: Who I am?

She who is going to punish you this very day
for trying to expel me from the land.

BLEPSIDEMUS: Wait a minute, aren't you the barmaid at the local pub

who always gives me short measure?

POVERTY: No, I'm Poverty, and I've been with you for
many a year.

BLEPSIDEMUS: Lord Apollo and ye gods, all of you,
what bolt-hold can one find?

CHREMYLUS: What a wimp you are! . . . Stay put.

BLEPSIDEMUS: That's the last thing I'll do.

CHREMYLUS: You must stay. Is a single woman going
to scare away a couple of men?

BLEPSIDEMUS: But she's Poverty, you shithead.

There's no one in the world so undermining.

CHREMYLUS: Stay, I beg you, stay.

BLEPSIDEMUS: So help me, Zeus, I won't!

CHREMYLUS: Believe me when I say

you'll be doing the most cowardly thing, running away
and leaving our god in the lurch
because we were afraid to put up a fight.

BLEPSIDEMUS: A fight? With what weapons, pray?

Is there a single breastplate or shield in sight
which this she-devil hasn't pawned?

CHREMYLUS: Bear up! I know this much:
our god will triumph over all her skulduggery.

POVERTY: You stinkers, you have the gall to bray
when you've just been caught in the very act of a
criminal deed.

CHREMYLUS: And you, you eyesore,
  bawling us out when we've not done a thing to hurt you.
POVERTY: No? Ye gods, aren't you aware
  that getting Wealth's eyesight back really does hurt me?
CHREMYLUS: How can it, when it's good for the whole
  of humanity?
POVERTY: What possible good? Can you think of a
  thing?
CHREMYLUS: Yes, if it means kicking you out of Greece.
POVERTY: Kicking me out of Greece?
  Poor humanity! Nothing could be worse.
    Let's examine that idea together right now
and if I can't prove to you
that I'm the source of every blessing
and that it's I who sustain you,
feel free to do with me whatever you like.
CHREMYLUS: You disgusting old crone, how dare you
  suggest such a thing!
POVERTY: Very well, pay attention for a moment.
  I think I can easily prove what a mistake you make
in promoting wealth among honest folk.
CHREMYLUS: Oh what would I not give right now for
  pillories and a cudgel?
POVERTY: There's no need to shout and swear before
  you've even heard me.
CHREMYLUS: Who can help shouting and swearing lis-
  tening to such twaddle?
POVERTY: Someone with sense.
CHREMYLUS: And if you lose the bet, what's your
  penalty?
POVERTY: Whatever you please.
CHREMYLUS: Right.
POVERTY: And if *you* lose
  that goes for you two too.

CHREMYLUS: [*to* BLEPSIDEMUS] D'you think twenty
  deaths would do?

BLEPSIDEMUS: For her, certainly,
  for us two is ample.

POVERTY: And you won't have to wait long: my brief's
  impregnable.

LEADER: [*to* CHREMYLUS] Go to it, marshal your ranks,
  trounce her in argument and don't expose your flanks.

CHREMYLUS:* So let's start with what I think everyone
                  fully agrees on:
  That it's perfectly fair that the good should prosper
                  and the bad suffer.
  That's what we wish and now we've been able
                  at last to find
  A nice device to bring this about;
                  it's simple and noble
  And'll stop Wealth staggering hither and thither
                  blind as a bat:
  It depends on his getting his eyesight back
                  so he'll be able
  To visit the good and boycott the bad
                  who do without God.
  That'll make everyone kind and rich
                  and godly too;
  Surely something that nothing could match
                  or ever outdo.

BLEPSIDEMUS: Absolutely, don't bother
                  even to ask her.

CHREMYLUS: You've only got to look at the condition
                  of the human scene
  Not to think it quite insane
                  and to wonder

*In the long anapestic passages that follow I have shortened the Greek
heptameter to hexameter, English being a slower language than Greek.

If it isn't some divine
    execration.
It hardly needs to be pointed out
    that some are rich
Yet without the smallest doubt
    acquired their loot
By swindling others, whereas some poor
    godly wretch
Is in a mess and ravenous
    and spends the year
Closeted with Poverty.
    That is why
If Wealth got his eyesight back
    and stymied her,
We'd need to have no further truck
    with trying to sustain
Human beings in trying to remain
    blessedly humane.
POVERTY: It amazes me how the two of you
    have fallen for
Such obvious fallacy, you two
    old dodderers,
Who surely must belong to the Order
    of Blabberers.
And if you ever get your dreams
    I tell you this,
They'll be different from what it seems,
    and be no use,
Because if Wealth does see again
    and can begin
To give himself to everyone
    equally,
No one will practice the arts and crafts
    ever again,

For once these have gone, who'll be
    at all ready
To ply the forge, to build ships,
    do tailoring,
Make wheels or shoes, do bricklaying,
    or come to grips
With washing clothes or leather tanning?
    Who will wish
To plough the earth and gather in
    the harvesting
Of Demeter's generosity
    once you can
Succumb to inactivity
    and do nothing?
CHREMYLUS: You're talking out of your hat because
    everything
Crossed off on your list'll be done
    by slaves of course.
POVERTY: And where will you get these slaves from?
CHREMYLUS: We'll buy them.
POVERTY: Yes, but who having money
    will want to sell them?
CHREMYLUS: Some businessman from Thessaly
    most probably
(That's where slaves are sold)
    hoping to make a profit.
POVERTY: But slave dealers won't exist,
    you've just implied
By your own premise. Would anyone
    take the risk
In that shady traffic? You
    yourself would have to

Sally forth to dig and plough
    and also do
Every kind of boring chore
    you don't do now.
You'll find life harder than it was before.

CHREMYLUS: God, I hope that happens to *you*!

POVERTY: What is more,
    Don't expect to sleep in bed
        or under a cover;
You won't find either. Who'd be so mad
        to toil and moil
When they've got it all? So when a bride
        is brought home
By her groom, she won't be sprayed
        with perfume
Or immediately arrayed
        in costly style
With divers colors and brocade.
        What use is money
When you have all that through me?
        Because of me
You get every necessity.
        I am she
Who by the pinch of poverty
        compels the hood
To earn his daily bread.

CHREMYLUS: And you, what usefulness can you
        direct our notice to
Except burns from heating baths
        and the hungry mouths
Of a horde of brats; and dismal hags,
        and swarms of gnats,
And lice and fleas: something that's
        beyond all count,
Which hum around our head
        or get us out of bed

As if they had but one intent
    and wished to hint:
"Get up or starve." But that's not all:
    you make us wear
The meanest rags instead of jackets,
    and sleep in foul
Bug-infested fiber mats
    instead of beds,
Where sleep's impossible for there
    moth-eaten sacks
Are made to do for proper blankets;
    no pillow either
but a hard and blocklike boulder,
    and for breakfast
No bread, but mallow leaves at best.
    No barley buns
But radish tops. And for our bums
    no decent chairs
But chipped old urns; and instead
    of a bowl for making bread,
A staved-in barrel, broken too.
    So let's say "Cheers!"
For all these "blessings" rained on us by you.
POVERTY: That's not my way of living,
    this litany of yours;
What you're simply giving
    is the life of beggars.
CHREMYLUS: But Poverty and Beggary are sisters,
    don't we say?
POVERTY: And aren't you the one who also says
    Thrasybulus*

---

*The point is that Thrasybulus, a hero of the democracy, recently killed in a campaign, could not be more different from Dionysius I, the stern tyrant of Syracuse, but some popular politician had evidently made the comparison. (Loeb)

Is no different from Dionysius?
    No way!
The life I stand for isn't like that
    and never will be.
What you're going on about so pat
    is beggary:
A life not owning anything,
    whereas poverty
Means owning something if only a little
    and being thrifty,
And working hard and scraping by,
    but not at all
Lacking what is really necessary.

CHREMYLUS: You make it all sound so nice,
    you do, by deuce:
The scrimping and slaving away
    till the final
Having nothing salted away
    for the funeral.

POVERTY: You're not serious and you think you're funny
    but you won't admit
That I raise better men than Wealth
    with all his money.
In mind and body they're much more fit;
    but with him,
They're gouty, have swollen limbs
    and bloated tummies.
They're also obscenely fat;
    but with me
They're slim, wasp-waisted and defeat
    the enemy.

CHREMYLUS: They get that wasp-waist by starvation,
    I would bet.

POVERTY: Let's take morals then,
    and I'll give a demonstration

That with me good conduct lies,
    with Wealth, conceit.
CHREMYLUS: Good conduct, I suppose, implies
    violence and theft.
BLEPSIDEMUS: And the modesty to keep out of sight
    while they abuse.*
POVERTY:† Just look at our politicians in every town:
  when they are poor they behave properly,
but after they've fleeced the exchequer and waxed
  wealthy
they change their tune,
undermining democracy and turning against the people.
CHREMYLUS: Well, you're right there and I won't quibble,
  though you're still a nasty old crone
and mustn't expect to get off lightly
after trying to make out that poverty
is superior to wealth.
POVERTY: But you've still given me no proof
  that I am wrong. All you've done
is wave your arms about and froth at the mouth.
CHREMYLUS: All right, but how come everyone
  avoids you?
POVERTY: Because I discipline them,
  and they react the same way that children do
when their fathers try to better them.
    Oh it's difficult to know what's best to do.
CHREMYLUS: No doubt you'll now say that not even
  Zeus
  knows what's best to do,
and he's endowed with wealth too.

---

*Bracketed by some editors as dubious.
†Aristophanes continues for another thirty-two lines with this sing-song repartee, however—*salva reverentia*—I can't help thinking that enough is enough, so at this point I am returning to his more straightforward manner.

BLEPSIDEMUS: And lets this old hag loose on us!

POVERTY: What blinkered ancient crocks you are—
both of you!
Actually Zeus is poor, which I can prove.
Why is it if he were wealthy
that when he gets everybody together
every fourth year for the games at Olympia
and he celebrates the triumphant athletes with
crowns of wild olive,
why isn't it with crowns of gold?

CHREMYLUS: That only shows that Zeus is thrifty and
not naive.
He has a great respect for wealth and doesn't
waste it:
he decorates the winners with trash and keeps the cash.

POVERTY: What you're really saying is that Zeus is
something worse
than poor—if he's really loaded
but behaves like the greediest thing alive.

CHREMYLUS: I hope that Zeus exterminates you after
crowning you with wild olive.

POVERTY: You've got a nerve,
going on implying that poverty's not the origin
of our every blessing.

CHREMYLUS: That's something that only Hecate can
answer:*
whether it's better to be rich or poor.
One thing she's bound to tell you
is that the rich put down a monthly meal for her
which the poor grab even before it hits the floor.
Now go to hell,
Stop whining and be off.

---

*Artemis in her moon personation: patroness of many departments
of life, including magic and witchcraft. Her statue was erected outside houses to ward off evil.

No matter what you say
I'll never see it your way.

POVERTY: City of Argos, are you there?*

CHREMYLUS: Call Pauson your messmate here.†

POVERTY: This is more than I can bear.

CHREMYLUS: Get lost and do it fast.

POVERTY: I am going, but going where?

CHREMYLUS: To the stocks. Go at last.

POVERTY: All right, but I want you to know:
One day you'll call me back—both of you.

[POVERTY *exits, as* CHREMYLUS *shouts after her*]

CHREMYLUS: Fine! we can wait till then.
Meanwhile, go to the dogs.
You can talk your head off, bitch,
But I'd rather be rich.

BLEPSIDEMUS: My God, you're right!
And as for me,
I'm going to luxuriate
Among my wife and kids and take
A bath, and I'll step out of it
All glisteningly
And fart in the face
Of Poverty.

CHREMYLUS: And now that we've got that hag to scram
Let's go as quick as we can,
The two of us, and lead the god
To Aesclepius' holy shrine
And there lay him down in bed.

BLEPSIDEMUS: Yes, so we mustn't tarry
Lest someone else arrives

---

*From Euripides' *Telephus,* fr. 713, a hyperbolic request for witnesses to an outrageous claim, cf. *Knights* 813. (Loeb)
†Gibed at for his mean way of living in *Acharnians* and *Women at
the Thesmophoria.*

And spoils our plans and makes us sorry.

CHREMYLUS: [*calling into the house*]

Cario, my lad, bring out the bedding
And bring out Plutus, the man himself,
As is only fitting;
Yes, bring everything.

[CARIO *and the other household servants bustle about
with bedding and baggage, then lead out* PLUTUS *for
the trip to the sanctuary of Aesclepius. All leave the
stage and the* CHORUS *performs an interlude with
dance and music, at the end of which* CARIO *enters.
It is the morning of the next day.*]

CARIO: [*beaming*] Hey, you oldsters, who at many
    a feast
for Theseus have slurped up bowls of soup
with crumbled bread, you are most fortunate—yes,
    truly blest,
like everyone who shares your fellowship.

LEADER: You best of all your fellow slaves, what's up?
    You look as though you come with happy news.

CARIO: My master's had a masterstroke of luck,
    or rather, Plutus has—oh yes,
no longer blind, with shining eyes he sees,
thanks to his healing by Aesclepius.

LEADER: This calls for cheers, this happy news.

CARIO: Cheer away, then, willy-nilly.

LEADER: [*breaking into song*]
    Blessed Aesclepius, let me raise
    For you and your children a shout of praise,
    You shining light for humanity.

[*the* WIFE *of* CHREMYLUS *comes hurrying out of the
house*]

WIFE: What's all the shouting about? Has somebody brought
   exciting news: something that I've yearned to hear,
someone I've sat waiting for?

CARIO: Quick, quick, bring out the wine, dear madame,
   you've got a good excuse because
I'm going to smother you with blessings.

WIFE: Where are they, then?

CARIO: You'll hear them from me in a moment.

WIFE: Very well, get on with it.

CARIO: Are you ready? I'll break the whole damn
   news to you from head to foot.

WIFE: Just the news, please. Keep it off my head.

CARIO: Even good news?

WIFE: Yes, stick to the facts.

CARIO: All right. . . . As soon as we had reached
   the shrine
   with the wretched wreck that's
now so glorious and happy,
the first thing we did
was take him to the sea and wash him.

WIFE: [*with withering sarcasm*]
   What a lovely idea, dipping an old man in the freez-
      ing sea!

CARIO: Then we went inside the god's holy home
   and after we'd burnt the offerings of cakes and barley
(excellent fuel for Hephaeston's flame),*
we tucked him up nicely in his bed
and lay down ourselves on our mattresses.

WIFE: Were there any other patients at the shrine?

---

*Probably the line is another quotation of a lost play of Euripides.
Hephaeston (the Roman Vulcan) was the god of fire and patron of
all artists working in metal. His mother, Hera, was so disgusted with
him when a baby that she tore him from her breast and he spouted
milk all over the heavens—the Milky Way.

CARIO: There was a certain Neocleides,*
  quite blind but with a sharper eye for theft than
    anyone with sight.
      There were many others too, all with different diseases.
      Then the temple warden put out the lights
and told us to go to sleep and not to speak
even if we heard noises.
      So we lay down dutifully but I couldn't sleep
because a pot of stew near some old lady's head
was driving me frantic
and the urge I had to crawl toward it was quite demonic,
but looking up I saw the temple steward
helping himself to cakes and figs from the sacrificial table
and then making the rounds of all the tables
to see what tidbits still remained:
which he duly dedicated to his sack.
      I couldn't help admiring his sense of dedication,
so I got up and made that pot of stew my destination.
WIFE: You scalawag, had you no fear of the god?
CARIO: Of course I had, I was terrified
  he'd beat me to the pot—
all garlanded and that.
      The priest had shown me what I could expect.
      When the old lady became alert
to the noise I was making she thrust her hand into
  the pot,
and I hissed and bit it like a snake.
      She pulled out her hand at once
and collapsed into total silence,
swaddled in her blanket and farting away with funk,
and stinking like a damned skunk.
      That's when I fell upon the stew,

*Not known. Probably one of Aristophanes' political hates.

and stuffed myself to the gills
until I was almost ready to spew.
WIFE: But didn't the god Aesclepius approach you?
CARIO: No, he was about to
  when a funny thing happened. He was all set,
when my overloaded stomach let out a snort.
WIFE: It must have filled him with disgust.
CARIO: No, but Iaso, who was behind him, blushed
  and Panacaea held her nose and turned away.*
    I don't fart incense, you know!
WIFE: Did the god too?
CARIO: He took no notice whatever.
WIFE: Are you stating the god's a clod?
CARIO: Not at all, only an excreta eater.
WIFE: You're such a card!
CARIO: After that I quickly went under cover,
  whilst the god methodically went his rounds,
inspecting every case.
    His assistant then produced a stone mortar,
a pestle, and a box.
WIFE: Of stone?
CARIO: No, that was the mortar.
WIFE: But you'd put yourself under cover, you liar,
  so how did you see all this?
CARIO: Through the chinks, of course,
  all those holes in my gown. . . . So first he pounds
a plaster for Neocleides
consisting of three cloves of Tenian garlic,†
a dash of fig juice and mastic spurge all mashed up in
  the mortar
and soused in Sphettian vinegar.‡

*The daughters of Aesclepius, god of healing. Iaso means "healer,"
and Panacaea "cure-all."
†From the little island of Tenos in the Aegean not far from Andros,
famous for its fountains, its wine, and its garlic.
‡Sphettus was a deme of Athens.

This he smears on the man's eyelids, turning them
    back
to make them smart the more.

Neocleides sprang up yelling
and tried to bolt, but Aesclepius just laughed and said:
"You're nicely plastered up. Stay where you are.

This will stop you making
a nuisance of yourself with your briefs in the Assembly."

WIFE: How patriotic and how knowing!

CARIO: Then he sat down next to Plutus and felt his
    head,
    and wiped his eyelids with a strip of clean linen
while Panacaea covered his face and head with a crim-
    son napkin.

Next, the god gave a whistle
and two snakes slipped out of the temple.

They were enormous.

WIFE: Good heavens!

CARIO: They slid silently underneath the napkin
    and as far as I could tell began to lick around the eyes.

Then, madame, before you could down a quart of
    wine,
good old Plutus stood up seeing.

I clapped my hands in delirious applause
and aroused my master as the god was disappearing
into the shrine, and the serpents too.

Imagine the joy of those who were reposing
next to Plutus, all those who
stayed up the rest of the night, embracing him and
    rejoicing
till the new day's light.

My admiration of the god knew no end,
both for giving Plutus back his sight
and making Neocleides more blind.

WIFE: What a show of power, O great Aesclepius, lord!

But now pray tell me, where is Plutus?
CARIO: He's coming, surrounded by a huge crowd:
  people who've lived good but stinted lives,
all dying to welcome him and shake his hand.

      There are also others, the rich and well endowed
who became so by dishonest ways;
these were scowling and wrinkling their brows.

      But the former were chasing along behind,
laughing and shouting out their gratitude
while old men drummed their shoes.

[*turning to the* CHORUS]

      So come along all of you: skip, strut, and dance
    in parade.
      Never again will you come home and find
there's not a grain to eat in your domain.
WIFE: Hurrah, holy Hecate!
      Brave bringer of such good news,
  I swear I could garland you with cakes!
CARIO: Don't hesitate,
  the crowds are almost on our threshold.
WIFE: Good, I'll go and get the birthday cookies
  to celebrate the born-again eyes.
CARIO: And I'll go to welcome the arriving crowd.

[*The* WIFE *goes into the house as* CARIO *takes up his position outside one of the gates. Meanwhile the* CHORUS *performs an interlude of dance and music, at the end of which* PLUTUS *enters. He looks like he has shed about twenty years and there is a spring in his step.*]

PLUTUS: First of all let me bow to the Sun,
  then Athena's glorious earth of Athens
and the whole of Attica.

      And now let me make it plain
how embarrassed I am by the way I used to batten
on the well-to-do, though I was unaware,

and how I kept aloof from those who merited my
    company.
    It's sad that I should have made
so glaring a mistake in both these matters.
    But now I intend to undo it
and demonstrate to all that I never meant
to give myself to such evildoers.

[CHREMYLUS *and* CARIO *appear:* CHREMYLUS *breathless and trying to get away from the crowds pursuing*
PLUTUS *and* CARIO *from the house*]

CHREMYLUS: Damn the lot of you!
    What an ordeal fair-weather friends can be!
    They appear from nowhere if you're doing well,
barging into you, bruising your shins, all
trying to show they're your bosom crony.
    There's not one who hasn't accosted me,
nor any of those old men in the market square
who hasn't tried to garland me.

[WIFE *comes out of the house with a tray of goodies*]

WIFE: You darling men, both of you, here you are!
    Now, Plutus, let me do what they always used to do
and hold you under a shower of candy.
PLUTUS: Please, I'd rather not:
    this is the first house I've entered with my born-
        again sight,
so it's not for you to bring anything out,
but for me to put something in.
WIFE: But wouldn't you like a cake?
PLUTUS: Yes, but not here—inside at the hearth.
    Let's tread the traditional path.
    That way we don't have to face all the silly slapstick
that goes on, with the producer chucking figs and things
at the audience to get a laugh.

WIFE: Hear hear! . . . Look,
Demetrius* has jumped up to scramble for figs.

[*all of them leave and the* CHORUS *performs another
inter-act, after which* CARIO *enters from the house*]

CARIO: How sweet it is, dear fellows, to lead a
blessed life,
especially when it costs us nothing!
An avalanche of good things
has fallen on this house even though we haven't
committed sins.
Oh, there's nothing like a life of wealth!
Good white barley fills our bins,
our casks are flush with dusky fragrant wines.
Our purses bulge with gold and silver past belief.
Our vats are full of olive oil, our jars with scent,
the loft with figs. Our plates and dishes,
pots and pans, now are brass or copper,
and those dreadful fish platters are gleaming silver;
and even our lamp all of a sudden went
ivory. And we servants play odds-or-even
with gold staters for our pitchers.
And instead of stones to wipe our bottoms with,†
now we are given
cloves of garlic every time.
At the moment our boss is in there garlanded and
busy
sacrificing pig and goat and ram,
but the smoke is terrible in there and has made me scram.
It stung my eyes and made me feel quite dizzy.

[*there enters an* HONEST MAN *with a boy carrying a
shabby cloak and an old pair of shoes*]

*Not known, possibly another politician.
†Not at all far-fetched: it's what they still do in the Indian
countryside.

HONEST MAN: Come on, lad, we'll go and see the god.

CARIO: Hi there, who are you, I wonder?

HONEST MAN: One whose life was crappy and now is happy.

CARIO: I can see that you're a gentleman.

HONEST MAN: Of course!

CARIO: And what is your pleasure?

HONEST MAN: I've come to thank the god because he's the cause
of my good fortune.
    You see, I was once flush,
with a handsome legacy from my father
and I decided to help my indigent friends;
considering that the decent thing to do, and . . .

CARIO: Don't tell me, it went in a flash?

HONEST MAN: Right. I imagined that the hard-up people one befriends
reciprocate if one falls upon hard times.
    But no, they turned their backs on me
as if I were invisible.

CARIO: Which they no doubt found quite risible?

HONEST MAN: Right. The drying up of my dimes
spelled my ruin. But that's all over now, so naturally
    I've come to pay my homage to the god.

CARIO: But what's the shabby garment for,
the one your boy is holding? Do tell.

HONEST MAN: That's the thing I've brought to give the god.

CARIO: You don't mean it's the one you wore
for your induction to the Mysteries?*

HONEST MAN: No, it's the one in which for thirteen years I froze.

CARIO: And the shoes?

---

*At the Eleusinian Mysteries the custom was to wear ragged garments and then dedicate these to the deities.

HONEST MAN: They shared in the freeze.

CARIO: And you're offering them to the god as well?

HONEST MAN: I am, by Zeus!

CARIO: I think the offerings you've brought the god
   are really swell.

[*a distraught* INFORMER *enters with a Witness*]

INFORMER: Hell's bells, I'm under a spell. I'm
      wretched and damned.
   Yes, with a triple, a quadruple, quintuple, duodecimal,
      umpteenesimal
doom I'm doomed.
      Put more water in the wine of my bad fortune.

CARIO: Healer Apollo and you benevolent deities,
   this fellow's disaster, we wonder what it is.

INFORMER: What it is! Just you tell me
   if it isn't something that nothing can match:
      I've lost everything at home, and that god is to
         blame,
the one who's going to be blind again
if the fucking courts are up to scratch.

HONEST MAN: Methinks I smell a rat.
   He may have fallen on bad times all right
but there's something fishy.

CARIO: In which case he deserves what he gets.

INFORMER: Where, I ask you, where is the one who
   all by himself promised to make everyone rich,
and in one stroke, if only
he could regain his sight?
      Instead, he's actually beggared quite a few.

CARIO: Really? Whom has he done that to?

INFORMER: Me, that's who.

CARIO: Which suggests that you were one of the hooli-
      gans
   who broke into houses.

INFORMER: God no! It's you people who are the villains,

and I think it's you who've gone off with my resources.

CARIO: Holy Demeter! He comes blustering in does this informer

as if he were suffering from bulimia.*

INFORMER: And you, I suggest that you go at once

and get put on the wheel in the marketplace.

That'll make you blurt out every misdemeanor.

CARIO: [advancing] For saying that, I'll make you wince.

HONEST MAN: I swear by our Savior Zeus that the whole of Greece

will be grateful to our god

if he brings these rubbishy informers to a rubbishy end.

INFORMER: So you too are siding with these men? And you think it fun. . . .

Wherever did you get that threadbare coat?

Yesterday I saw you in a suit.

HONEST MAN: You're not worth worrying about.

Besides, I'm wearing a protective amulet

I got from Eadmus† for a drachma.

CARIO: I doubt it'll protect you from an informer's bite.

INFORMER: Must you be so beastly rude?

Laugh at me if you dare

but you haven't confessed yet

what you are doing here.

I warrant you're up to no good.

CARIO: Not where you're concerned. You are right there.

INFORMER: That's for sure. It's my money that's paying for your dinner.

---

*It is obvious from the following conversation that a big meal is in the offing.
†Unknown.

HONEST MAN: Dinner? I hope that you and your witness will explode.

CARIO: Yeah, bursting with nothing!

INFORMER: [*sniffing*] Admit, you swine: in there aren't they cooking
a whole range of fish and meats. . . . Yum yum!

CARIO: Smell something, hyena?

HONEST MAN: In that moth-eaten coat, I expect he caught a cold.

INFORMER: Ye gods and Zeus, I am
flabbergasted by their behavior . . . absolutely riled
that an upstanding patriot like me should be subjected
to such abuse.

HONEST MAN: You, an upstanding patriot?

INFORMER: No man more.

HONEST MAN: In which case let me ask you this . . .

INFORMER: Right, get on with it.

HONEST MAN: Are you a farmer?

INFORMER: D'you think I'm off my rocker?

HONEST MAN: Well then, in business?

INFORMER: When it suits me, yes.

HONEST MAN: In any particular trade?

INFORMER: Of course not!

HONEST MAN: Then how do you live if you have no livelihood?

INFORMER: I operate in a private and public capacity.

HONEST MAN: You do? How?

INFORMER: I offer my services.

HONEST MAN: Your services, you toad?
You mean your meddling in what's none of your affair?

INFORMER: None of my affair, goose, when I do all in my power
to benefit the State?

HONEST MAN: So being a tiresome busybody benefits the State?

INFORMER: No, by promoting law and order
and cracking down on every transgressor.

HONEST MAN: I thought the State appointed justices to take care of that.

INFORMER: Yes, but who does the prosecuting?

HONEST MAN: Whoever's willing.

INFORMER: That's me, surely. And the reason why the State's affairs are my affair.

HONEST MAN: And the reason why the State's got such a poor protector.
Come now, wouldn't you rather
leave well enough alone and live in tranquillity?

INFORMER: That's a sheep's life, dull with complacency.

HONEST MAN: Wouldn't you prefer it?

INFORMER: No, not if you gave me Wealth himself
and all of Buttus's harvest of Silphium.*

CARIO: Take off that coat right now.

HONEST MAN: He's speaking to you.

CARIO: Your shoes too.

HONEST MAN: He's still speaking to you.

INFORMER: OK, come out and get me. . . . Any offers?

---

*ΣΙΛΦΙΟΝ, Latin *Silphium* (later confused with Laserwort or Asafoedtida) was a wonder plant that grew wild in Libya and apparently resisted attempts at cultivation. It was thought by many to be worth its weight in gold and was used as a food, a cure-all and, it seems, an abortifacient (from a tea brewed from its leaves). Silphium was often represented on Greek and Roman coins and looked a little like celery with side shoots. Indeed, like celery and fennel, it belonged to the genus *Ferula* (the umbelliferous family). Several North African cities controlled the Silphium trade and many men built their wealth upon it, like Buttus—a North African millionaire who founded the city of Cyrene. Silphium became extinct through overharvesting during the reign of Nero (A.D. 54–68). Is it possible that it still exists somewhere? My guess is it does, perhaps on some remote Indian plain fed by the Ganges.

[CARIO *rushes at him, whips off his coat, and grabs his shoes*]

INFORMER: Help! I'm being stripped in broad day.

CARIO: That'll teach you to batten on the life of others.

INFORMER: [*to Witness*] Look what he's doing. You're my witness.

[*Witness runs off*]

CARIO: Your precious witness is too scared to stay.

INFORMER: Don't I know it! I'm all alone.

CARIO: Boohoo! Boohoo!

INFORMER: I'm in a real mess.

CARIO: [*to* HONEST MAN] Give me the coat.
I'm putting it on the informer.

HONEST MAN: Don't do that,
it's destined for Plutus.

CARIO: But it's perfect for this kind of rotter.
Plutus deserves something much better.

HONEST MAN: And the shoes, what's to be their purpose?

CARIO: Let me have them. I'll graft them on to his
head like a wild olive.*

INFORMER: I'm going. I know I'm no match for you two,
but if I can find an ally—no matter how good-for-
nothing—
I'll bring an action against that mighty god of yours
this very day
and indict him with intent, single-handedly, to remove
the face of democracy and with no attempt to bow
to the national Council or Assembly.

[INFORMER *leaves in high dudgeon*]

---

*Almost all fruiting olive trees are grafted on to a stock of wild
olive, which gives the tree the energy to live for hundreds of years,
provided that the suckers of wild olive that sprout below the graft
line and threaten to take over are removed regularly.

HONEST MAN: [*shouting after him*] Go on, beat it to
    the public baths,
  dressed up as you are in the things I wore.
      And while getting warm get yourself called boss.
      That was my position once.
CARIO: More likely the bath attendant'll grab him by
    the balls and throw him out.
      He'll recognize a scumbag at the first glance.
      Now let's go inside
and you can say your prayers to the god.

[CARIO *and* HONEST MAN *enter the house. There follows an interlude of music and dance by the* CHORUS,
after which an OLD WOMAN *arrives with an attendant
carrying a tray of cakes and eatables.*]

OLD WOMAN: My dear old men,
  have we come to the home of the new deity
or have we taken the wrong turn?
LEADER: Dear girl, you're at his very door . . .
  I can't help but call you girl, you ask so prettily.
OLD WOMAN: Fine. Let me summon someone out here.
CHREMYLUS: [*coming out of the house*] No need, I was
    coming out anyway.
  Tell me, please, why you're here.
OLD WOMAN: I've been through a terrible time, dear man,
  and it's most unfair.
    My life's been unlivable ever since the day
the god got his eyesight back again.
CHREMYLUS: In what way?
  You're not by any chance a female version of
    informer?
OLD WOMAN: Certainly not.

CHREMYLUS: Perhaps you did some wine tasting in the courts without a ticket?

OLD WOMAN: You're teasing me, and I'm in a miserable state.

CHREMYLUS: Miserable? In what way?

OLD WOMAN: Listen. I had a boyfriend, a sweet lad, not a cent to his name
but upright, honest, and extremely handsome.
He did whatever I asked. He really suited me
and I pleased him.

CHREMYLUS: What sort of thing did he expect from you?

OLD WOMAN: Not much. He had a real regard for me.
He might ask for thirty silver drachmas for a cloak,
or for a pair of shoes size eight;
and for his sisters a frock or two,
or a shawl for his mum,
and four bushels, say, of wheat.

CHREMYLUS: My word, that was modest of him!
It's practically nothing.

OLD WOMAN: And he'd make a point of saying
that it wasn't greed that prompted him to ask for anything
but sheer affection, because he always thought of me
when he wore the cloak.

CHREMYLUS: There's a fellow head-over-heels in love.

OLD WOMAN: Oh, but now that's not the way the bloke has come to behave.
He's completely changed.
Do you know, when I sent him this tart
and these other goodies on this tray
with a note saying: "I'll visit you tonight" . . .

CHREMYLUS: I'm all agog. Exactly what?

OLD WOMAN: He sent the whole thing back, including the cheesecake,

  saying that he never wanted to see me again
and that once long ago the Milesians were brave.*
CHREMYLUS: That shows he isn't really a bad character,
 only that now he's rich he can do better than eat
   pea soup.
  Before, he'd eat anything . . . when he was poor.
OLD WOMAN: Absolutely! Every day he'd be at my door.
CHREMYLUS: Hoping for a funeral and a feast.
OLD WOMAN: Not in the least. He just wanted to hear
 my voice.
CHREMYLUS: And see what he could pick up.
OLD WOMAN: And when he saw I was in the dumps
 he'd cuddle me and call me his little duckling, his
  turtledove.
CHREMYLUS: And no doubt ask for a pair of shoes.
OLD WOMAN: And at the Mysteries once
 when someone made eyes at me as I rode past in
  my chaise,
 he beat me black and blue.
  That's how jealous my joyboy was.
CHREMYLUS: He obviously wanted to eat you on his own.
OLD WOMAN: And he said I had lovely hands.
CHREMYLUS: Especially when they held out twenty
 drachmas.
OLD WOMAN: And he said he loved the fragrance of
 my skin.
CHREMYLUS: Especially when you were pouring Tha-
 sian wine.†
OLD WOMAN: And that the look in my eyes was
 sweetly bland.
CHREMYLUS: Yes, he could tell, the fellow was no fool:
 he knew how to sponge on a randy old dame.

---

*A metaphor for "Once upon a time" or "Things change" or "So what?"
†From Thasos, an island in the Aegean famous for its marble quar-
ries, its gold and silver mines, and its red wine.

OLD WOMAN: And this, dear sir, is where the god is
   not fulfilling his role.

   He's supposed to come to the rescue of people in
   distress.

CHREMYLUS: What d'you want him to do? He'll do
   whatever you tell him.

OLD WOMAN: Well, it's only right and proper that the
   man

   I treated nicely should treat me nicely in return.

   Or am I to be left without redress?

CHREMYLUS: But didn't he treat you nicely every night?

OLD WOMAN: Yes, he said he'd never leave me as long
   as I live.

CHREMYLUS: Quite right, but now he thinks you no
   longer live.

OLD WOMAN: Dear man, I'm pining away in a terrible plight.

CHREMYLUS: [to himself] No, rotting away I'd say.

OLD WOMAN: Why, you could pull me through a ring.

CHREMYLUS: [aside] If the ring were the size of a hoop.

OLD WOMAN: Look, here comes the young man now,
   the very one I've been accusing.

   He's probably on his way somewhere to whoop it up.

CHREMYLUS: Well, he's garlanded and his torch is
   blazing.

[the YOUNG MAN approaches and peers at the OLD
WOMAN's face by the light of his torch]

YOUNG MAN: Greetings!

OLD WOMAN: What's he saying?

YOUNG MAN: Good heavens, my antique girlfriend,
   you've turned gray!

OLD WOMAN: Poor me, that's hardly a polite thing to
   say!

CHREMYLUS: It appears that he hasn't seen you for
  years.

OLD WOMAN: Nonsense! He was with me only yesterday.

CHREMYLUS: In which case, unlike with most people,
  drink's given him keener vision.

YOUNG MAN: [*holding torch up to* OLD WOMAN's *face*]
  Holy Poseidon, King of the Fathoms, and every an-
    cient deity,
how her countenance is wizened!

OLD WOMAN: I'll thank you to keep that torch away
  from me.

CHREMYLUS: Sound idea! One spark and she'll flare
  up like a withered wreath.

YOUNG MAN: Would you like a little . . . fun 'n' games
  with me?

OLD WOMAN: But where?

YOUNG MAN: Why not here?
  We could use these nuts as counters.

OLD WOMAN: What for?

YOUNG MAN: A guessing game . . . about the number
  of your teeth.

CHREMYLUS: My guess is four.

YOUNG MAN: Wrong! Pay up! Only one, a molar.

OLD WOMAN: You monster! You're insane!
  Drenching me in shame before all these men!

YOUNG MAN: A little drenching's not a bad idea.

CHREMYLUS: A very bad idea!
  Wash off that rouge and you've got a gargoyle.

OLD WOMAN: [*glaring at* CHREMYLUS] Obviously old
  age has made you senile.

YOUNG MAN: Perhaps he fancies you
  and would like to get his fingers round your boobs . . .
while I'm not looking.

OLD WOMAN: Not a chance, the brute!

CHREMYLUS: By Hecate, I'd be raving!
  All the same, young man, I can't let
you despise this maiden.

YOUNG MAN: Me? I worship her.

CHREMYLUS: But she blames you.

YOUNG MAN: Blames me for what?

CHREMYLUS: For being so brazen,
  and for saying: "Once long ago the Milesians were
    brave."

YOUNG MAN: Well, I won't fight you for her.

CHREMYLUS: Oh?

YOUNG MAN: No, I give way to your seniority and age.
  I wouldn't be so generous to any other.
    So, with my best wishes, take the maiden and go.

CHREMYLUS: I know what you're thinking:
  I know you're thinking that perhaps she's not
    worth having.

YOUNG MAN: True, I for one wouldn't:
  I wouldn't want a woman who's been on offer for
    about thirteen thousand aeons.

CHREMYLUS: All the same, if you've sipped the wine
  it's only fair that you should drain the dregs.

YOUNG MAN: Maybe, but these dregs are prehistoric
  and stink.

CHREMYLUS: You can use a strainer as a dredge.

YOUNG MAN: [*shrugging*] I'm off to the god.
  I'm going to dedicate these garlands to him.

OLD WOMAN: I too have something to say to the god.

YOUNG MAN: Then I'll not budge.

CHREMYLUS: Bear up, don't be afraid.
  She's not going to rape you.

YOUNG MAN: I'm relieved to hear it;
  I've been plugging the old tub long enough.

OLD WOMAN: Off with you now. I'm right behind you.

[*the* YOUNG MAN *goes into the house with the* OLD WOMAN *close behind him*]

CHREMYLUS: My word, great Zeus, in very truth
   as clamped as a limpit the old baggage sticks to
      the youth!

[*an interlude follows of dance and music by the* CHORUS, *after which* HERMES *appears and knocks at the door, then slips behind a pillar*]

CARIO: [*coming out of the house*] Who's been bashing
   at the door?
   [*seeing nobody*] That's queer!
      Door, I'm going to give you what for
if you bark and there's no one there.
HERMES: [*stepping into view as* CARIO *is about to turn
   back to the house*]
   Hey, Cario, wait!
CARIO: So it's you that was breaking down our front
   door?
HERMES: Not really, but I was getting ready to if you
   hadn't opened up.
   Now listen, go like a shot and get your boss, Mr. Big,
and his wife and his brats and his servants and his dog
and, why not, the family pig.
CARIO: For heaven's sake, what's going on?
HERMES: It's Zeus, you scamp,
   he's in a terrible temper and ready to pound you
      all in the same bowl
and chuck the mash onto the Deadman's Dump.
CARIO: "For bad news cut out the messenger's tongue."*
   But why does Zeus want to mash us up?

*A proverbial saying.

HERMES: Because you've committed the most hei-
   nous crime.

Ever since Plutus was able to see again

no one's bothered to sacrifice anything at all to any
   of us divine:

no incense, sweet bay, barley cake, slaughtered beast—
not a bloody thing.

CARIO: And about time!

Nor will they because in the past

you never bothered to care for us.

HERMES: I'm not so worried about the other gods as
   for myself. I'm lost.

CARIO: Shows good sense.

HERMES: In the old days, as early as dawn, barmaids
   would bring me bites:

brandy cake, honey, figs—oh lots!—

all the things that Hermes likes,

but now I'm sprawled out hangdog and quite ravenous.

CARIO: Well it's because of what you've done.

Didn't you sometimes come the heavy on these
   very folk that gave you bites?

HERMES: It's sad. What a loss!

No more ritual cake on the fourth of the moon.*

CARIO: "You pine for me no longer here, you call for
   me in vain."†

HERMES: I pine for the ham I used to down.

CARIO: You could ham it up right here in the open
   air.‡

*Hermes' monthly birthday.
†From a lost tragedy probably by Euripides in which Heracles be-
moans the death of Hylas, a beautiful youth whom Heracles took
to Colchis (in search of the Golden Fleece).
‡In the Greek there is a play on the words κωλη (*kōlē*) and Ἀσκωλι-
αζω (*Askōliazō*), to hop about at the festival of Askolia. I have stolen
Jeffrey Henderson's clever solution of the problem with "ham it up."

HERMES: The fried livers and kidneys I used to dispatch.

CARIO: For which your own kidneys and liver seem to groan.

HERMES: And the wine, half-and-half, I used to pour down the hatch.

CARIO: [*offering a pail of slops*]
Here, have a sip of this, then go to hell.

HERMES: Can't you help me, your old pal?

CARIO: Depends what kind of help you want.

HERMES: How about some bread fresh from the oven, and a chunk of steak from your sacrifice in there?

CARIO: Hey, this isn't a carryout.

HERMES: Remember
how I used to help you swipe a platter from your master.

CARIO: Provided you got your share.
Steak and puffed pastry were your delight.

HERMES: Of which you certainly had a bite.

CARIO: But you never shared the whipping I got when I was caught redhanded in the act.

HERMES: Can't you be magnanimous now that you've got Phyle?*
For God's sake let me join your party.

CARIO: You mean you want to leave Olympus and live here?

HERMES: Well, you people are certainly sitting pretty.

CARIO: But don't you think it ungrateful to desert your country?

HERMES: One's country is wherever one does well.†

CARIO: But will *we* do well if you come down here to settle?

*A bellicose village near Athens, captured by Thrasybulus in 404/3 B.C.
†Probably another quotation from a lost tragedy.

HERMES: I can be the lintel god of your front door.

CARIO: Lintel god? We don't need a lintel.

HERMES: Your business-god-adviser then?

CARIO: We're rich. We don't need a Hermes middle man.

HERMES: All right, your god of expert trickery.

CARIO: God of expert trickery? Certainly not.
Now that we've mended our ways tricks are out.

HERMES: God of guidance, then?

CARIO: We have a god who sees again
and have no need of one who guides.

HERMES: Then let me be your competition god.
What's wrong with that?
Athletic and artistic contests are right up Plutus' street.*

CARIO: [*to the audience*] Hasn't he fixed himself up cleverly with tags?
He's made a profession of it.
It's not surprising that jurymen hype
themselves on to a similar list of pegs.†

HERMES: It's agreed, then, that I may take my place inside?

CARIO: You may. So go to the sink and wash some tripe
and install yourself as servant god.

[HERMES *follows* CARIO *into the house. A* PRIEST *arrives*]

PRIEST: Can anybody tell me where Chremylus is?

CHREMYLUS: [*coming out of the house*] How goes it, my good man?

---

*It was the wealthy citizens who paid for much of civic entertainment.
†Volunteers for jury work were parceled off among an assortment of courts and received payment.

PRIEST: What else but terrible.

I'm dying of starvation
ever since Plutus got his sight back again.

    I've simply not a thing to eat. I, Zeus the Savior's
    priest!

CHREMYLUS: You don't say! And what's the reason?

PRIEST: Nobody sacrifices. Nobody takes the trouble.

CHREMYLUS: Why not?

PRIEST: Because everybody's rich.

  In the days when people had nothing, the businessman
safely home from his trip
would offer a sacrifice in thanks:
so would the man acquitted in court,
and the sacrificers would ask me to be the priest.

    But not so now:
no one offers a thing or sets a foot
inside the temple except to find a loo,
and these are numerous too.

CHREMYLUS: A loo? Not exactly the place to get your cut!

PRIEST: So I'm saying good-bye to Zeus the Savior and
  settling here.

CHREMYLUS: Bear up! God willing, all will be well,
  for Zeus the Savior is here. To come was his own idea.

PRIEST: So with you everything is hunky-dory?

CHREMYLUS: Yes, we're just about to set up Plutus here—
  oh, don't go!—exactly where he was before he
stopped being treasurer-in-residence in the temple
    of Athena.

    So, as soon as someone brings the lighted flares
you can lead the god's parade.

PRIEST: I'm full of gratitude.

CHREMYLUS: Somebody go and call Plutus here
  outside.

[*the* OLD WOMAN *arrives*]

OLD WOMAN: And what about me?

CHREMYLUS: See these vessels we're using for the in-
stallation of the god,
carry them on your head in solemn style . . .
I say, your getup's good!

OLD WOMAN: That's not why I came.

CHREMYLUS: Not to worry, everything's arranged:
your young man will come to you tonight.

OLD WOMAN: All right,
since you assure me this is so I'll settle to carry
these vessels.

CHREMYLUS: [*watching her balancing the vessels on
her head*]
How extraordinary, the behavior of these pots is
really rum:
with other pots the scum
comes to the top, but with these the pots
come on top of the scum.

[*To the sound of gong and triumphal music* PLUTUS
is led in by the rest of the household and the PRIEST
*marches the whole company off in solemn procession
to the Acropolis, where* PLUTUS *will be restored as
treasurer-in-residence in the temple of Pallas Athena.
Meanwhile, the members of the* CHORUS *line up for
their own procession as they chant the envoi.*]

CHORUS: Now is not the time to be lagging
so let us start following,
Forming up behind them and singing.

Classics from
Ancient Greece

THE ILIAD
trans. W.H.D. Rouse   527372
This very readable prose translation tells the tale of Achilles,
Hector, Agamemnon, Paris, Helen, and all Troy besieged by the
mighty Greeks. It is a tale of glory and honor, of pride and
pettiness, of friendship and sacrifice, of anger and revenge. In
short, it is the quintessential western tale of men at war.

THE ODYSSEY
trans. W.H.D. Rouse   527364
Kept away from his home and family for 20 years by war and
malevolent gods, Odysseus returns to find his house in disarray.
This is the story of his adventurous travels and his battle to
reclaim what is rightfully his.

THE AENEID
BY VIRGIL. *trans. Patric Dickinson*   622774
After the destruction of Troy by the Greeks, Aeneas leads the
Trojans to Italy where, according to Virgil, he re-founds the city
of Rome. And begins a dynasty to last 1,000 years. This, Virgil's
greatest triumph, was seen by many Medieval thinkers as linking
Rome's ancient past to its Christian future.

THE GREAT DIALOGUES OF PLATO
trans. W.H.D. Rouse   527453
Here are some of the most influential texts in Western Literature.
From Classical times till now, these have been considered funda-
mental texts that every learned person should have read. This
volume includes the complete texts of *The Republic*, *The Apology*,
Crito, *Phaedro*, *Ion*, *Meno*, *Euthydemus*, and *Symposium* in a widely-
acclaimed translation.

To order call: 1-800-788-6262